BUILD SHIPS!

BUILD SHIPS!

Wartime Shipbuilding Photographs
San Francisco Bay: 1940-1945

by

Wayne Bonnett

WINDGATE PRESS: SAUSALITO, CALIFORNIA

Left: SS *Mormacsun*, Moore Dry Dock Company, August 28, 1940.
Previous page: SS *Alcoa Pioneer*, Bethlehem Shipbuilding.

Copyright © 1999 Wayne Bonnett. All rights reserved. No part of this work may be reproduced or used in any form or by any means; graphic, electronic, or mechanical, including photocopying, digital scanning, or information storage and retrieval systems without written permission of the publisher. Windgate Press, P.O. Box 1715, Sausalito, CA 94966.

ISBN: 0-915269-20-1

Tanker *Mission Santa Barbara*, Marinship, June 8, 1944.

★ ★

BETHLEHEM ★ BASALT ★ BELAIR ★ COLBERG ★ CLYDE W. WOOD ★ D.W. NICHOLSON ★ GENERAL ENGINEERING ★ FULTON ★ HICKINBOTHAM BROS.★ HUNTERS POINT ★ KAISER ★ KYLE ★ POLLOCK-STOCKTON ★ WESTERN PIPE & STEEL ★ INDEPENDENT IRON WORKS ★ HURLEY MARINE ★ JUDSON-PACIFIC ★ MARE ISLAND ★ MARINSHIP ★ McDONOUGH STEEL ★ MOORE EQUIPMENT ★ MOORE DRY DOCK COMPANY ★ STEPHENS BROTHERS ★ UNITED ENGINEERING

★ ★

WARTIME SHIPBUILDING PHOTOGRAPHS

Introduction	6
Prelude	9
Early Steel Shipbuilding: 1885-1915	10
World War I Program: 1916-1921	12
Between the Wars: 1922-1936	18
The Buildup: 1936-1941	24
America at War: 1941-1945	28
New Wartime Shipyards	32
Kaiser, Marinship, Belair, Stockton	
Building Ships	46
Liberty Ships, Yard Layout, Shipyard Cranes	
Ship Launching	84
Outfitting	92
Small Yards	104
Wooden Craft	108
Shipyard Morale	115
Housing and Transportation	120
Special Vessels	124
Landing Craft, "Pint-size" Liberties, Balloon Barges, Floating Dry Docks, Barges	
Repair and Conversion	138
Winding Down and Victory	148
Vessel Types	154
Index	167
Acknowledgments	170

★ ★

BETHLEHEM ★ BASALT ★ BELAIR ★ COLBERG ★ CLYDE W. WOOD ★ D.W. NICHOLSON ★ GENERAL ENGINEERING ★ FULTON ★ HICKINBOTHAM BROS.★ HUNTERS POINT ★ KAISER ★ KYLE ★ POLLOCK-STOCKTON ★ WESTERN PIPE & STEEL ★ INDEPENDENT IRON WORKS ★ HURLEY MARINE ★ JUDSON-PACIFIC ★ MARE ISLAND ★ MARINSHIP ★ McDONOUGH STEEL ★ MOORE EQUIPMENT ★ MOORE DRY DOCK COMPANY ★ STEPHENS BROTHERS ★ UNITED ENGINEERING

★ ★

INTRODUCTION

WINDGATE

Golden Gate and San Francisco from the Marin Headlands, c.1968.

In 1940, it took fourteen months to build a typical cargo ship; in 1945, it took eight weeks. In the decade prior to 1940, America launched only twenty three ships. In the five years after 1940, American shipyards launched more than 4,600 ships. Bay Area shipbuilders produced almost forty-five percent of all the cargo shipping tonnage and twenty percent of warship tonnage built in the entire country during World War II. The war lasted 1,365 days. In that span of time Bay Area ship-yards built 1,400 vessels— a ship a day, on average. How was it possible?

Standing today on the steep Marin Headlands overlooking the Golden Gate, one can see into the past; with a little imagination, back to 1942. The Pacific Ocean, a broad sheet of blue extending to the horizon, certainly looks the same; the scudding clouds and distant fog bank might be typical of a spring day almost sixty years ago. The great bridge spanned the Golden Gate as it does now; the graceful curve of San Francisco's shoreline remains the same. The pastel clutter of North Beach and Russian Hill is similar and so are the green-blue pines and eucalyptus of the Presidio. Only recent highrises of the financial district and the omnipresent Sutro Tower jolt one's consciousness back to the present.

While the setting is little changed today, the emotions of those now distant days are difficult to conjure up except for those who experienced them firsthand. America was at war. Americans were shaken as never before by events of the previous months beginning in December, 1941, the Japanese attack on the naval base at Pearl Harbor in the Hawaiian Islands and simultaneous attacks on American military bases in the Philippines. San Franciscans shared the anger and shock of the rest of the country, the heart-wrenching anguish and desire to strike back. But more than most Americans, San Franciscans felt vulnerable, poised as they were on the edge of a continent, the brink of a thinly defended ocean.

Rarely has American thought galvanized so quickly around a simple fact: The war that had been Europe's problem had become overnight America's problem too, a struggle for survival. Today, standing near time-ruined concrete bunkers in the Marin Headlands, one senses that past era when coastal artillery lay in wait for an unseen enemy that never came. The massive naval rifles and mortars once mounted here were almost all that stood between San Francisco Bay and a potential invader. The most recent fortifications were part of an elaborate plan worked out in the 1930s for Pacific Coast defense. After December 7, 1941, that plan disintegrated as the ships and planes essential to its success lay shattered in Pearl Harbor. National defense ceased to be theoretical and overnight had become deadly serious.

One thing had not changed: America's strategy in fighting a Pacific war before and after Pearl Harbor relied on seizing the offensive. Military and civilian resolve, as it had been before Pearl Harbor, was to drive back and crush the enemy. America's ability to do that, however, had suffered a setback. America would have to transform herself from peace to war, personal goals and ambitions set aside, sacrifices made. For many, the price would be high. America would have to build the weapons of war in quantities never before thought possible. And if the war was to be carried to the enemy, America must build ships; warships, cargo vessels, troop transports, invasion craft. The shape of the war would be determined by America's ability to take it to the enemy on the decks and in the hulls of American made ships.

America's rearmament program was already under way when the nation was thrust into war. The pace quickened and prodigious production goals were set, then set higher, then higher still. Bay Area shipyards met the challenge as workers from all parts of the country flowed into California.

The great armada that set a wartime course from here a half-century ago valiantly served its purpose and most of the vessels returned through the Golden Gate to tumultuous welcome. Now, save for a few preserved as museum ships, they have gone to the ship breakers, their work completed, their victories and losses entered in the pages of history. The Americans who sailed the ships, served on them, and built them have passed from center stage to the eventide of their lives. Their numbers dwindle. The shipyards of San Francisco Bay have all but disappeared, themselves scrapped or put to other uses. The story of those shipyards, however, and the ships, the workers, the miraculous achievements remain vivid in photographs and documents and in memories of the remaining survivors of that era.

The photographs of World War II shipbuilding in this book were taken, for the most part, to document day-to-day efforts, the works-in-progress in Bay Area yards. They were taken by professional photographers commissioned by the shipyards or the Navy or U.S. Maritime Commission as part of contractual requirements. Others were taken for promotional purposes within the strict wartime censorship code. Some still bear the wartime admonition, "Not to be released for publication." The censors were fully aware of how well the photographers had captured the essence and minutiae of shipbuilding, information they didn't want to fall into enemy hands. Since unauthorized photography was forbidden in and around wartime shipyards, these and other similar photos and motion pictures comprise the visual record of that time and place. Now, as that war recedes in history, the photographic record increases its documentary value, reminding us of those heady days when over 200,000 Bay Area residents worked in shifts around the clock to produce an armada such as the world had never seen and will not see again.

WINDGATE

Pearl Harbor, December 7, 1941; destroyer *Shaw* explodes, battleship *Pennsylvania* silhouetted at right.

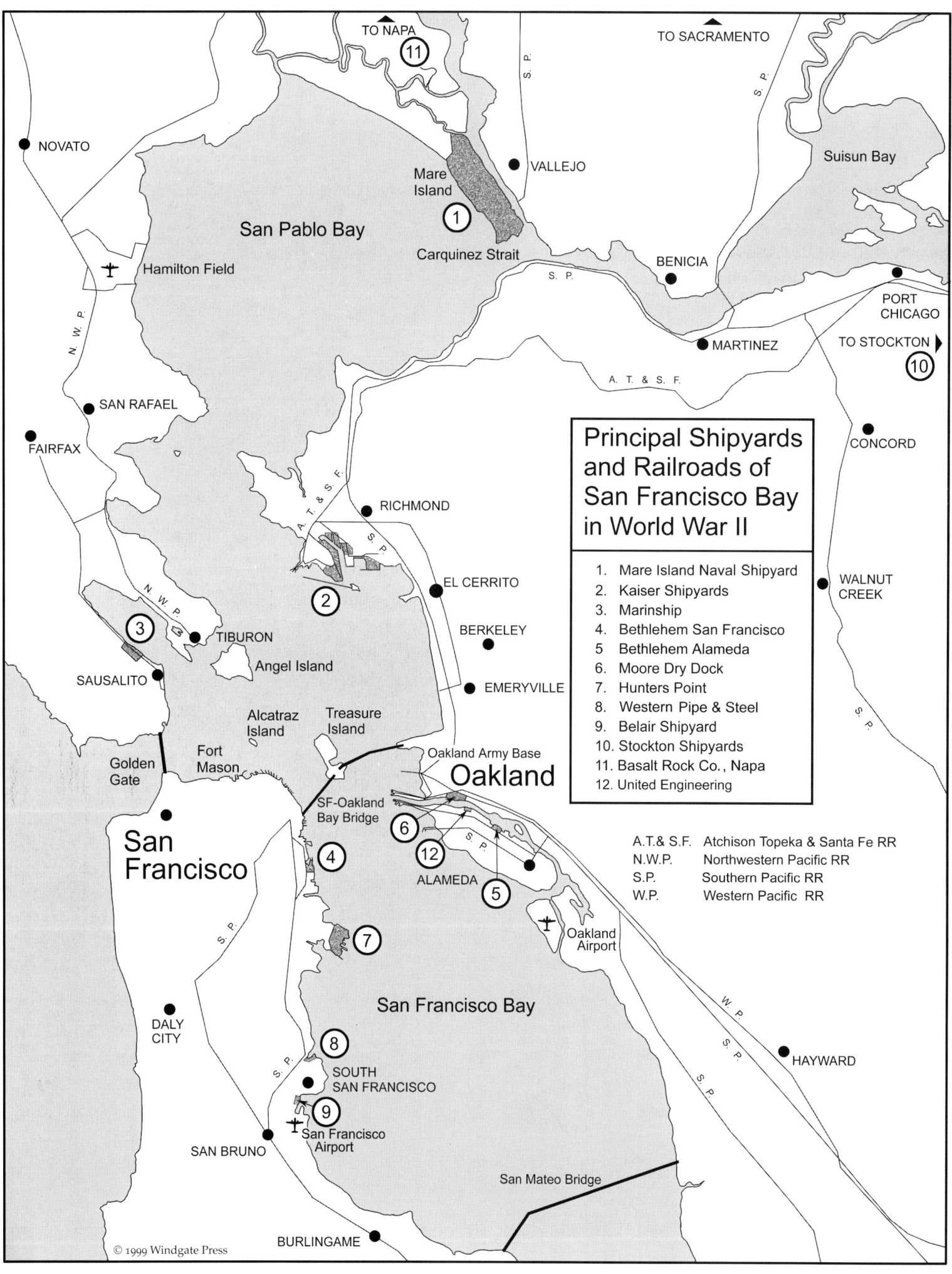

PRELUDE

San Francisco Bay is one of the finest natural harbors in the world. In 1940, the essential mix of industry and population, existing shipyards and potential sites for new ones made the Bay Area an ideal shipbuilding center. The map at left shows the widespread nature of Bay Area shipbuilding near the end of World War II. At the time, the Bay Area was the greatest concentration of ship repair and construction facilities in the world, with thirty separate shipyards under Naval control or supervision. A single command at Mare Island Naval Shipyard controlled that yard plus the Hunters Point Naval Drydocks, and supervised Navy contract work at 28 other yards. Some of those yards plus scores of small shops and machine facilities also produced vessels and parts for the United States Maritime Commission. The Bay Area web of shipyards, repair facilities, part suppliers, contractors and sub-contractors was so vast that a complete list of all who participated would be all but impossible to compile. In fact, almost everybody and every business in the Bay Area was somehow involved, directly or indirectly, in contributing to the war effort. A look at Naval and Maritime Commission records reveals the complexity of contacts let, completed, modified, canceled; the maze of vessel types and sub-types. Company records, where they exist, are similarly complex, with code names given to parts and sub-assemblies. Added to normal government complexity in record keeping was the unintentional but unavoidable confusion born of haste and the need for secrecy. War work often was done in secrecy or, at least, semi-secrecy. Shipyard workers and low-level management often had an inaccurate picture of their participation in the grand scheme.

Photographers, too, were somewhat in the dark. They photographed what they were told to photograph. In most cases, the subject matter was obvious; sometimes less so. One photographer at Marinship shot the insides of every freight car that arrived at the yard, before and after it was unloaded. He thought he was documenting attempted sabotage when in reality he was recording the effectiveness of various methods of packing parts. Often photographers were sent aloft in shipyard cranes to take pictures of general or specific activities. As each hull rose in the shipway, a photographer was sent aloft in sunshine, rain, cold or wind to make a daily record of progress. Of course, every vessel launch was well recorded. At other times, photographers labored over repetitive mundane but vital shots of parts and more parts. In spite of the repetitive and technical nature of much of the assigned photography, a good number of shots rise above the ordinary. A few photographers created works of astonishing drama and aesthetic brilliance, testimony to the skill and craftsmanship they brought to the assignment.

As with most industrial photography, the camera records unintended detail that enriches the subject. The background reveals an unidentified vessel, a familiar shoreline. Dockside and shipway scenes contain tools and machines, men and women at work. This is true not only of World War II maritime photographs but of those taken during World War I and earlier.

The Bay Area was fortunate in one respect; two major local shipyards had gained valuable experience in large-scale rapid production during World War I and had on hand core management and labor groups when needed for World War II. These two yards, Bethlehem Shipbuilding Corporation and Moore Dry Dock Company, had long histories in steel shipbuilding and had managed to survive the depression years of the 1930s, a period when American shipbuilding all but ceased. In addition to these yards, Mare Island Naval Shipyard and Hunters Point Dry Docks provided well-established repair and shipbuilding facilities when the need arose.

Industrial expansion and population growth since 1900 had given the Bay Area untapped resources at the outset of World War II. One reason the Bay Area was selected as the site of the Kaiser yards and Marinship was availability of workers. Big shipyards along the northeast seaboard of the United States drew on the dense population of that region for workers. By the time America entered the war, those yards were operating at capacity and local skilled labor was fully employed. The Bay Area had also many miles of relatively undeveloped shoreline that contained several excellent shipyard sites. Smaller existing yards and potential sites existed along the deep-water channel in Stockton, accessible to the worker population of the Central Valley.

Proximity to the Pacific war made the Bay Area a logical ship production site. Victory in the Pacific depended on ships; all men and material had to reach the war zone by ship. Aircraft at the time had insufficient range to operate from mainland bases and the only way to get air bases nearer to Japan was to build them on islands seized by force through amphibious landings. San Francisco's Fort Mason was a well-established port of embarkation and Oakland had large (and expandable) army and navy shipping facilities. Fortunately, America's rail network in 1941 was intact, although it had suffered in the depression. Because of direct rail links between the Bay Area and industrial centers in the Midwest and East, a steady flow of steel and other material could sustain massive ship-building.

These four components, local experienced yards, ready labor supply and building sites, proximity to pacific war, and established transcontinental railroads set the stage for what would become the largest concentrated outpouring of ships in the history of the world.

EARLY STEEL SHIPBUILDING: 1885-1915

Steel shipbuilding was well established in the Bay Area by the start of World War II, largely through the early work of Union Iron Works. Two brothers, Peter and John Donahue, came west in 1849 like so many others to find gold. They found instead a dire need for their talent and experience, respectively, as a machinist and boiler maker. With $500 in pooled capital, they set up a blacksmith shop in San Francisco. By the Spring of 1850 their expanded operation, Union Iron and Brass Foundry, was making iron castings and working a blacksmith's forge and a small lathe. Their first iron casting was a spring bearing for the propellor shaft of the steamer *John S. McKim*. (First propellor-driven commercial vessel built in the United States.)

Within a few years Peter Donahue was sole proprietor of Union Iron Works. His shop built the machinery for the *Saginaw*, first Naval vessel built on the Pacific Coast. Although this little side-wheel steam gunboat gave Union Iron Works valuable shipbuilding experience, the main part of the business was in producing castings for a variety of steam engines, saw mills, grist mills, even cast iron store fronts, railings, balconies and fancy staircases. After 1860 the bulk of Union Iron Work's business stemmed from the great silver Comstock Bonanza.

Under the leadership of Irving M. Scott, Union Iron Works branched out after decline of the mining industry around 1880. Competition for agricultural machinery and railroad products was intense, so Scott turned to shipbuilding and moved Union Iron Works to thirty-two acres of land in San Francisco's Potrero District. Because of San Francisco's distance from eastern sources of parts, steel and machinery, Union Iron Works became a complete plant capable of making everything needed in a ship. From the company's first vessel in 1885— the 750-ton collier *Arago*— until 1902, the yard built seventy-five vessels. Between 1902 and the beginning of World War I, Union Iron Works merged with adjoining Risdon Iron Works, repaired ships, and built small craft and gold dredges. In October, 1917, the combined plants became Bethlehem Shipbuilding Corporation, Ltd.

SAN FRANCISCO MARITIME NHP P79-242x

Battleship *Oregon* at the outfitting dock, Union Iron Works' Potrero yard, San Francisco, near 22nd Street and 3rd Street. 1898.

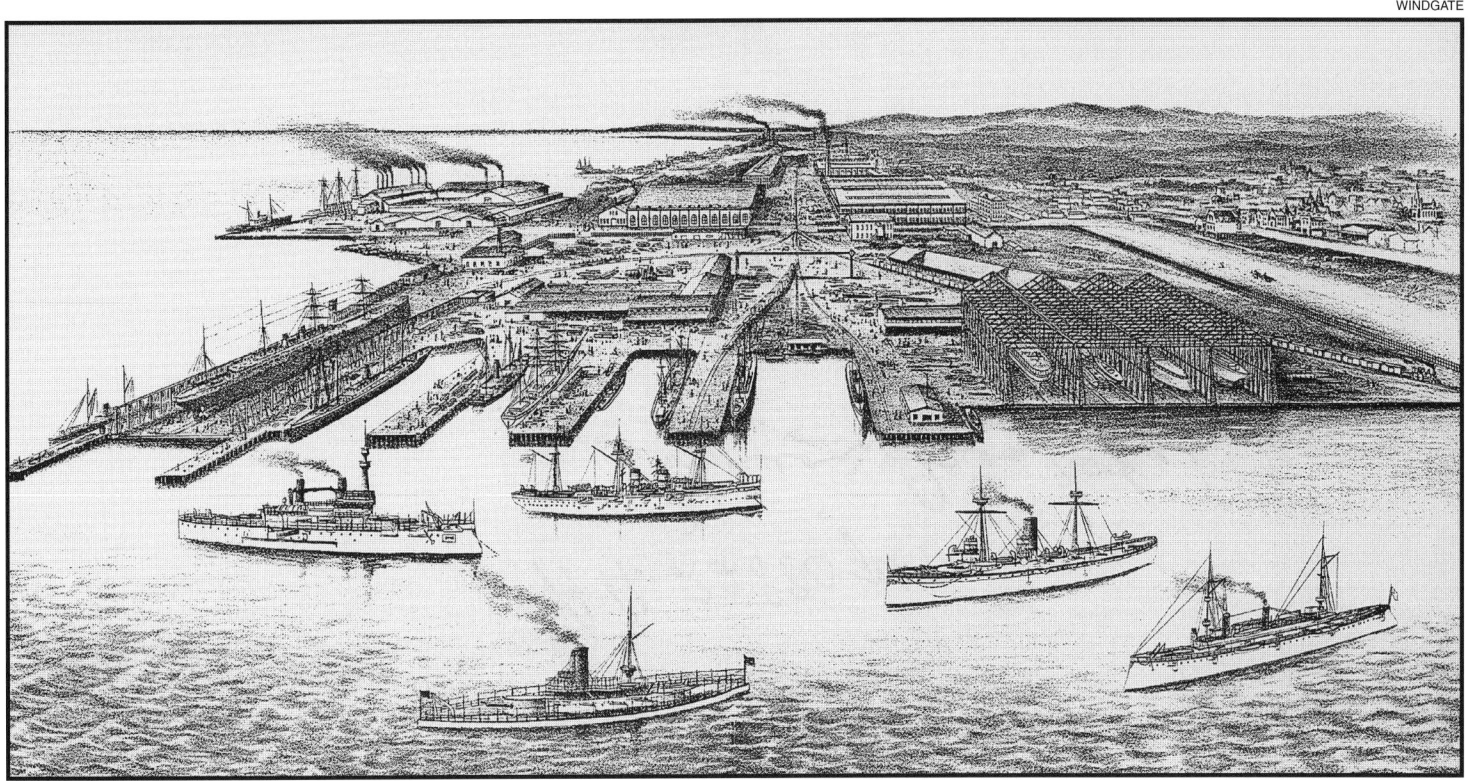

Above: Union Iron Works, San Francisco, looking south c.1900. Vessels in foreground are, left to right, battleship *Oregon*, monitor *Monterey* (front), cruiser *San Francisco*, cruiser *Charleston*, and cruiser *Olympia*.

Below: Union Iron Works, San Francisco, 1885.

Above: The tow boat *Dauntless* ready for launch at Risdon Iron Works, San Francisco, November 12, 1902.

Right: Another product of Union Iron Works was the cruiser *Olympia*, launched in 1892 and shown here at Mare Island's dry dock in 1895 before joining the Asiatic Fleet. *Olympia* was Admiral Dewey's flagship at the battle of Manila Bay in 1898.

WORLD WAR I PROGRAM: 1916-1921

When war broke out in Europe in 1914, America remained neutral, determined to stay out of the conflict. Within a year, the land war in Europe settled into an extended siege while war at sea consisted mainly of the British and German naval fleets fighting for dominance of the seaways. Both nations relied on maritime commerce for survival. Germany attempted to strangle England by sinking merchant ships of any nation destined for England. This unrestricted submarine warfare ultimately turned the tide of American opinion from neutrality to hostility. America entered World War I in 1917 on the side of Great Britain and France.

In many ways, America's wartime experience foreshadowed World War II twenty years later. Congress authorized an emergency Naval program of more and bigger battleships and warships of all types (396 in all, many completed after the war had ended). Merchant convoys to supply Britain became necessary and, for them to succeed, more submarines and destroyers were needed to protect them from German submarines. Wooden "subchasers," mine layers and minesweepers were hastily built in American shipyards.

Congress set up an emergency merchant shipbuilding program that delivered over 3,000 seagoing ships between 1917 and 1922. In the Bay Area, Moore & Scott and a few other established shipyards participated by building freighters and tankers, and Mare Island and Bethlehem built warships. Bethlehem in San Francisco began a major expansion. The old Risdon Iron Works yard, which had been taken over by Pacific Rolling Mills, became the United States Destroyer Plant, operated by Bethlehem for the Navy. Called the Risdon Plant, this section of Bethlehem turned out destroyers at the rate of three per month. The parent company became the Bethlehem Shipbuilding Corporation, Ltd. in 1917 and consolidated all operations at the Potrero plant. In all during the World War I program, Bethlehem, San Francisco, produced sixty-six destroyers and eighteen submarines. The last vessels were not delivered until 1924, six years after the armistice.

Above: One of sixty-six destroyers built by Bethlehem's Potrero yard during the wartime naval expansion between 1917 and 1924. With each launch, Bethlehem issued an official "medley" photograph showing the vessel, the sponsor and suitable decorations. January 15, 1919.

SS *Fresno*, built by Moore & Scott, on sea trials, June 20, 1918. This Oakland shipyard delivered 42 freighters and tankers to the U.S. shipping Board between 1917 and 1921.

WINDGATE

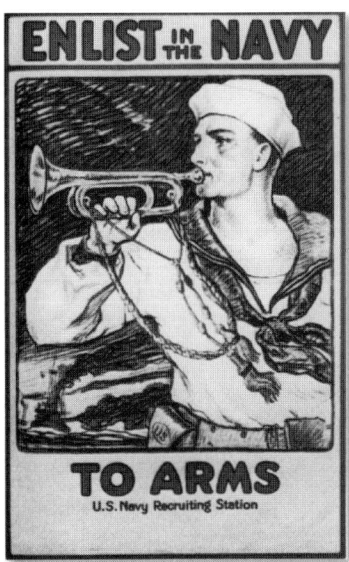

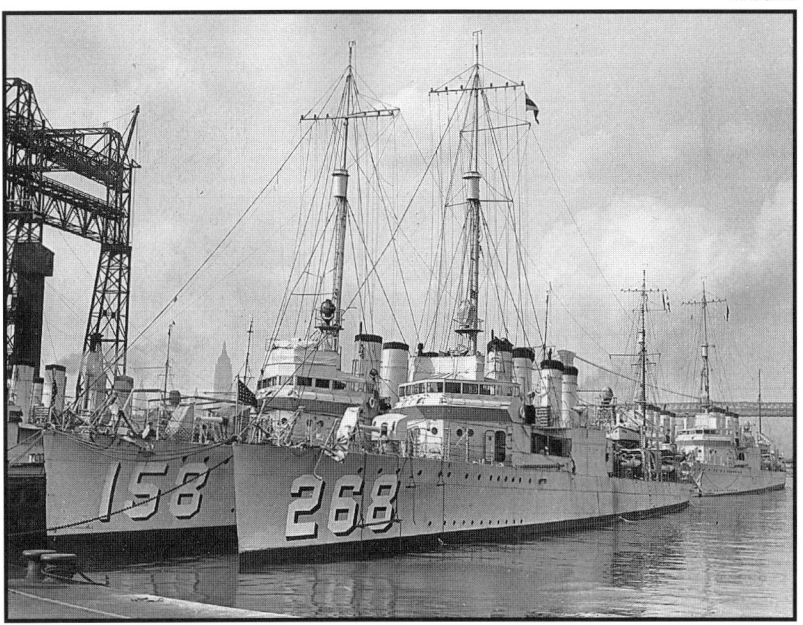

Above: Both Bethlehem and Mare Island Naval Shipyard built flush-deck "four piper" destroyers, the mainstay of America's destroyers forces in World War I and the years between the wars. At the outset of World War II, fifty of the old ships were sent to England as part of the "lend-lease" program, others served in World War II in various capacities including as minesweepers. Here, the USS *Leary* and USS *Shubrick* among others await their fates at the Brooklyn Navy Yard, 1940. *Leary* was scrapped in 1956, *Shubrick* was sunk by a German submarine in 1943.

SAN FRANCISCO MARITIME NHP P79-071a Scr55:c pl.779

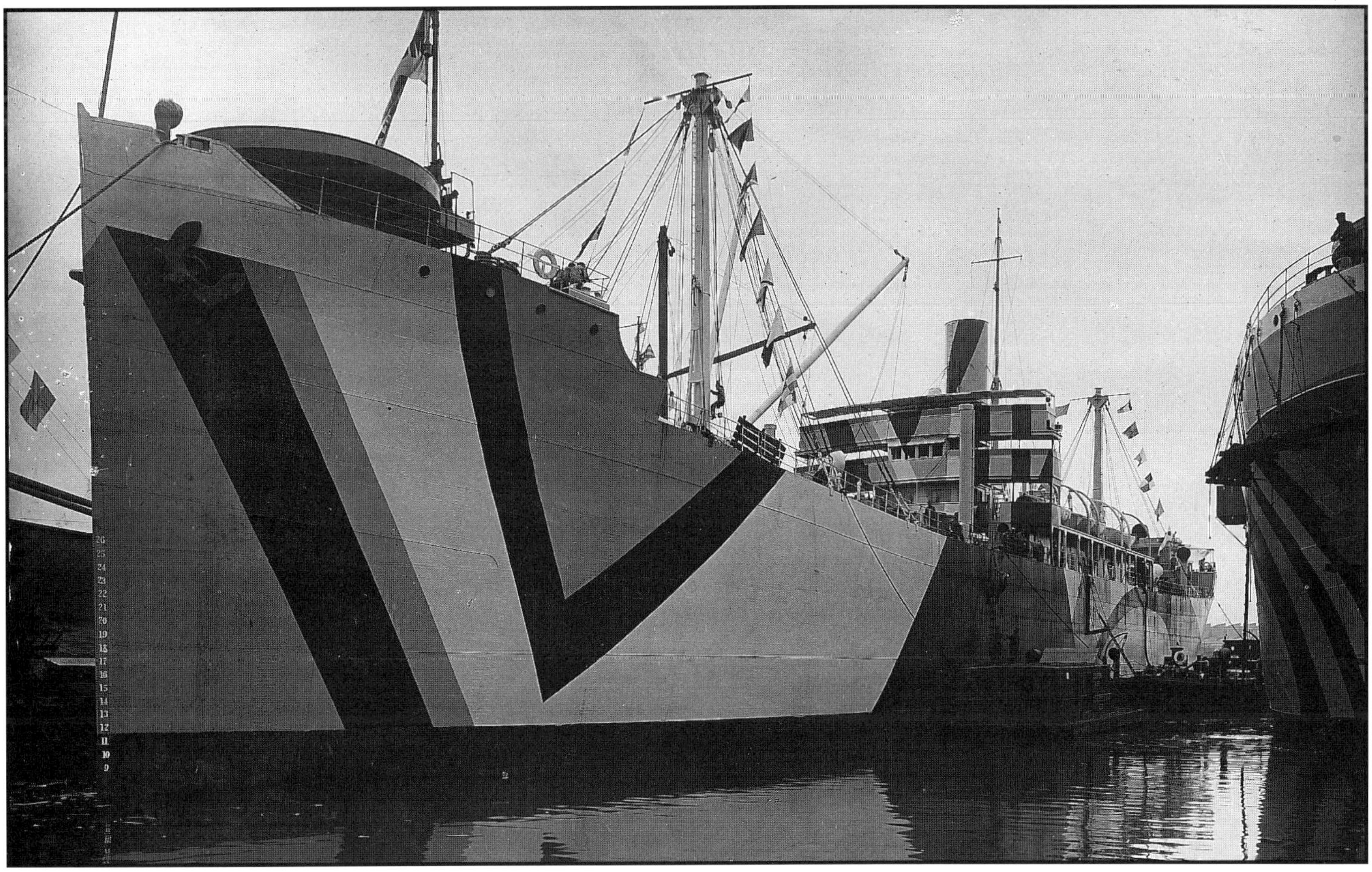

SS *Alloway*, July 3, 1918. Moore-built 9,400-ton freighters were 402 feet long by 53 feet beam. Merchant vessels and warships alike were delivered painted in dazzle camouflage. The striking bold blue, gray and deep red patterns were intended to present a confusing silhouette to the enemy.

SAN FRANCISCO MARITIME NHP P79-071a Scr55:a pl.355

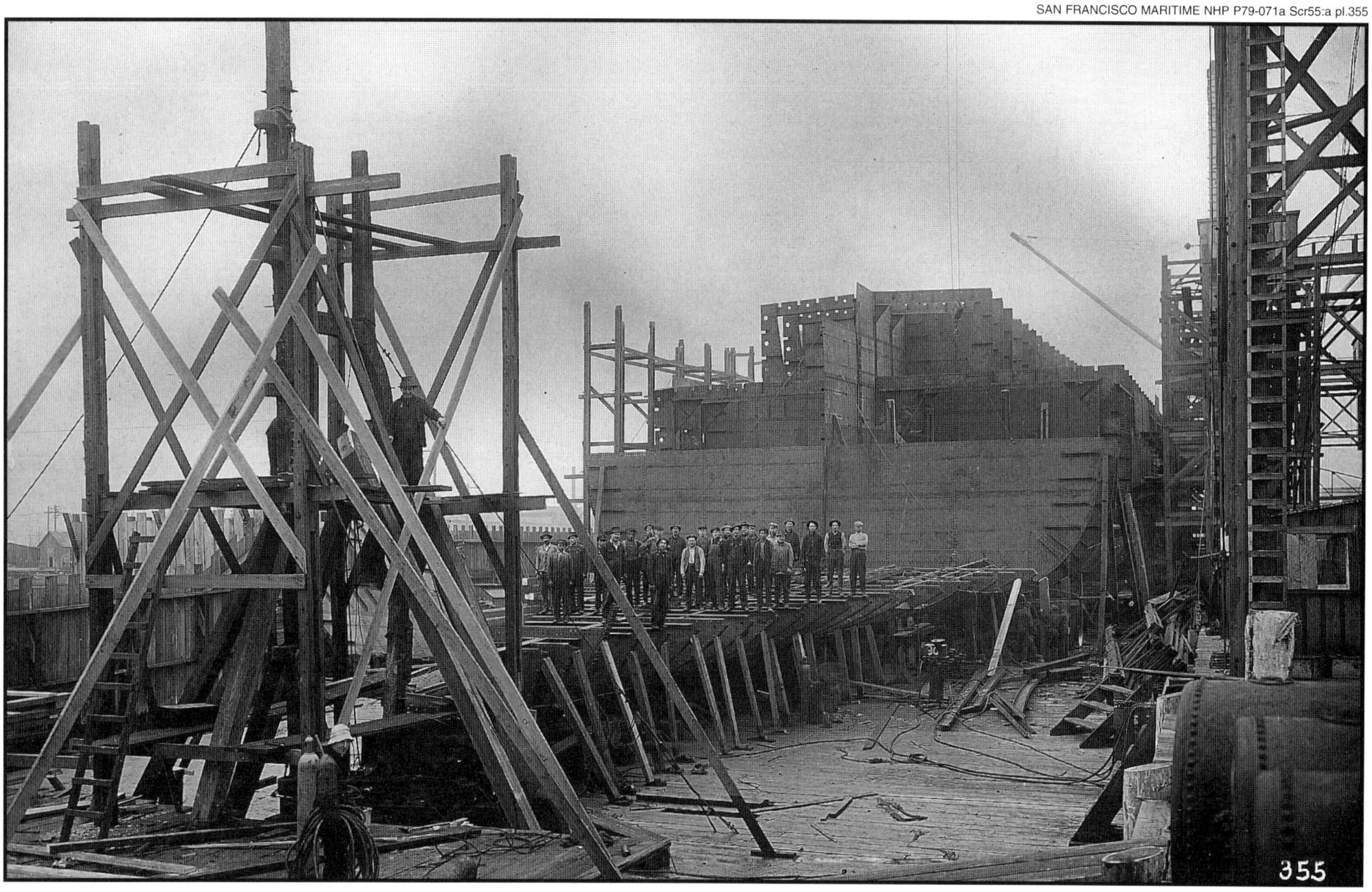

Isherwood-type tanker *Frederic R. Kellogg* under construction at Moore & Scott, January 11, 1917.
(Moore & Scott became Moore Shipbuilding in January, 1918.)

Moore & Scott built tankers during World War I, some using the Isherwood System, an English development of 1906. Isherwood hulls had a series of transverse bulkheads with hull plating riveted to longitudinal stringers. The system lent itself well to tankers since the hull compartments served as ready-made oil tanks. From the exterior, an Isherwood ship looked no different from one built using traditional methods. A similar system of transverse bulkheads was incorporated in tankers built in World War II at Marinship (See Page 69).

SAN FRANCISCO MARITIME NHP P79-071a Scr55:a pl.443

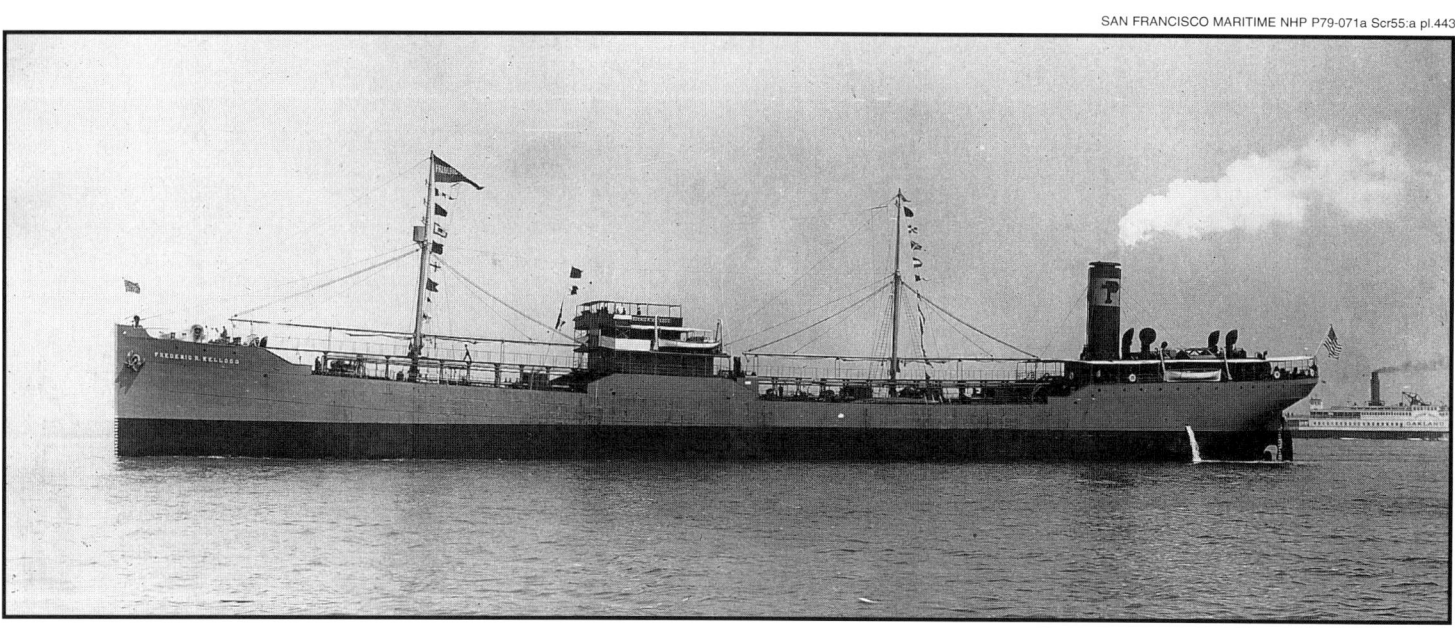

Frederic R. Kellogg, built for Pan American Petroleum & Transport Company at 10,447 deadweight tons, considered large by World War I standards. July 28, 1917.

SAN FRANCISCO MARITIME NHP P79-071a Scr55:b pl.922

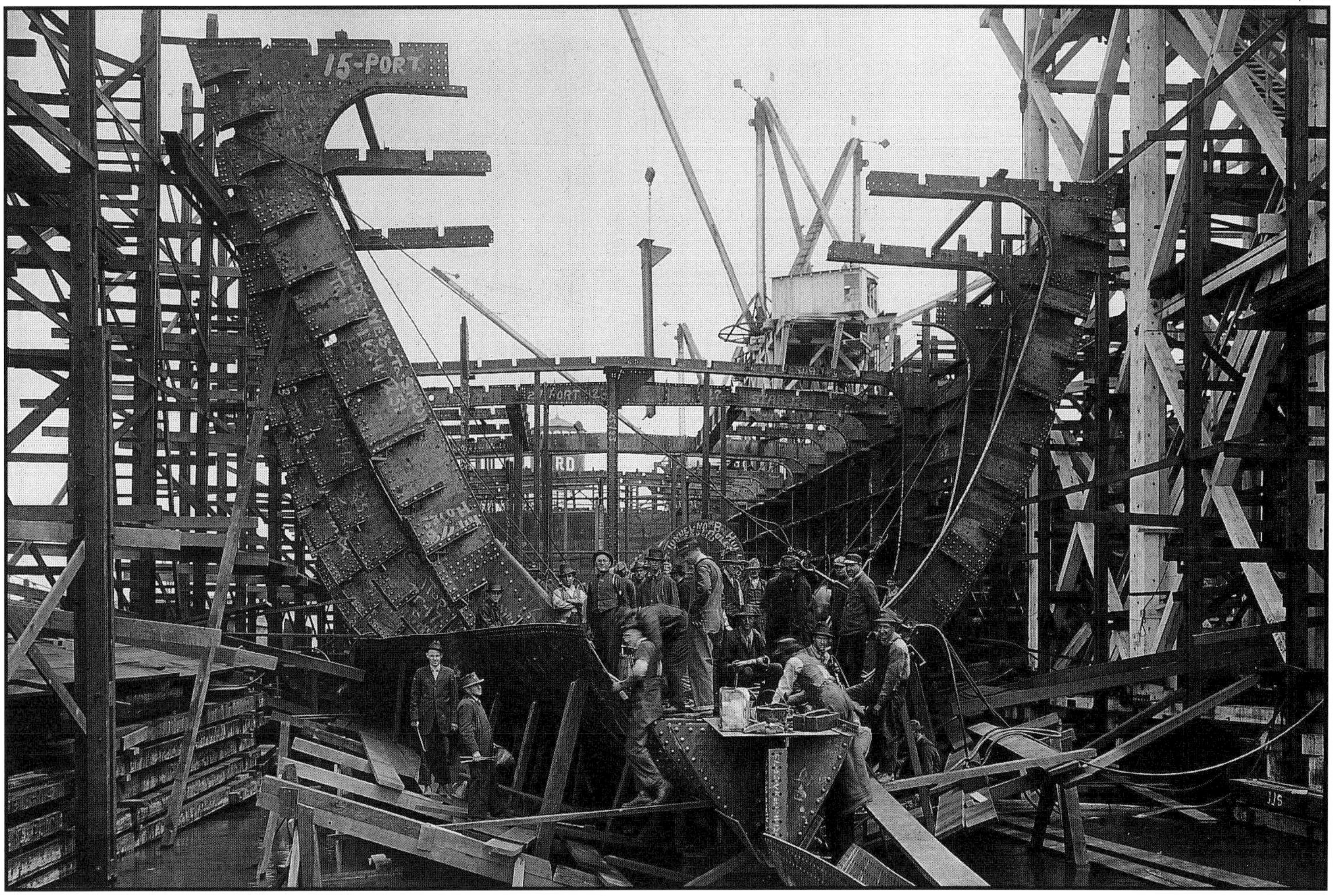

Stern view, freighter SS *Yaquina* at Moore Shipbuilding Company, May 8, 1918.

Traditional steel shipbuilding in World War I was little changed except for materials since the days of wooden ships. Hull plates were riveted to closely-spaced frames, as shown above, forming a large cargo space within the frames. For tankers built this way, storage tanks had to be placed within the hull, adding weight and cost.

Early in the program, a ship typically took twelve to fourteen months from keel-laying to delivery. In 1920, Moore delivered a tanker in 100 days, a record for World War I. Moore also set a record on October 11, 1919, by launching six ships on a single tide, an event that presaged the output competition of World War II shipyards.

SAN FRANCISCO MARITIME NHP P79-071a Scr55:d pl.1096

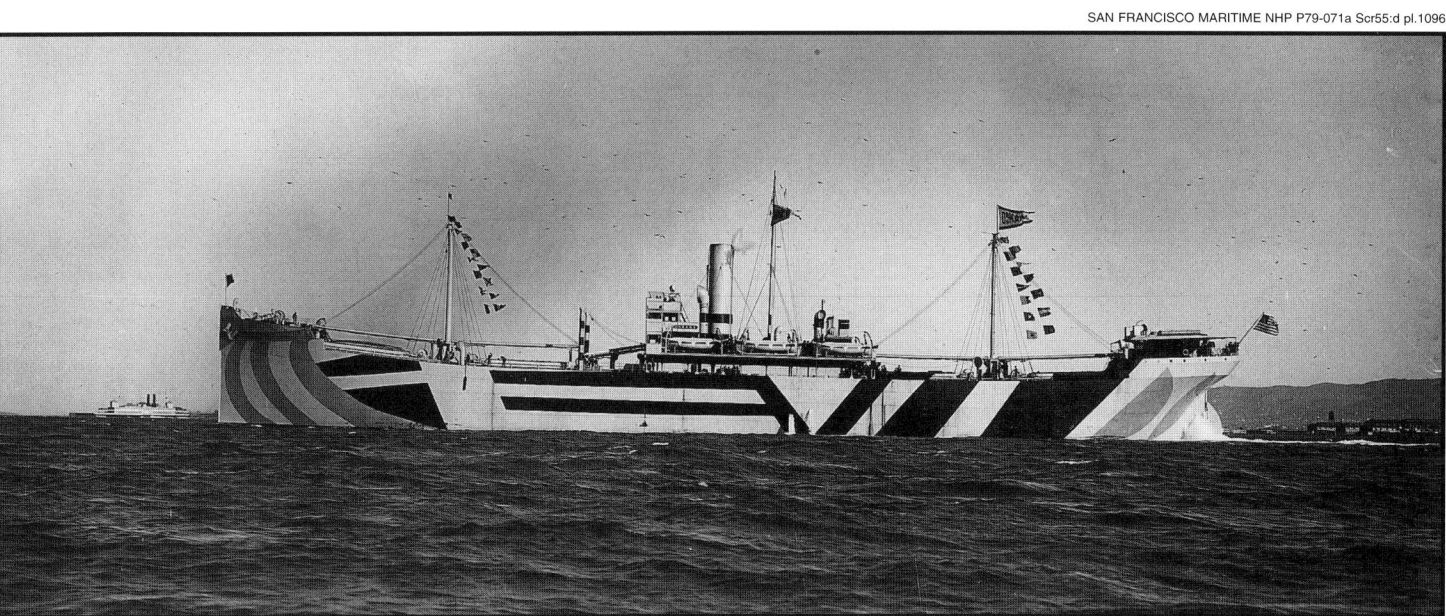

Traditional plate-on-frame freighter SS *Oskawa*, Moore Shipbuilding, December 29, 1918.

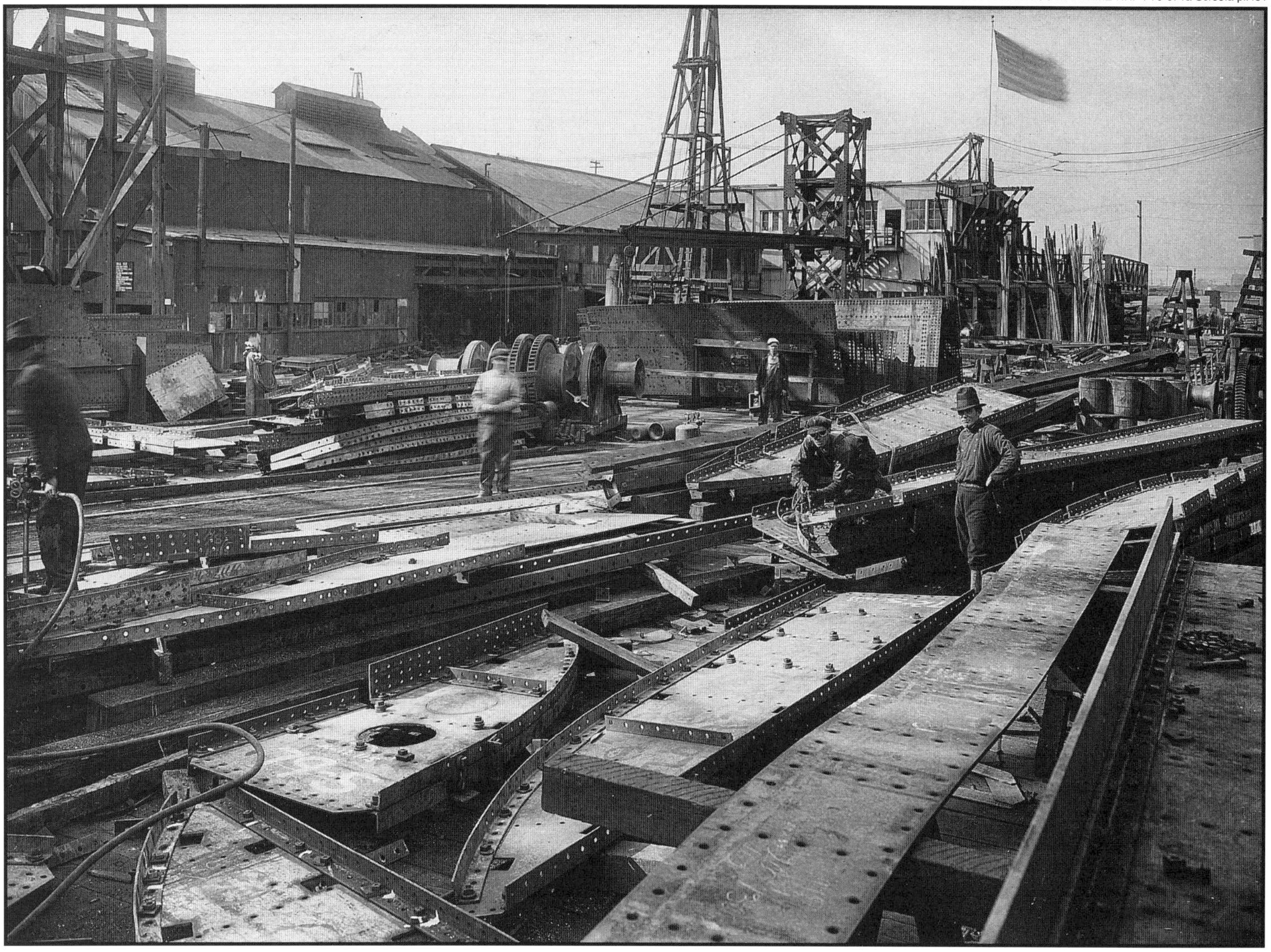

Thousands of rivet holes characterized World War I ship construction. Here, curved floor pieces for the inner-bottom and hull plates of Hull 115 (SS *Yellowstone*) are racked for installation, Moore & Scott, August 23, 1917.

Ships in World War I took longer to build than in World War II primarily because they were riveted rather than welded. Welding was introduced in American ships prior to World War I although none had an entirely welded hull. Riveted ships were strong and durable, and their steel framing and bulkheads created large cargo spaces. But riveted hulls had drawbacks. Chief among them, the man-hours required. To place each rivet took two workers, one on either side of the plates being fastened. But to reach that point required the efforts of at least two other workers. A "driller" had to position each hole in the proper place and drill through the one-inch-thick hull plate. After the plates were aligned on the frames they seldom matched precisely the pre-drilled or punched holes, so a "reamer" had to enlarge the holes to eliminate overlap. The weight of rivets needed to fasten hull and deck plates could add over 300 tons to a ships hull thus decreasing the vessel's payload. Strong as they were, rivets could pop loose under stress or when hull plates were damaged. Unless the exterior heads of the rivets were flush with the hull, they added drag that could slow the ship at sea.

A bull riveter heating rivets in a gas-fed forge, Moore Shipbuilding, July 26, 1919. A rivet-making machine produced the approximately 150,000 rivets needed for each hull but each rivet had to be driven individually by a team of workers.

SAN FRANCISCO MARITIME NHP P79-071a Scr55:h pl.2198

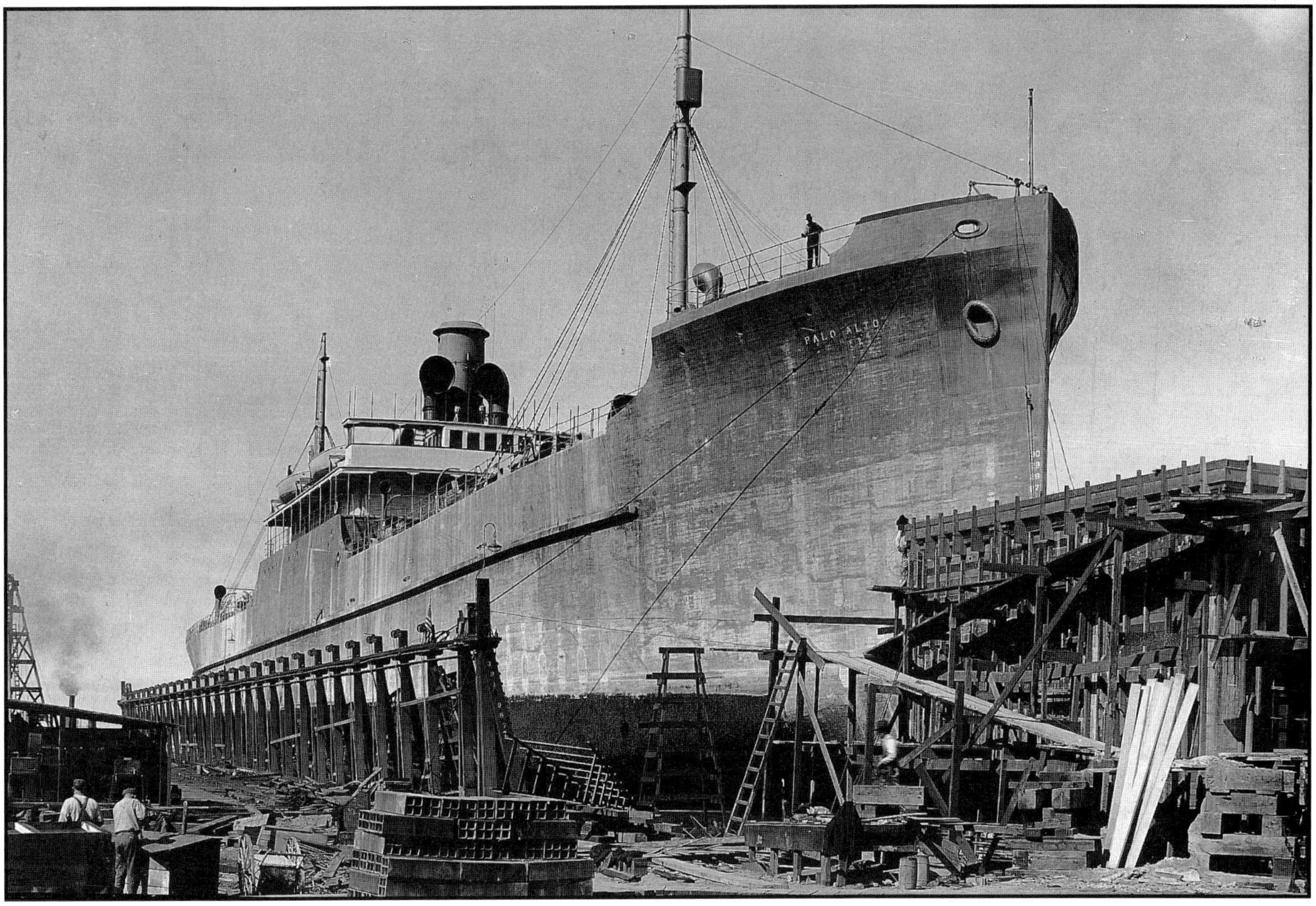

Oil tanker *Palo Alto*, shown here in Moore's dry dock, June 18, 1920, was built that year by the San Francisco Shipbuilding Company in Oakland for the U.S. shipping Board. She was, at 7,500 tons, the world's largest concrete-hulled ship at that time.

Pacific Coast yards constructed both wooden sailing vessels and steam powered wooded freighters during World War I. Although steel ships had largely replaced wooden ships in ocean-going commerce by 1916, many shipwrights and carpenters experienced in wooden shipbuilding were available and suitable timber was abundant in America's forests. The Emergency Fleet Corporation decided to build 700 wooden steamers as part of America's "bridge of ships" to aid our European allies. Of the total, 334 were to be built on the Pacific Coast, mainly in the Northwest. Of approximately 30 Pacific Coast yards building wooden vessels for the Emergency Fleet Corporation, seven were old-time yards, ten were established for the civilian boom in wooden ships of 1916, and thirteen were built solely for Emergency Fleet ships. In the Bay Area, Benicia Shipbuildng Company, the old Matthew Turner yard in Benicia, completed three vessels. Additionally, hundreds of wooden barges and wooden sailing vessels were built along the Pacific Coast. The wooden ship program was heavily criticized after the war for producing ships that were obsolete for peacetime merchant marine purposes.

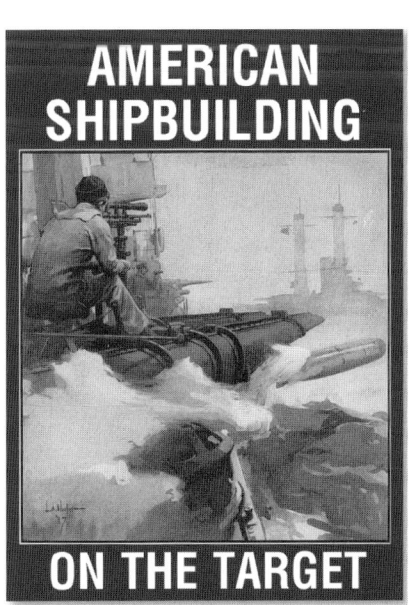

Making vessels from concrete rather than steel was an idea that emerged from the Emergency Shipbuilding Program of World War I (and reintroduced in World War II). Poured concrete hulled vessels proved durable and economical but slow to complete. After the war, little demand remained for new ships, concrete, wood or steel.

BETWEEN THE WARS: 1922-1936

Shipbuilding in America languished after World War I. The merchant marine in 1920, ten times the size of that of 1914, was left with far too many ships for existing commerce, and the Navy had too many warships to maintain. Bay Area shipyards finished their wartime contracts then turned to repair and maintenance or struggled to find other means to make ends meet. The huge emergency shipyard at Hog Island, near Philadelphia, had turned out 122 freighters, all too late for the war. The ships were laid up or sold to high bidders for a fraction of their cost. Hundreds of other merchant ships were cut up for scrap, sold to other countries, or laid up in reserve. A national shift to disarmament throughout the 1920s resulted in a greatly reduced Navy.

With the depression in 1929 came even greater cutbacks in maritime trades as worldwide trade dwindled. Between 1922 and 1937, only two ocean-going dry cargo freighters, a handful of tankers and about twenty passenger/cargo ships were built in American shipyards. Naval construction, limited by international treaty, slowed considerably. Mare Island Naval Shipyard, one of the few U.S. Navy yards nationwide, built between 1922 and 1936, one submarine, two destroyers, two heavy cruisers and a garbage lighter.

WINDGATE

The combined Battle Force and Scouting Force of the United States Fleet gathered at Coco Solo Naval Base at the Panama Canal during fleet maneuvers, 1933.

Above: Two-year-old battleship USS *Mississippi* at Hunters Point in 1919. This ship and several others of the fleet shifted their home bases from the Atlantic Coast to the Pacific after World War I. San Diego was developed into a major Navy base in the 1920s, bringing more maintenance and repair business to Bay Area shipyards. *Mississippi* was home-ported at San Pedro from 1919 to 1923 and spent most of her career operating in the Pacific. She was present in Tokyo Bay for the Japanese surrender in 1945.

Left: The 73 vessels present at Coco Solo, almost half of all the Navy ships in commission at the time, included the aircraft carriers *Lexington* and *Saratoga* and the old *Langley*, nine battleships, twelve heavy cruisers, thirty-eight destroyers, and eleven auxiliaries. Twelve years later at the end of World War II, the Navy had grown fifteen-fold and was the largest, most modern fleet in the world.

THE HAGGIN MUSEUM

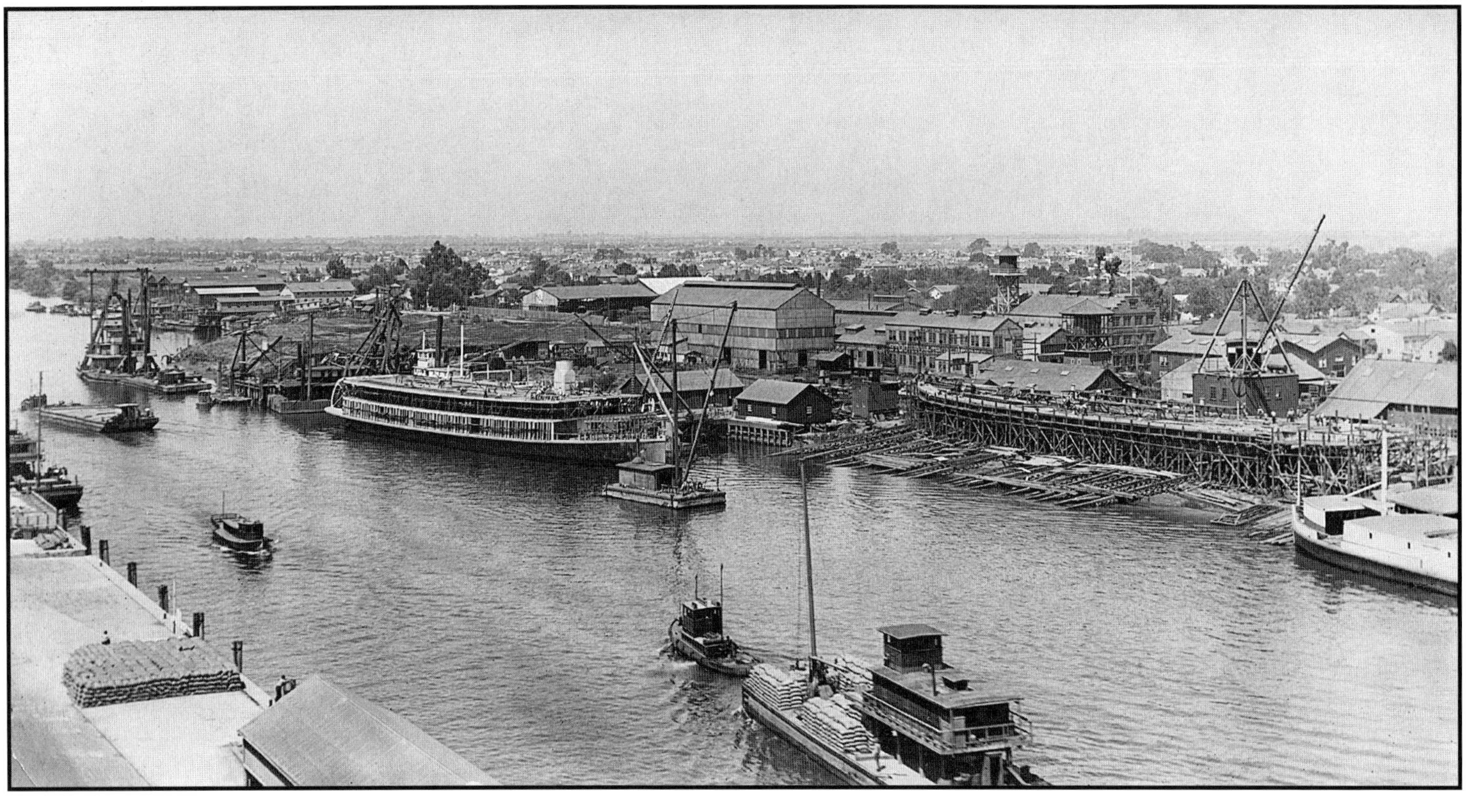

Riverboats *Delta King,* left, and *Delta Queen* under construction at the California Transportation Company's Harrison Street yard on the Stockton Channel, c.1926. Both vessels served in World War II ferrying troops to and from ships in San Francisco Bay.

SAN FRANCISCO MARITIME NHP P85-100.84pl

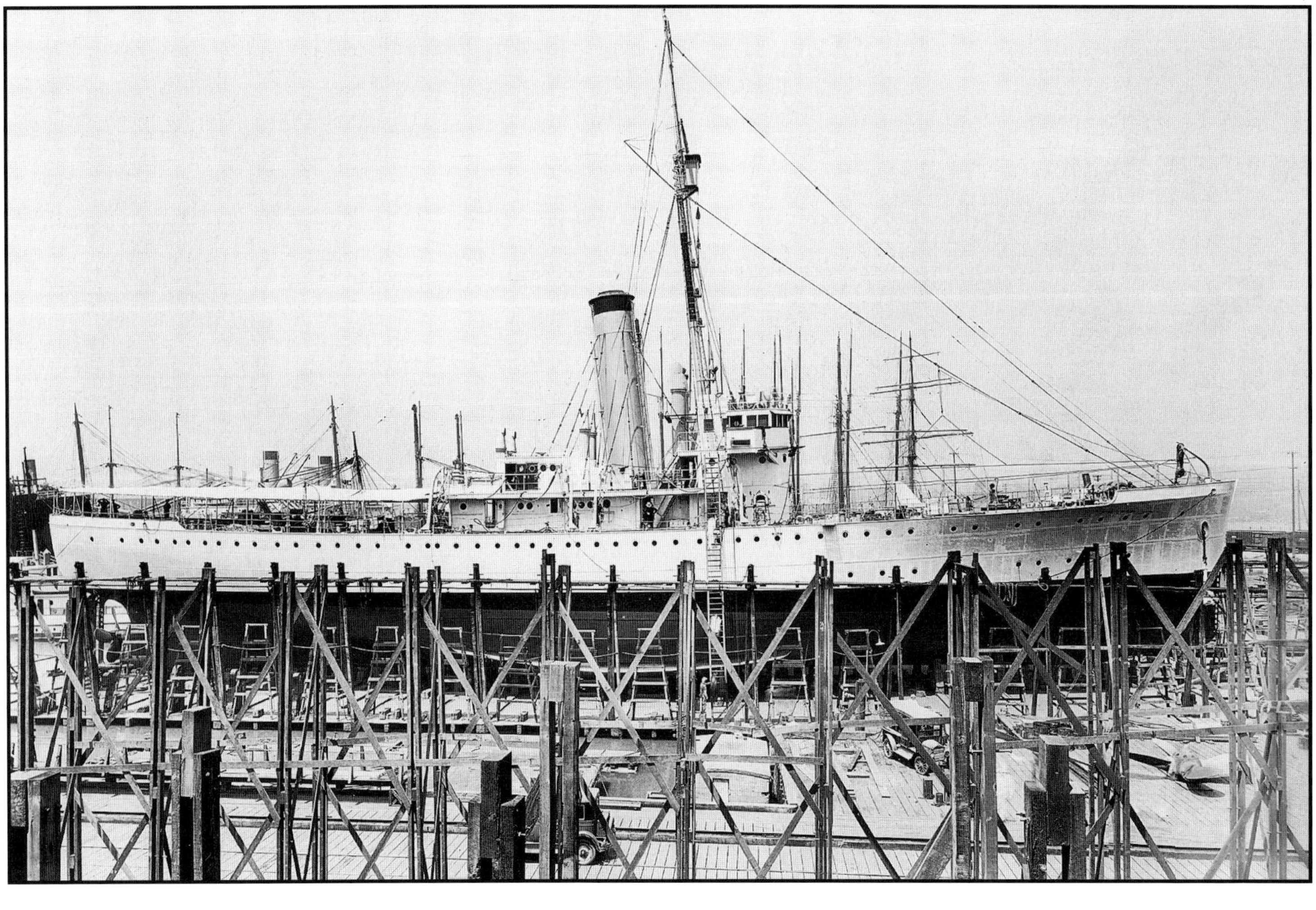

The 250-foot Coast Guard cutter *Sebago,* built by General Engineering & Dry Dock Company in 1930, was one of eight cutters built by the company during the 1930s.

Although shipbuilding in the United States slowed to a crawl between the wars, technical developments advanced the state of ship design and construction. Coal-burning ships were phased out in favor of oil-burners. Diesel engines and turbo-electric drives were improved and applied to more types of vessels. Ships got faster and safer, with better radio and other electronic navigation. Steam boilers became more efficient with higher pressures and operating temperatures. New types of vessels, such as aircraft carriers and small landing craft, were developed that would later play important roles in World War II.

SAN FRANCISCO MARITIME NHP P85-100.294pl

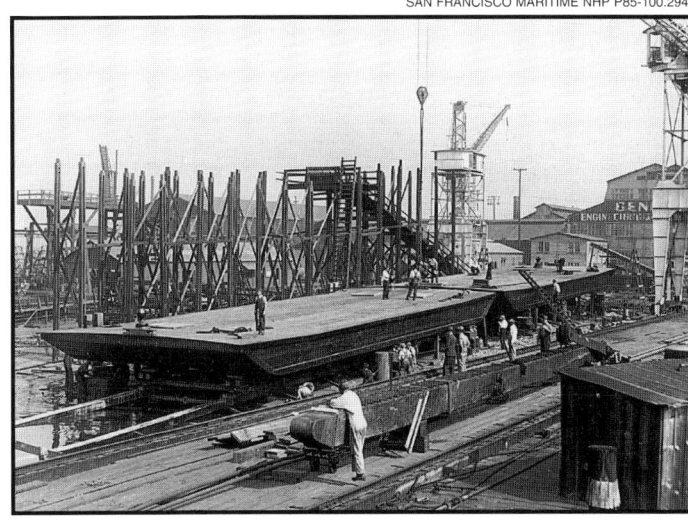

Right: Like most other shipyards during the depression, General Engineering welcomed any contract. Here, two barges occupy a shipway prior to launch in the mid-1930s.

WINDGATE

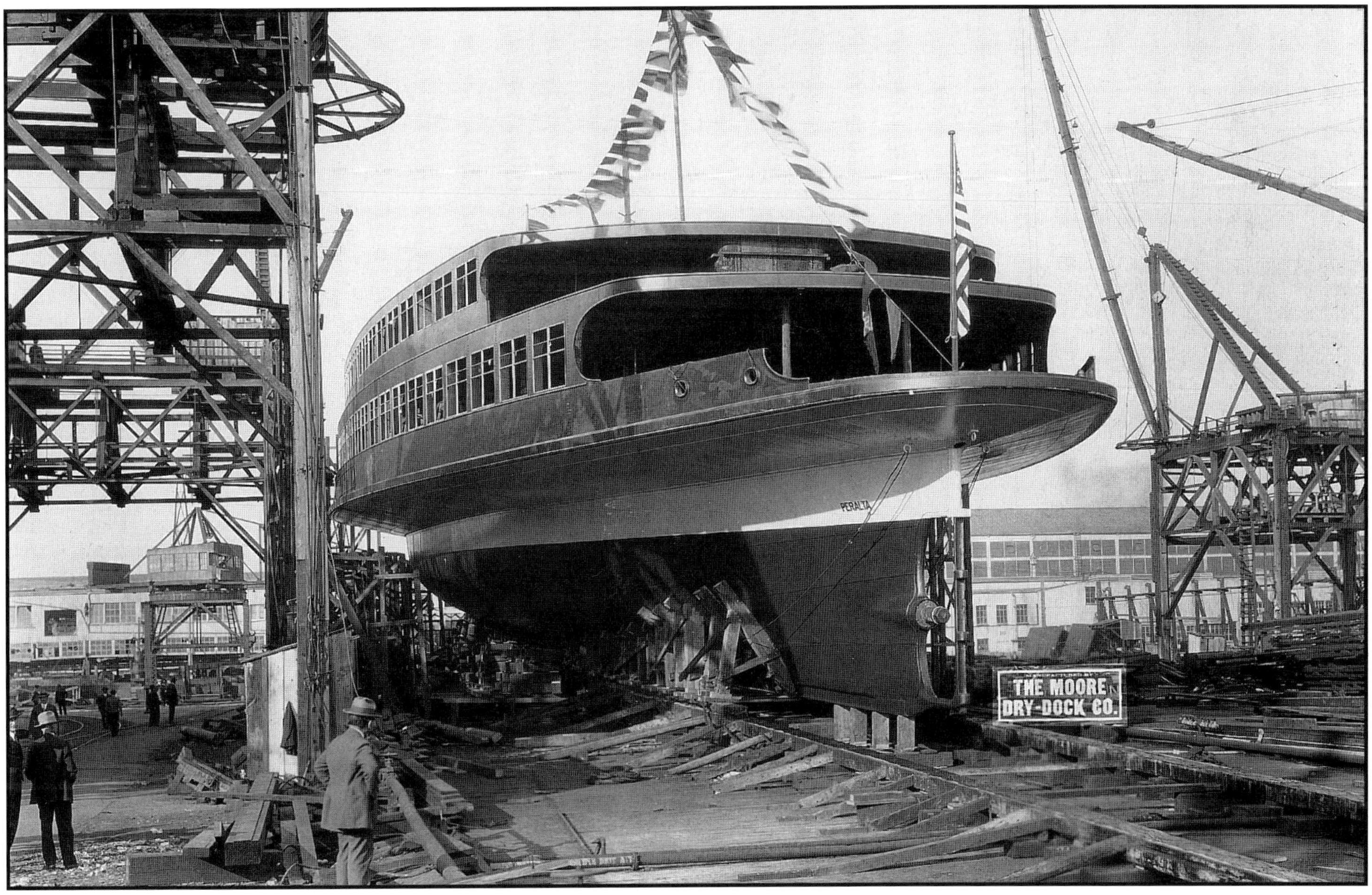

Moore Dry Dock Company built barges and dredges in the 1920s and early 1930s, plus several ferry boats including the *Peralta*, shown here October 14, 1926.

Above: The USS *California*, launched in 1919, was the only battleship ever built at Mare Island. She was damaged at Pearl Harbor but, after repairs, served throughout the Pacific war.

Mare Island became a key Naval installation on the Pacific Coast and gave the Bay Area more of a strategic position in the event of a Pacific war. Although most naval construction in the 1930s took place in eastern yards, both Mare Island and Bethlehem built warships.

Below: Mare Island Naval Shipyard, seen from across the strait in Vallejo. The two old protected cruisers in the background, *Cincinnati* and *Raleigh*, were sold by the Navy in 1921, the probable date of this photo.

Above: the new Northampton Class heavy cruiser *Chicago*, launched at Mare Island Naval Shipyard in 1930 was one of two cruisers built there in the 1930s. The other was the Astoria Class USS *San Francisco*, launched in 1933. Both ships, and the *California*, saw heavy action in World War II (*California* was damaged at Pearl Harbor, *Chicago* was sunk in the Solomon Islands, 1943, *San Francisco* damaged at Guadalcanal).

Below: A flush-deck destroyer, left foreground, almost hidden in the dry dock at Mare Island in the 1930s.

THE BUILDUP: 1936-1941

Hitler's rise to power in Germany in the 1930s and the rapid buildup of naval forces by Japan, Germany and Great Britain prompted major revaluation of America's ability to fight another war. Recognition that success in any future war would depend on America's naval and merchant marine superiority, Congress and President Roosevelt, revitalized American shipbuilding. In 1936 Congress passed the Merchant Marine Act, followed immediately by formation of the United States Maritime Commission, in part with an eye toward the possibility of a future war. The new commission's mandate was "to develop and maintain a merchant marine sufficient to carry a substantial portion of the water-borne export and import foreign commerce of the United States on the best-equipped, safest, and most suitable type of vessels owned, operated and constructed by citizens of the United States, manned with a trained personnel and capable of serving as a naval and military auxiliary in time of war or national emergency." The first act in 1937 of the new commission authorized a long-range program, construction of fifty new vessels a year for the next ten years.

The five men appointed to the Commission well remembered America's experiences in World War I, just fifteen years earlier, when merchant ships could not be produced in sufficient numbers quickly enough to affect the outcome of the war. This time, they determined, America would not be caught unprepared. While a threat of war existed in 1936, no one could have foreseen the magnitude of the Commission's responsibility over the next decade.

Congress also greatly increased Naval appropriations; Navy yards were reactivated and expanded. Although the number of new warships produced in the 1930s was small compared to wartime production, the vessels were modern and greatly improved over their World War I counterparts. Even newer and superior designs were under review and consideration when the war began. On the eve of World War II, the United States Navy was large by standards of the time but far from modernized. As of December 7, 1941, the Navy comprised fewer than 200 combat vessels on active duty and approximately another 100 smaller craft and auxiliary vessels. Of the combat vessels, only sixty-two could be classified as major warships. Of 17 battleships, all but two (*North Carolina* and *Washington*) had been designed prior to World War I. Of 171 destroyers in commission in 1941 (only 71 on active duty), over one third were of World War I vintage. Over half of American submarines were World War I types, and had been in reserve during the 1920s and 1930s and recalled to active duty in 1941.

Reinvigorated shipbuilding beginning in 1936 brought new life to Bay Area shipyards and gave them a running start before World War II. Government contracts enabled local yards such as Moore and Bethlehem to modernize and expand. The big northeastern shipyards,

SAN FRANCISCO MARITIME NHP P79-071a Scr55:p pl.4383

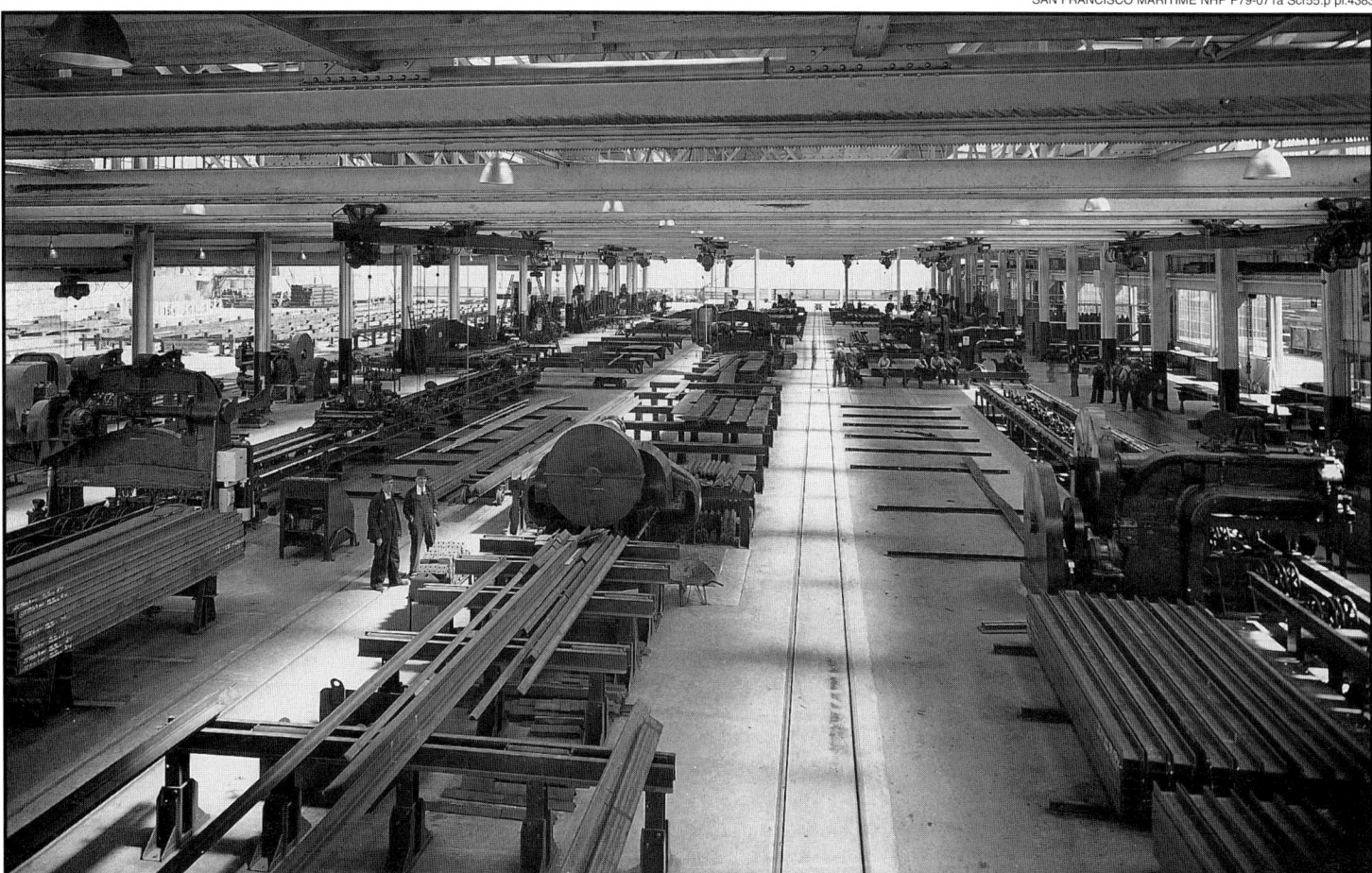

Moore Dry Dock Company, September 15, 1937. Expansion included this new steel fabricating shop. In 1939 keels for two C3 freighters were laid, first of over 100 Moore ships for the Maritime Commission and Navy.

Newport News, Federal, New York, Sun, and Bethlehem, got the first round of Maritime Commission contracts in 1937, but the Bay Area was represented soon after. Late in 1938 Moore received the first Maritime Commission contract placed with a Pacific Coast yard. Western Pipe and Steel reopened and expanded the yard in South San Francisco where cargo vessels had been built during World War I.

In 1940, Congress boosted the original Naval production goal of America's shipyards by seventy percent, adding to the already busy workload of shipyards. Bethlehem in San Francisco, revived by Maritime Commission contracts, was assigned to do Navy work exclusively. Moore Dry Dock, busy with Maritime Commission work, began to receive Navy contracts as well. Although adequate supplies of steel existed to meet new orders, machinery necessary for fast modern ships was in short supply. Congress gave the Navy top priority for turbine engines and other scarce components and tools. In June, 1940, only six private shipyards nationwide were working on Navy contracts. The Navy program was expanded again after Pearl Harbor. By the spring of 1942, there were over sixty yards engaged in Navy work.

By the time the Maritime Commission began its emergency program in late 1940, layered atop its 1937 long-range program, America's shipyards were at full capacity. Added to an order for 200 new ships was a British order for 60 cargo ships to help compensate for their heavy losses. By December 7, 1941, the emergency program had been expanded three times before even the first ship had been launched. The only way to accommodate the increased demand was to build more shipways. That meant adding more ways to existing yards and building entirely new yards.

As the pace of shipbuilding in the Bay Area and nationwide increased, advances made in shipbuilding techniques between the wars came into play. Steel pre-fabrication and pre-assembly of major parts of a ship's hull increased in importance as ship types became more standardized. Interchangeability of parts and assembly-line methods common to other manufacturing operations could be applied effectively to shipbuilding only when the rate of production accelerated. Shipyards saved time because the Maritime Commission ships generally were standardized and contracts for them were awarded in groups of four or six vessels rather than one at a time.

Moore Dry Dock Company, April 29, 1937, shows the variety of work in progress. At left are two floating dry docks. Wartime expansion of the yard took place to the left (west) of this photo.

SAN FRANCISCO MARITIME NHP P79-071a P82-125a.3958nl

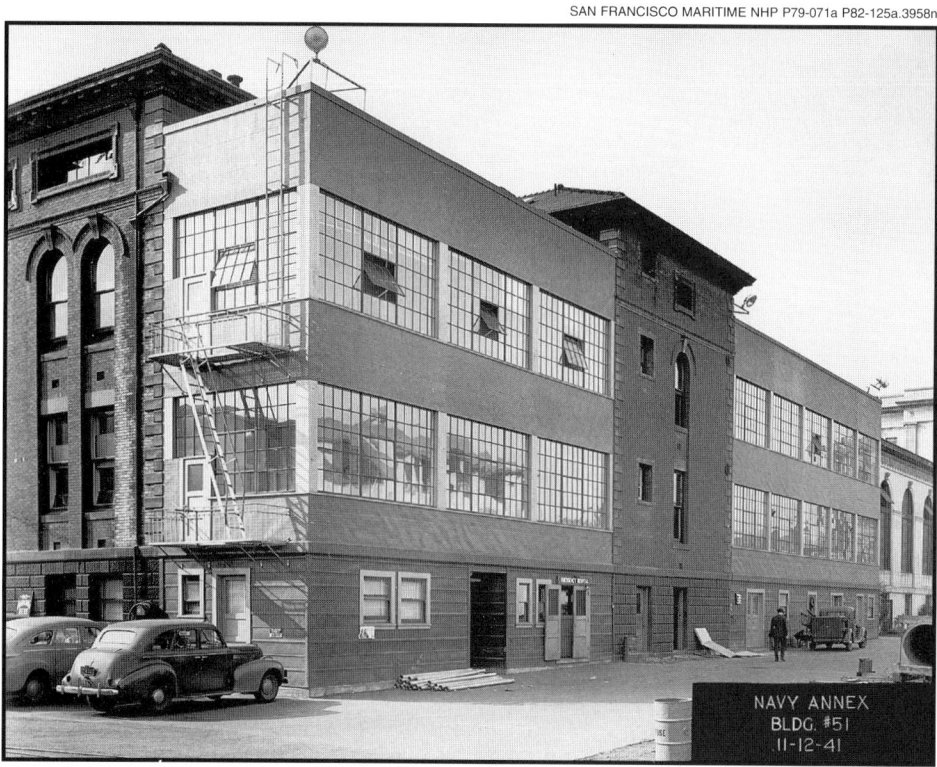

Right: Bethlehem, San Francisco, added this new yard hospital wing to an older brick building in 1941, seen here just days after the attack on Pearl Harbor.

SAN FRANCISCO MARITIME NHP P83-119.8pl

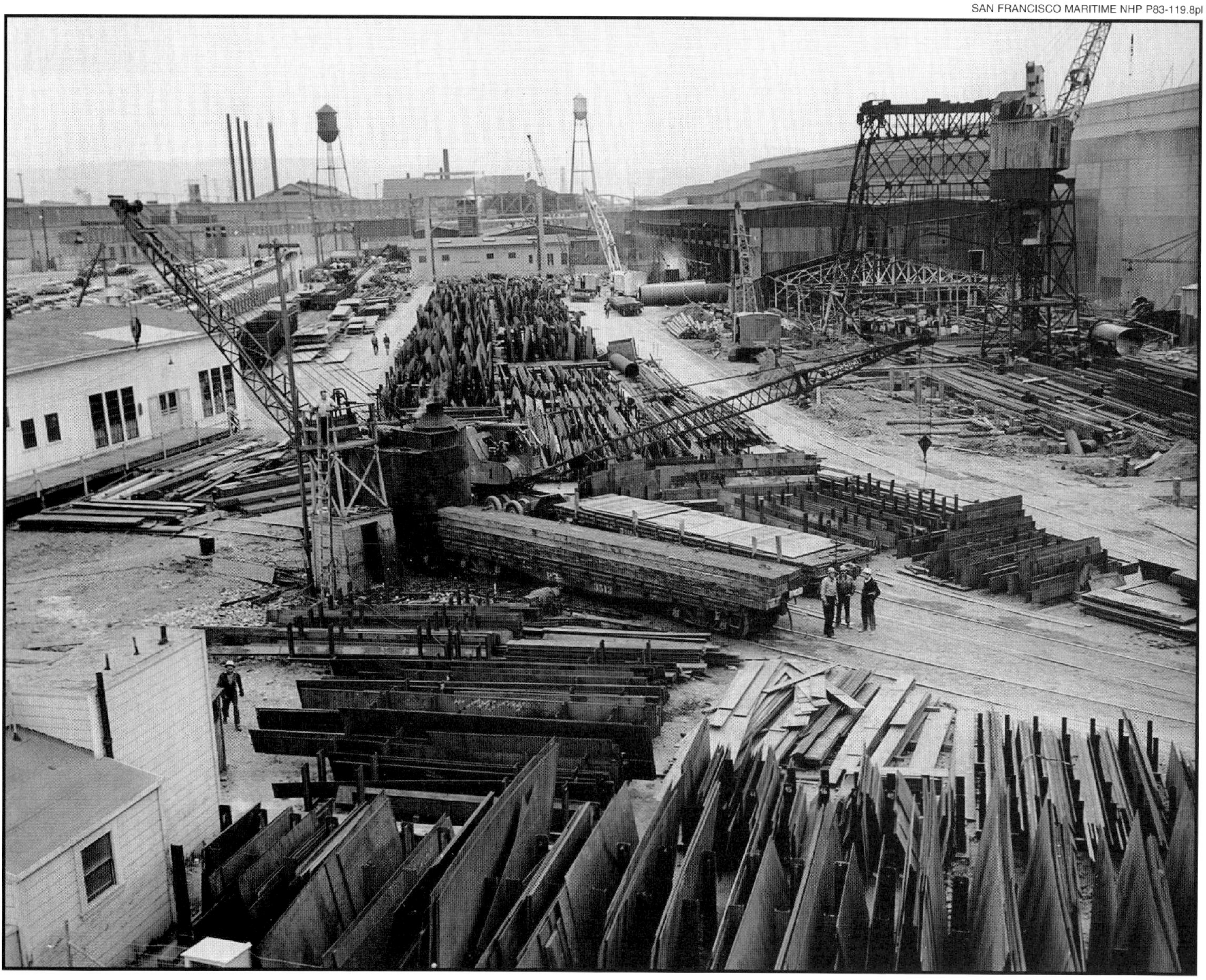

Western Pipe and Steel storage yard, 1941, filled with steel plate for new cargo ships as new plate shop rises at right.

As shipyard expansion continued, the Navy and the Maritime Commission competed for available ways. In March, 1941, a Presidential conference sorted out competing interests and assigned certain yards to Navy work, others to Maritime Commission work, and still others to a combination of the two. Moore Dry Dock and Western Pipe and Steel were in the latter category.

Western Pipe and Steel Company, located in Richmond before World War I, made sewer and water pipe, storage tanks and other steel structures. During World War I the company opened a plant in South San Francisco and built eighteen cargo ships between 1918 and 1920. The yard remained open between the wars but conducted little business. A Maritime Commission order in 1940 for five C-1 freighters followed by an order for five C3's rejuvenated the yard. New contracts came thereafter in rapid succession and the company built a second side-launch shipway. In September, 1940, a contract came for four C-3's for Isthmian Lines but these were completed for the Navy. A contract in May, 1941, called for 17 C3 hulls modified for various special uses; two Army, nine Navy and six Maritime Commission. Of fourteen more C3's, six were completed as APA attack transports. The final vessels at Western Pipe and Steel were six A4's completed in 1945-6 for American President Lines. The company also had a yard in San Pedro to build ships for the Navy, including ice breakers and amphibious landing craft.

Western Pipe & Steel's new side-launch ways under construction for expansion program. July 24, 1941.
After the war Western Pipe and Steel became Consolidated Western Steel Corporation.

SAN FRANCISCO MARITIME NHP P82-125a.5456pl

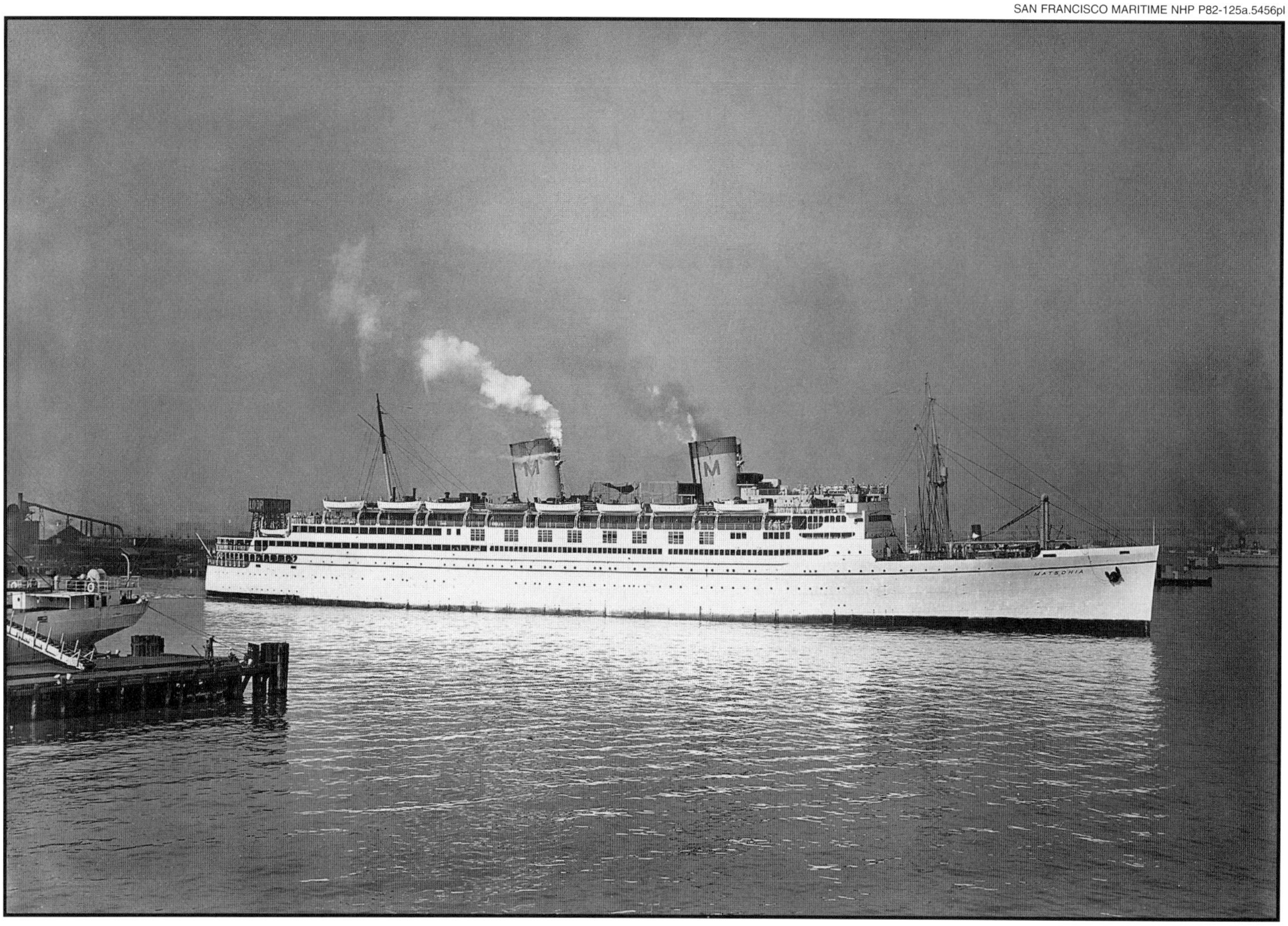

Matson Line's SS *Matsonia* in her pre-war livery promised adventure and luxury between San Francisco, Hawaii and Asia. She served Matson as *Malolo* from 1927 to 1937 when she was reconditioned and renamed *Matsonia*. January 5, 1937.

1st EXTRA Evening Telegraph 1st EXTRA

WAR!

SAN FRANCISCO, Dec. 7.—President Roosevelt announced this morning that Japanese planes had attacked Manila and Pearl Harbor.

JAPANESE PLANES BOMB HAWAII

LATEST WAR BULLETINS Page 2

Battleship Oklahoma is Sunk, Manila, Guam Attacked

AMERICA AT WAR: 1941-1945

WINDGATE

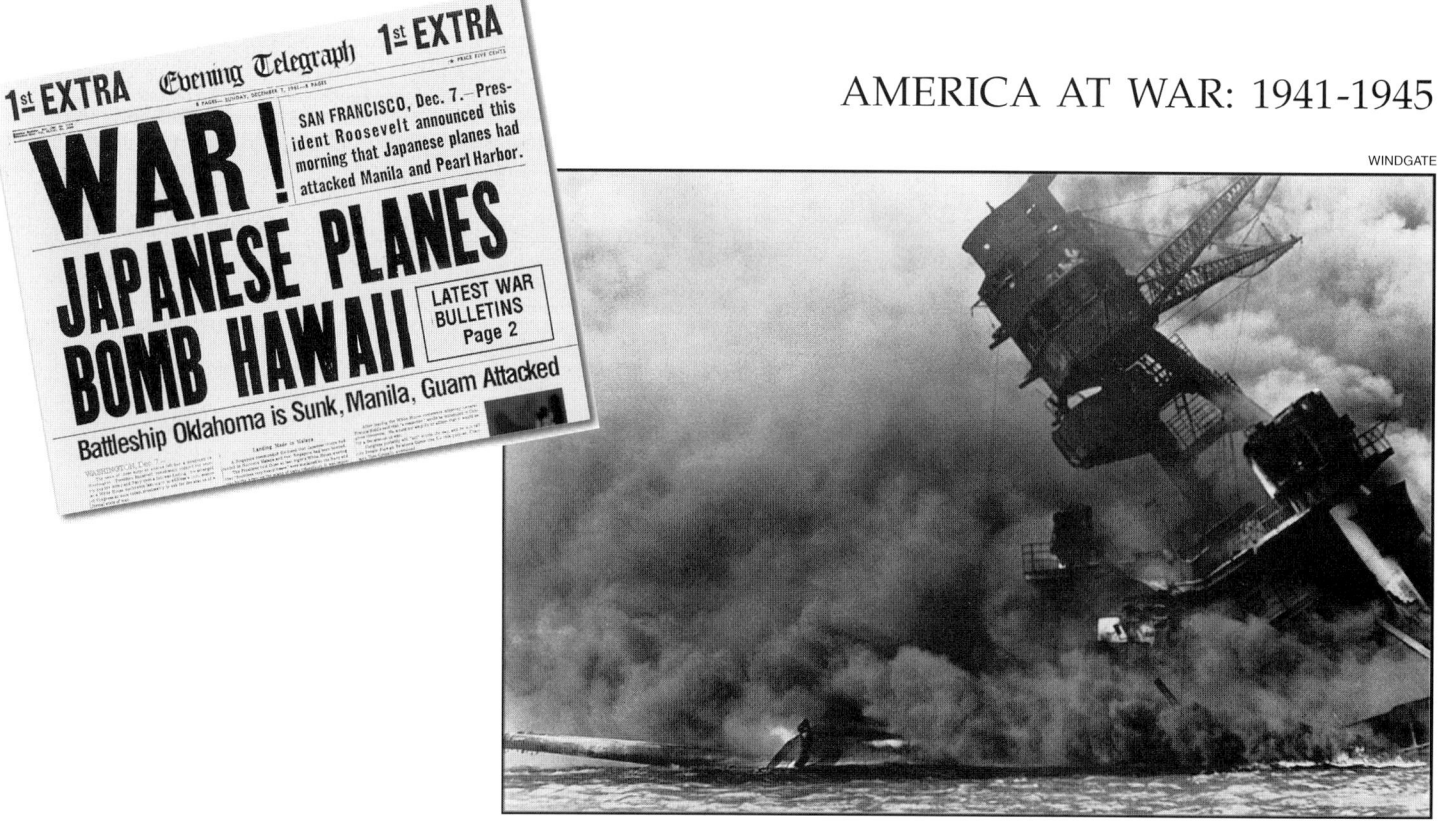

Battleship *Arizona,* sunk and burning, Pearl Harbor, December 7, 1941.

The *Matsonia* in dry dock at Bethlehem, San Francisco. She was converted to a troop ship just weeks before Pearl Harbor and served throughout the Pacific war transporting, soldiers, civilians, cargo and munitions. After the war, she was returned to Matson Lines.

When Pearl Harbor was bombed Sunday morning, December 7, 1941, the nation was stunned and electrified. In the Bay Area, tension mounted as residents realized the full implications of the attack and the vulnerability of California's coast. All military personnel were called to immediate active duty, police and firemen were put on full-time alert. Armed guards were placed at all defense plants, bridges, railway crossings, and airfields.

Monday morning found all shipyards in the Bay Area open for business as usual but with tightened security. All employees arriving for work were scrutinized more carefully than usual as rumors of attempted sabotage circulated. All gates were manned by soldiers and private guards, creating an air of uncertainty and urgency not previously experienced. Shipyard management teams met in closed meetings to evaluate the situation.

Over the next few days as reports of catastrophic damage came in from the Pacific, some glimmers of light were mixed in with the gloomy news. Although the Battle Fleet lost most of its battleships at Pearl Harbor, the U.S. Navy was not decimated. In terms of the battleship-dominant pre-war tactics, the Navy indeed was dealt a crippling blow. But in terms of the way the war actually was fought over the next three years, the losses at Pearl Harbor were of far less tactical importance. The navy's six aircraft carriers, for example, unscathed in the attack, came to replace the battleship as the nucleus of battle task forces. Because of Japanese determination to destroy the American battleships, the submarines and submarine repair facilities were ignored during the attack. Likewise vital oil storage facilities at Pearl Harbor were not bombed. This oversight or miscalculation proved to be a major mistake from the Japanese perspective.

In the days following the attack, ships at sea returned to San Francisco and some underwent immediate conversion to military needs. The government seized all enemy shipping in American ports and commandeered all American-owned vessels that might be useful to the war effort. Private yachts, coastal liners, fishing trawlers, ferryboats, even aging river boats were reviewed for their potential usefulness. Luxury ocean liners became troop transports, many small vessels filled in as coastal patrol boats until they could be replaced with new boats built specifically for that duty.

In the weeks following Pearl Harbor, as workers and management alike learned of the deaths of friends and family members, Bay Area shipyards dug in for the long battle of production that lay ahead.

With America in the war, Germany and Japan openly attacked American ships wherever they were encountered. Losses quickly mounted, particularly along the Atlantic coast where German submarines operated almost with impunity. British shipping already had suffered huge losses by the time America entered the war. American convoys to Britain had to make the two-way voyage unescorted most of the distance. Little was said publically about early American losses but, for a time in 1942, the struggle to supply Britain by sea seemed in doubt. Quite simply, German U-boats were sinking ships faster than America and Britain could build them. Even with the running head start American shipbuilders had with the Maritime Commission programs beginning in 1937, increased ship production was vital.

In the early weeks and months of 1942, the U.S. Navy struggled to consolidate and regain naval strength. After the initial losses at Pearl Harbor, the Pacific Fleet regrouped around aircraft carrier task forces, using the few cruisers and destroyers on hand as escorts for the carriers.

In addition to the merchant losses indicated in the chart at right, the U.S. Navy and Coast Guard lost over 360 ships between Pearl Harbor and the Japanese surrender.

Natural isolation and updated defensive installations around the Bay Area gave war planners confidence that the Bay Area could handle increased wartime production. Defense planners felt that the narrow entrance of San Francisco Bay, with careful preparation, could be protected from submarine, surface and air attack.

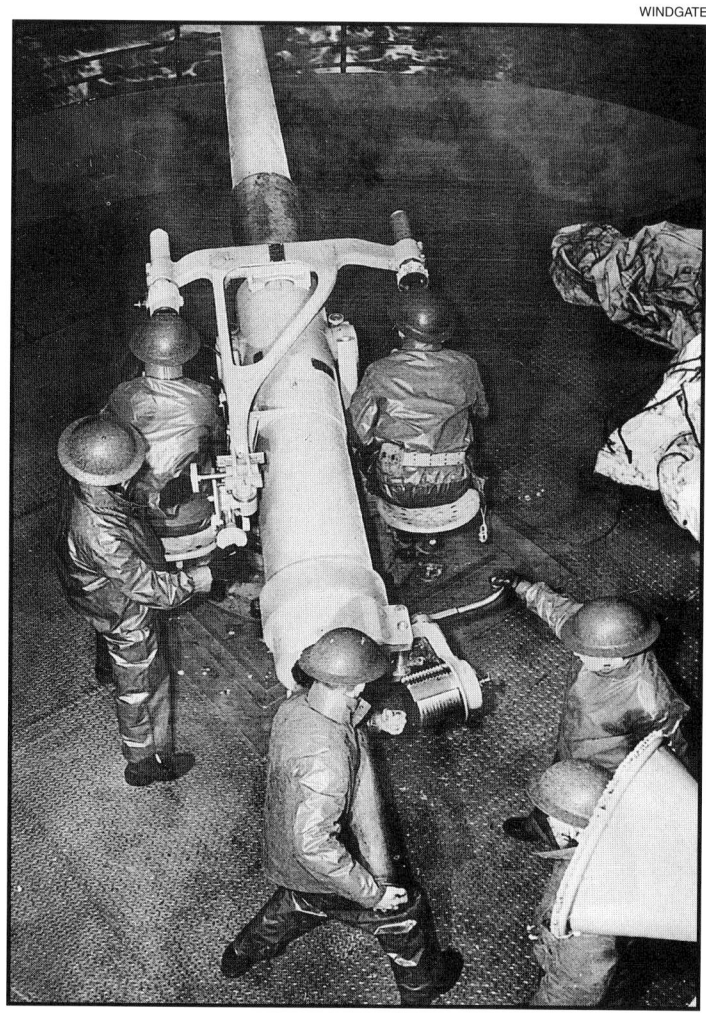

Big naval rifles capable of reaching twenty miles at sea were installed in coastal fortifications around San Francisco Bay. This one being unloaded from a truck is bound for Fort Cronkhite, 1939.

Left: Test firing a twelve-inch mortar at Fort Cronkhite, Marin Headlands, c.1941.

Far left: In the early month of World War II, cargo vessels were armed with guns of World War I vintage as defense against submarines.

In the first seven months of 1942, 281 American ships totaling over 6 million deadweight tons were sunk or damaged, mostly by German submarines operating off the east coast. British and allied shipping losses were even greater. If that loss rate had continued much longer, England would have been starved into submission and the outcome of World War II might have been significantly different. The two-part solution was to build more ships and simultaneously improve defenses against Axis submarines. Both were accomplished by 1944.

U.S. Flag Merchant Ships Lost or Damaged From All Causes During World War II												
	Jan	Feb	Mar	Apr	May	Jun	Jul	Aug	Sep	Oct	Nov	Dec
1940	0	0	0	0	0	0	0	0	0	0	0	1
1941	0	0	0	0	1	0	0	0	1	1	0	16
1942	18	30	35	42	52	56	48	17	22	24	20	9
1943	22	21	37	13	18	11	22	10	14	14	6	16
1944	15	8	11	10	1	7	9	4	4	5	13	16
1945	10	9	10	15	4	3	6	3	0	(764 total)		

This aerial view of Richmond, looking northwest around 1930, shows the marshy area south of Cutting Boulevard that would become the Kaiser shipyards. Richmond before the war was a small industrial town with a Standard Oil refinery (in the distance), a Ford assembly plant, a Pullman Company repair yard and a dredged seaport under development.

NEW WARTIME SHIPYARDS: KAISER

The name Henry J. Kaiser more than any other stands out in any discussion of Bay Area shipbuilding. Indeed, Kaiser gained national and worldwide recognition during World War II for his contribution to Allied victory. His maritime achievements are the more remarkable considering that before 1940 he had never built a ship or a shipyard. By 1945 he and his associates had built seven shipyards and delivered 1,490 ships, 747 at the Richmond yards alone. The four Kaiser yards in Richmond comprised the largest shipbuilding operation on the Pacific Coast.

Prior to the war, Kaiser was known in construction circles as a tough, competitive highway contractor and builder of massive dams. Through his work on Hoover Dam, Grand Coulee Dam and Bonneville Dam in the 1930s, Kaiser had developed working partnerships with Bechtel Corporation and others that would prove invaluable during the war.

Kaiser entered the shipbuilding arena in 1940, joining with Todd Shipyards, one of the nation's most experienced shipbuilding companies. Todd knew how to run a shipyard, Kaiser knew how to build one. Jointly, Kaiser and Todd formed the Seattle-Tacoma Shipbuilding Corporation and successfully bid a Maritime Commission contract to build five C-1 freighters. Simultaneously in 1940 the same group created the Todd-California Shipbuilding Corporation to build emergency freighters for the British. Kaiser and his engineers had scouted Richmond and concluded that the mudflats facing San Francisco Bay made an ideal shipyard site.

With the British contract, construction of the Kaiser yard in Richmond began. Thirty of the vessels were to be built at Richmond, and thirty on the east coast by Kaiser in partnership with Bath Iron Works in Maine. As the Maritime Commission shipbuilding program expanded in 1941, Kaiser and his partnership group responded by building additional shipyards in Oregon and Richmond.

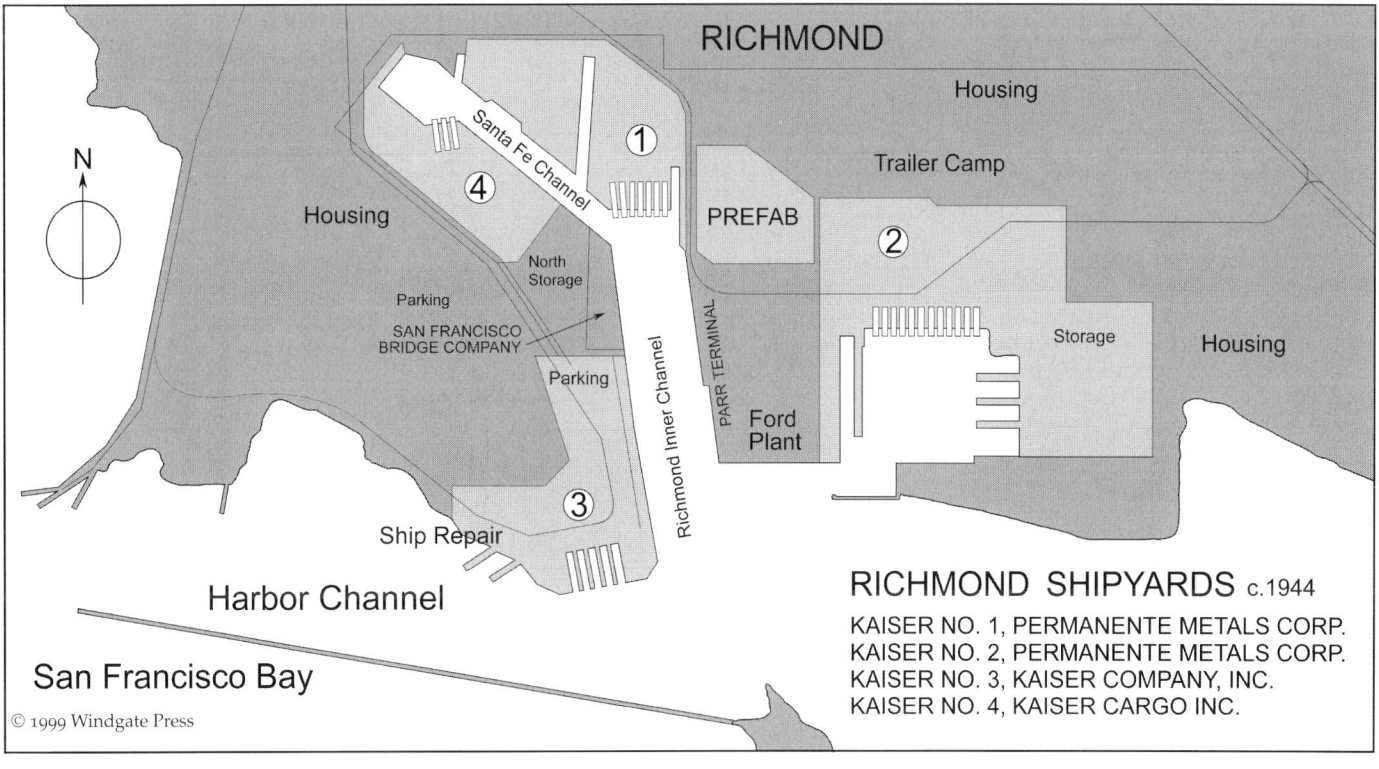

The four Kaiser yards with 27 shipways, seen here at the peak of production in 1944, and accompanying wartime housing transformed Richmond forever.

RICHMOND SHIPYARDS c.1944

KAISER NO. 1, PERMANENTE METALS CORP.
KAISER NO. 2, PERMANENTE METALS CORP.
KAISER NO. 3, KAISER COMPANY, INC.
KAISER NO. 4, KAISER CARGO INC.

Above: Marinship site March 24, 1942. looking north to Mount Tamalpais. The Northwestern Pacific Railroad tracks lie across a tidal marsh that will be filled for the shipyard. American Distilling Company buildings at left.

Above: Marinship's bi-weekly newspaper points up a worker shortage in 1944.

MARINSHIP

In 1941, the W.A. Bechtel Company, one of Henry Kaiser's partners in dam building and the first Kaiser shipyards, built an emergency shipyard at Los Angeles, the California Shipbuilding Company, called Calship. Three months after Pearl Harbor, Bechtel was asked by the Maritime Commission to build another new yard on the Pacific Coast. In less than a day, March 12, 1942, Bechtel had selected Sausalito on Richardson's Bay as the site. Most of the developed waterfront of Los Angeles and San Francisco Bay was already congested with war industry, but Marin County was relatively untouched so far by the war. The yard was to build Liberty ships on six ways that could be extended later to accommodate tankers. Ground was broken March 28 and the first keel laid on June 27, before the yard was fifty percent complete. For expediency, steel for the first six ships was prefabricated at Calship in Los Angeles then shipped north.

The new yard began as the "W.A. Bechtel Co., Marin Shipbuilding Division" but it quickly became "Marinship." Experience gained in other yards was applied to Marinship, which became a speed record-setting producer of tankers. Originally contracted to build 100 vessels, Marinship built 93 (the last seven were canceled at war's end). Workers were proud that only one of their products, Liberty ship *Sebastian Cermeno*, was lost to enemy action.

Shipyards in the Bay Area seemed to spring up almost overnight in the early days of World War II. Because of wartime secrecy, most Bay Area residents were uninformed about production goals, output or even the exact nature of work being done. Some residents naturally objected to the upheaval of their neighborhoods and the dramatic changes taking place. But as the war progressed, upheaval became the norm and the sights and all-night sounds of heavy industry on San Francisco Bay became more accepted.

SAUSALITO HISTORICAL SOCIETY

Marinship looking north in 1943 when the yard was in full swing with tankers on the ways. The large building at center is the sub-assembly shop with the plate shop behind it.

SAN FRANCISCO MARITIME NHP P82-019a.4117pl

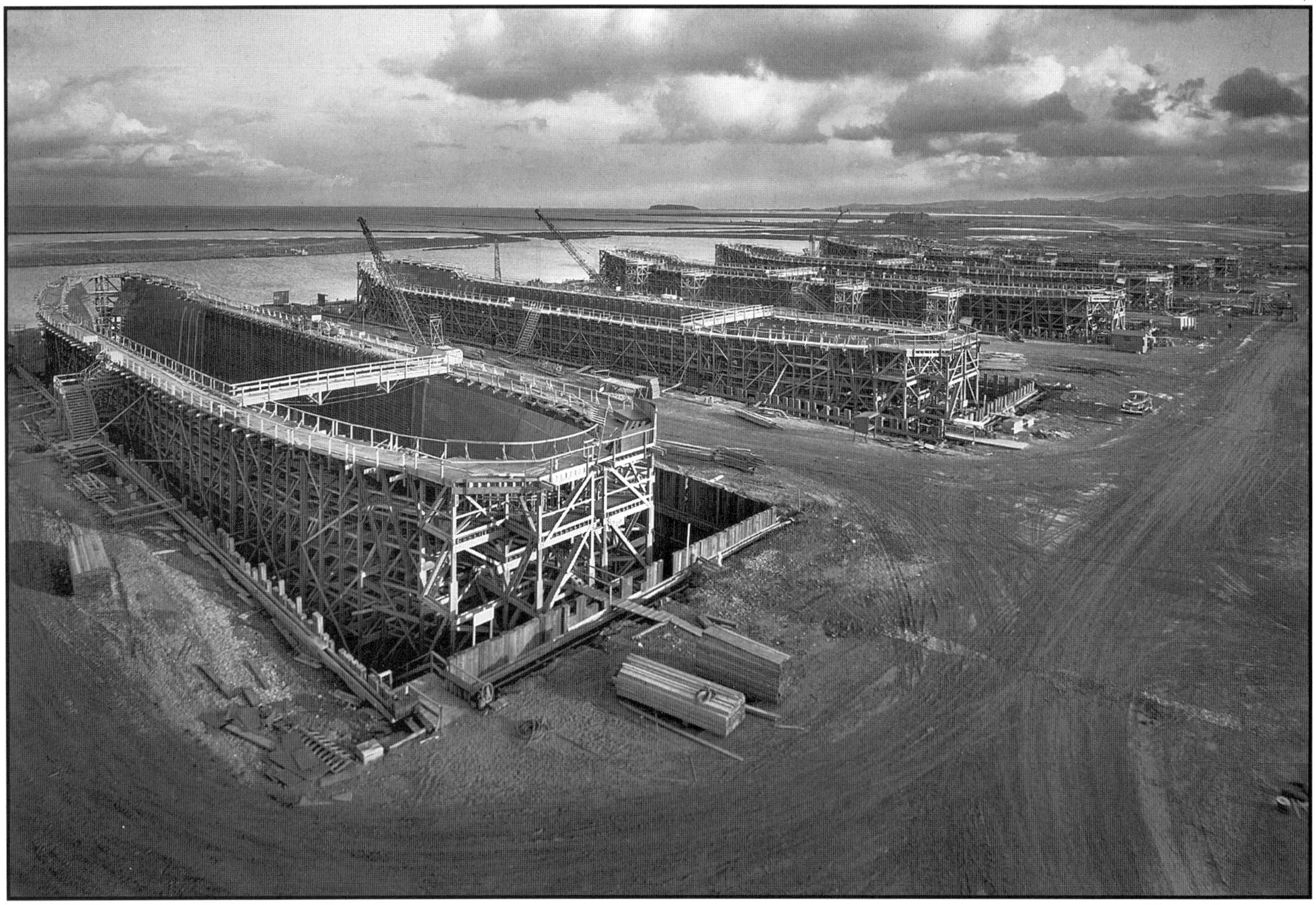

Belair lay just north of the San Francisco airport. The seven graving docks, all that remains of the shipyard, are visible today from the air. February 8, 1943.

SAN FRANCISCO MARITIME NHP P82-019a.1808pl

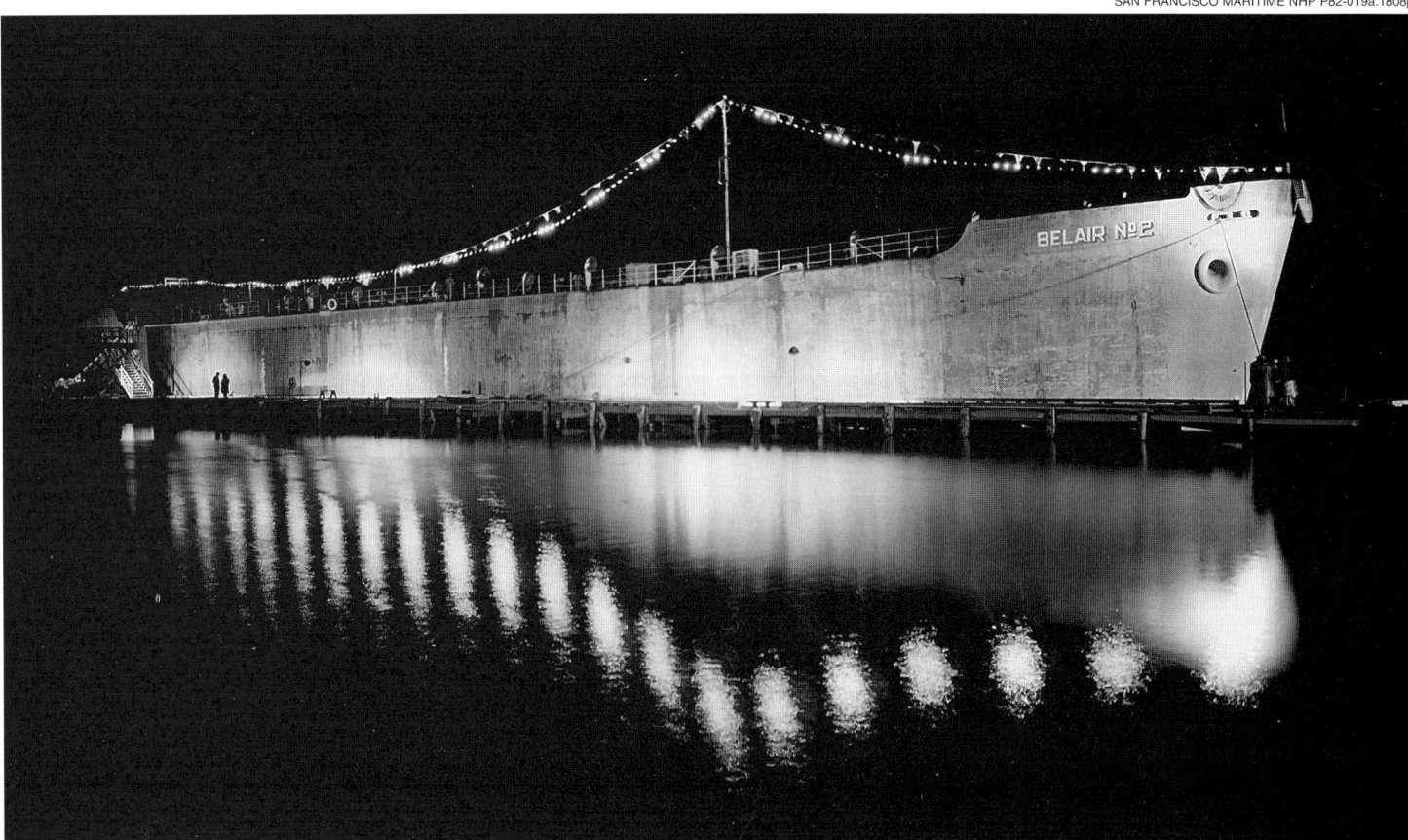

A concrete hull before addition of warehouse structure. Each hull had living space for ten men and small engines to operate generators and winches. June 29, 1943.

BELAIR

Prior to World War II, Belair Island was a small rise in the mud flats near the San Francisco Airport. The Maritime Commission in 1942 selected the site for a new specialty shipyard. Barrett & Hilp, San Francisco contractors, were directed to excavate seven 400-foot graving docks in the marsh to accommodate construction of concrete barges. The idea behind the concrete vessels was, as in World War I, to save plate steel. The hulls were made of "Haydite," a lightweight aggregate poured in plywood forms to form steel reinforced walls six-inches thick. Towed in pairs by a single tug, they were designed to haul cargo between North and South America. Belair Shipyard delivered twenty concrete hulls, each 365 feet long, 56 feet wide and 38 feet deep. By the time they were completed, war needs had changed and the hulls were converted to floating warehouses and towed to the South Pacific to follow the island invasion forces. They served variously as tankers, repair barges, and refrigerated barges complete with ice machines

Similar concrete hulls were built near San Diego by Conship (Concrete Ship Constructors). Although concrete hulls proved durable and seaworthy, their construction proved time consuming and the amount of steel used in their steel-reinforced construction equaled almost 60 percent of that used in conventional steel hulls.

The first concrete hull ready for launch at Belair, June 17, 1943.

THE HAGGIN MUSEUM

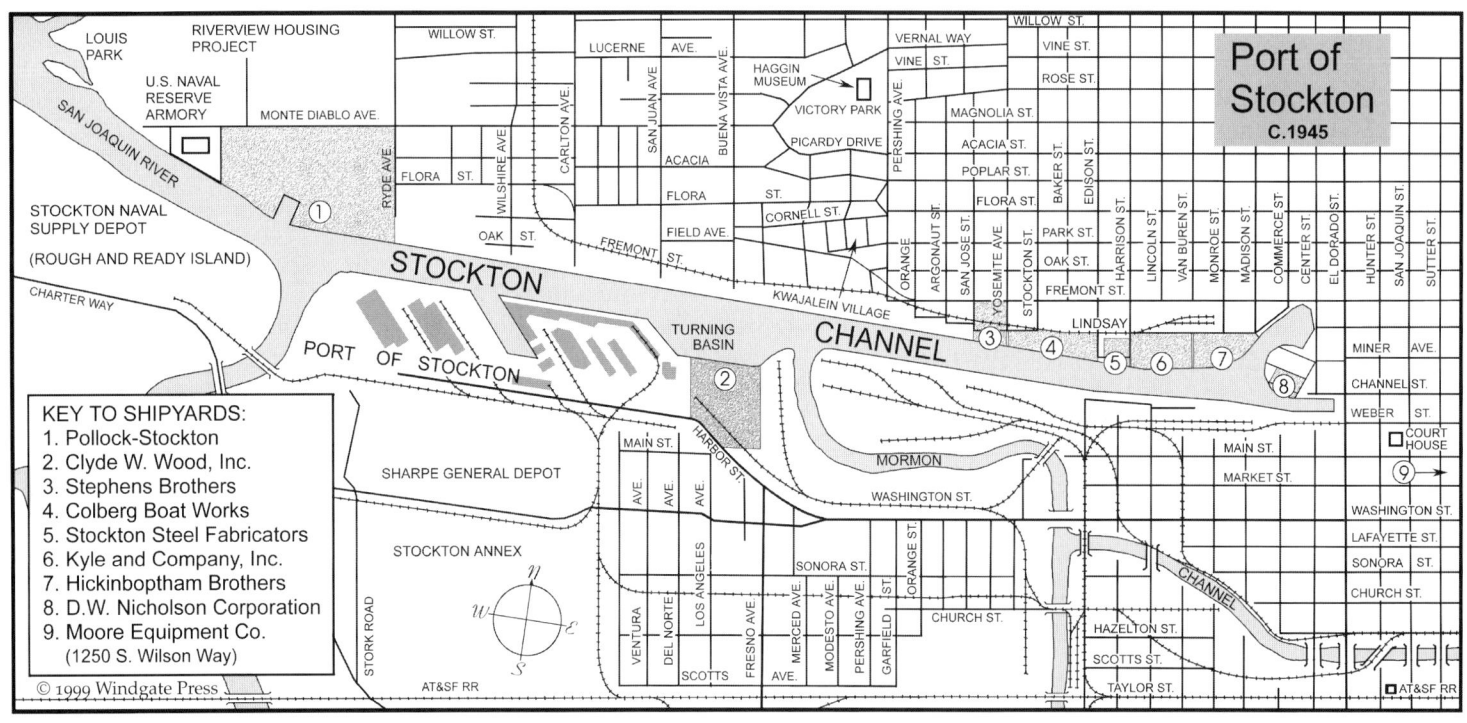

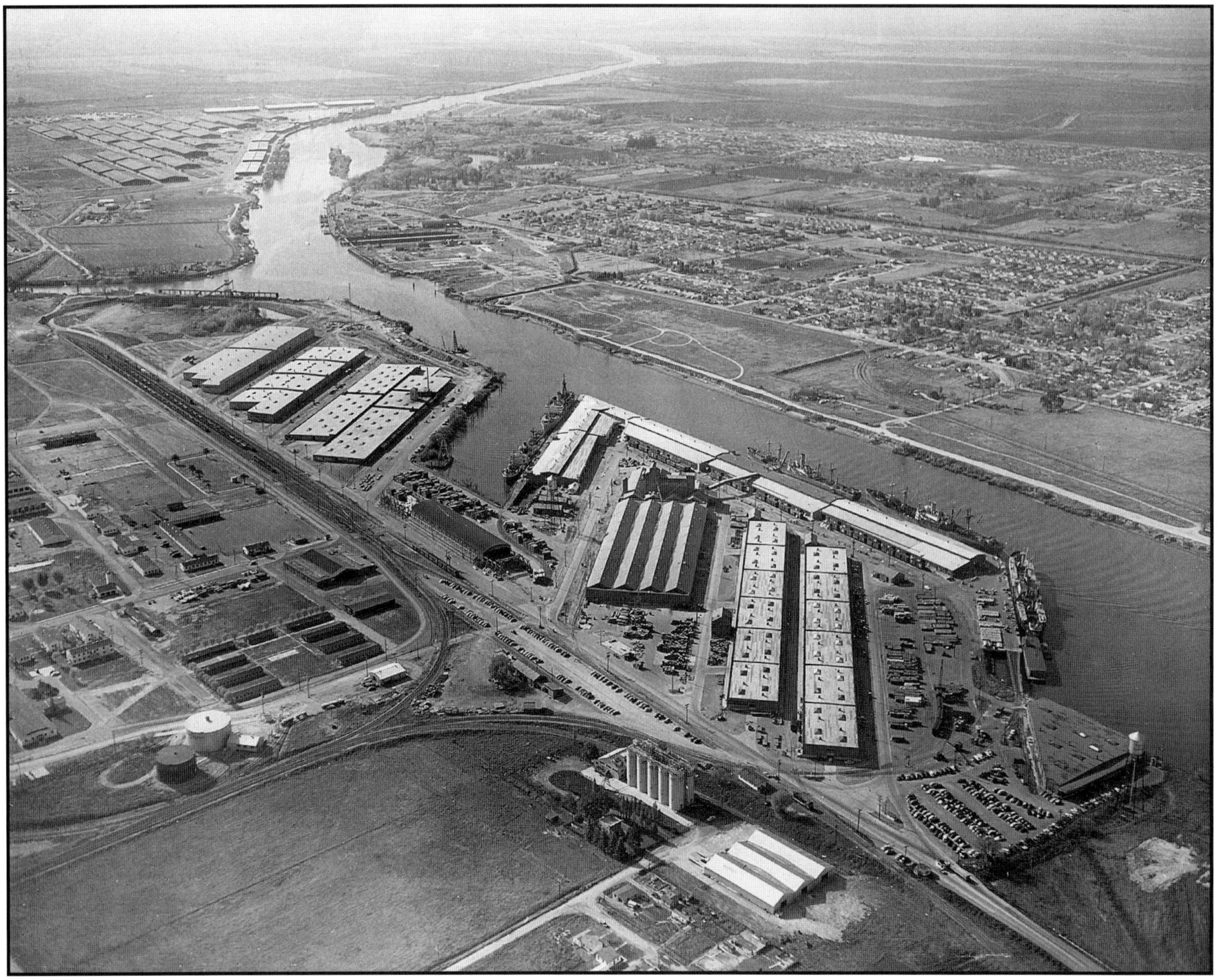

Port of Stockton, looking west, down river, c.1945.

STOCKTON

Stockton became a major contributor to Bay Area shipbuilding during World War II. Located some 100 miles up the San Joaquin River from San Francisco, Stockton had been a transportation hub since gold rush days when it was a supply base for the southern mines in the gold country. The natural sloughs at Stockton were dredged into a channel that served river boats and local waterborne commerce. In the 1930s major deepening of the channel and dredging in the San Joaquin River created a long-sought seaport at Stockton to accommodate large deepwater steamers. Further dredging in 1940 plus construction of a belt line railroad that gave channel access to all three transcontinental railroads made the Port of Stockton a strategic site for wartime industries.

In World War II the Port of Stockton fell under Army jurisdiction; Rough and Ready Island became a naval supply depot. The airport became a Air Corps training field and thousands of war workers streamed into Stockton. Local farm equipment manufacturers soon were busy with war work as were the city's machine shops and construction companies.

It was Stockton's potential as a maritime center, however, that caught the attention of the U.S. Maritime Commission. Of fourteen defense plants in and around Stockton, nine were shipyards. Stockton was considered by the Bechtel company as a site for the shipyard that eventually became Marinship. But the narrow channel at Stockton was better suited to building smaller craft where several shipyards could operate in tight quarters and "side launch" into the restricted waters. Within a year after Pearl Harbor, the Inland Shipbuilding Association had formed around the six largest shipyards, employing over 3,500 people. Before war's end, Stockton shipyards employed over 10,000 men and women in shipbuilding.

THE HAGGIN MUSEUM

Looking east up the Stockton Channel, Stephens Brothers compact boatyard lies just above the Texaco tank in foreground and beyond that is Colberg Boat Works, c.1945.

Stephens Brothers boatyard in more placid times, c.1915.

Seaport cities on both coasts vied for new shipyard construction as the word went out in 1940 and 1941 that more shipways were urgently needed. Site selection criteria, however, dictated that no new yard would drain off the labor supply from an existing yard or overcrowd existing yards' supply channels. For that reason, the Pacific Coast got a large share of new shipyard construction. Stockton linked California's Central Valley population and industrial capacity to shipbuilding. Defense work other than shipbuilding focused on Stockton and Sacramento for the same reason.

Some of the boatyards in Stockton had been in business since the beginning of the century, building and repairing boats that served local needs. In 1902 Theodore and Roy Stephens built a 33-foot sloop in the back yard of their family home, an effort that launched a successful business. Their subsequent boats, both pleasure craft and work boats, became known for their quality of design and workmanship. During World War I Stephens Brothers built boats for the Navy. After demand for Delta work boats declined in the 1920s due to highway construction, Stephens Brothers turned to fast pleasure craft. Their most successful model was an all-teak speedster, the Stephens 26, which became popular on Lake Tahoe and along the coast. The boats grew larger until the 48-foot power cruiser became the company's flagship of the 1930s. Their customers included wealthy yachtsmen from around the world as well as the United States.

In 1940, Stephens Brothers and Colberg Boat Works, in business since before 1900, were awarded a joint contract for six wooden minesweepers. After Pearl Harbor, Stephens Brothers expanded their operation to fill the small site on the Stockton Channel, with over 450 employees producing over 125 vessels, minesweepers and salvage boats, tugs and rescue craft for the Navy and Army, and picket boats for the Coast Guard. Both yards won Army-Navy "E" production awards.

Hickinbotham brothers John and Edwin, originally carriage makers, began business in Stockton in 1852. The family business evolved into a hardware and building materials supplier and, after World War I, Hickinbotham Brothers moved into steel and iron industrial supplies, welding supplies and hardware. After Pearl Harbor, the company joined with Guntert & Zimmerman, another local firm, to open a shipyard called Hickinbotham Brothers Construction Division. The site was the former Banner Island at the head of the Stockton Channel, used in the 1930s as an unoffical city dump. The yard built ten types of vessels for the Army and Navy, from crane barges to 176-foot supply vessels and was awarded the Army-Navy "E".

The city of Stockton's geographical position made it strategically important as a rail center as well as the head of navigation on the San Joaquin River. Lathrop, the little town nine miles south of Stockton became the Lathrop Holding and Reconsignment Point (later Sharpe General Depot), a major rail shipping and distribution center for the Central Valley with over 1,400 employees. At peak times over 6,000 freight cars per month were unloaded or discharged in Lathrop.

When the Army in 1942 took over the Port of Stockton, a good portion of the port became the Stockton Subdepot of the Benicia Arsenal, called locally the "Stockton Ordinance Depot." As the neighboring shipyards on the Channel turned out military vessels, the depot received, warehoused and shipped vehicles, parts and military ordinance. The round-the-clock activity made the narrow channel a far busier place than these wartime photographs suggest.

Before and after: the unofficial city dump became Hickinbotham Brothers shipyard. The top view shows the site in February, 1942. Below is the yard in February, 1945, after scores of vessels have slid down the launching ways at left.

Right: Publicity photos such as this one at Marinship were meant to reassure newly recruited women workers that they would be instructed patiently by skilled men welders. By 1944, over 40 percent of all shipyard workers in the Bay Area were women.

Below: James R. Moore, left, vice-president of Moore Dry Dock Company, is joined by the manager of naval construction to inspect Air Raid Shelter No. 5 at the shipyard, July 26, 1942.

THE HAGGIN MUSEUM

The booklet at left, "How to Train Workers Quickly," underscores a critical problem of World War II shipbuilding. All experienced workers in the Bay Area already were hard at work when America entered the war. Tens of thousands of unskilled men and women, recruited to meet demands of new emergency shipyards, had to be trained. Years of training and experience necessary to make a journeyman shipyard worker could not be condensed into a matter of days or weeks, yet the war would wait for no one. The solution was to break the complex job of building a ship into the smallest possible components, teach workers to do that specific task and let them gain experience through repetition. Trade unions objected strenuously to this practice, giving rise to deep conflicts between unions and shipyard management that remained unresolved throughout the war.

Below: Wartime shipyards set up on-site training schools to help get new workers up to speed. This welding school is at Moore Dry Dock, September 12, 1941. Kaiser even set up a welding school aboard a ferry that transported workers to Richmond.

SAN FRANCISCO MARITIME NHP P79-071a Scr55:s pl.5298

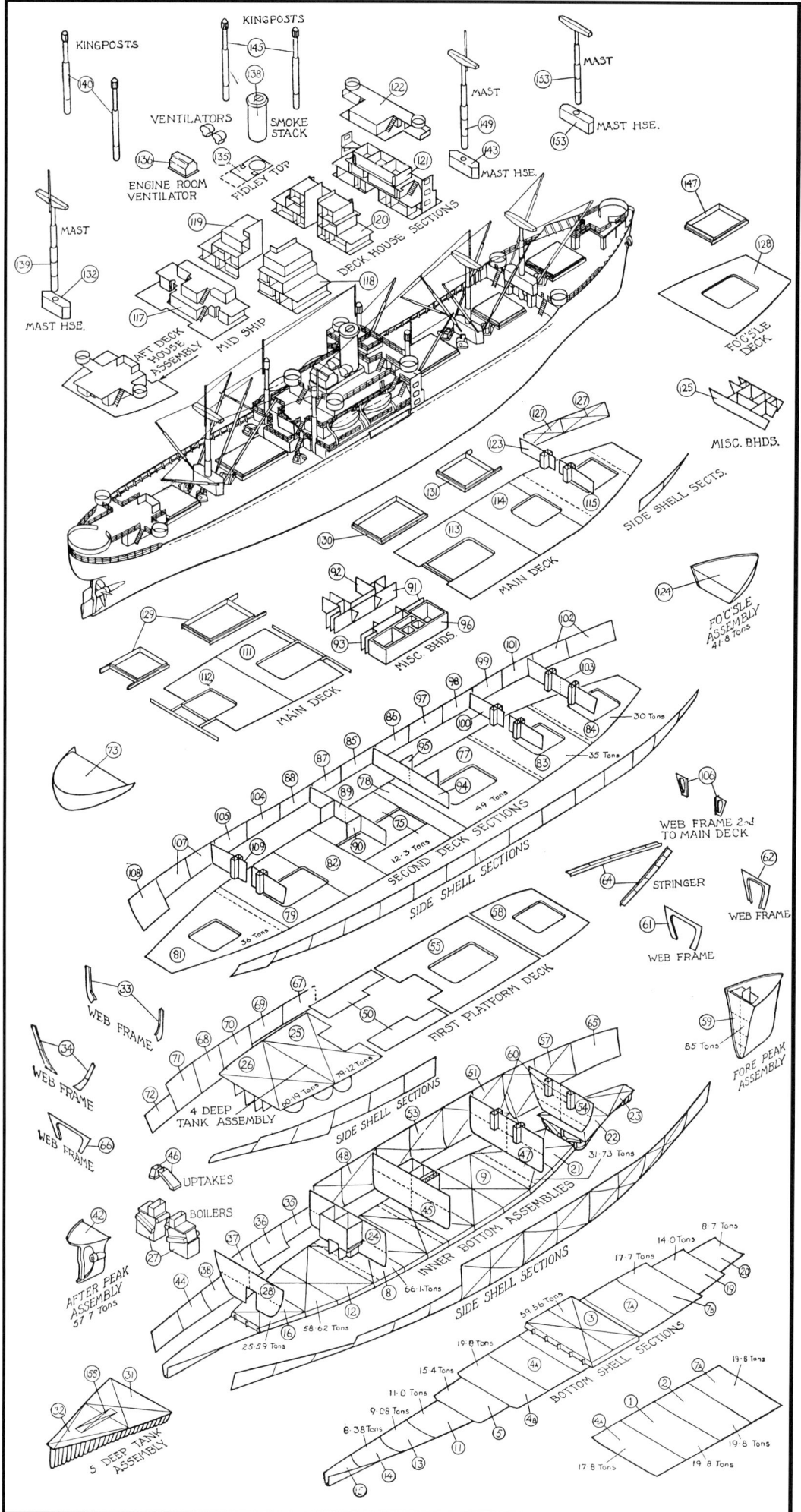

TRAINING AIDS

Charts like the one at left and cutaway models simplified for new workers the complex nature of ship construction. While no single worker was expected to understand all that went into the vessel, he or she benefitted from seeing how one person's effort fit into the "big picture." Each shipyard built its own models and some devised ingenious devices to train workers for specific tasks. Once trained, workers seldom changed jobs. This chart shows major sub-assemblies for a Victory ship typical of those built at Kaiser in Richmond.

KEY TO DRAWING:

Bottom Shell: 1, 2, 4, 5, 7, 11, 13, 14, 15, 19, 20
Double Bottom Units: 3, 8, 9, 12, 16
Transverse Bulkheads: 24, 28, 45, 47
Brackets: 60
Deep Tank Assembly: 31, 32, 155
Side Shell: 35, 36, 38, 44, 48, 51, 53, 57, 65
Forepeak assembly: 59
Boilers and Uptakes: 27, 46
Aft Peak Assembly: 25, 26
Deep Tank Assembly: 25, 26
First Platform Deck: 50, 55, 58
Stringer: 64
Web Frames: 33, 34, 61, 62, 66, 106
Side Shell: 67, 68, 69, 70, 71, 72
Second Deck: 75, 77, 78, 79, 81, 82, 83, 84
Transverse Bulkheads: 89, 94, 100, 103, 109
Longitudinal Bulkheads: 90, 95
Side Shell: 85, 86, 87, 88, 97, 98, 99, 101, 102, 104, 105, 107, 108
Fo'c'sle Assembly: 124
Stern Assembly: 73
Machine Casing: 91
Misc. Bulkheads and spaces: 92, 93, 96
Main Deck: 111, 112, 113, 114, 115
Transverse Bulkhead: 123
Hatch Coaming: 129, 130, 131
Side Shell; 127
Misc. Bulkheads; 125
Fo'c'sle Deck: 128
Hatch Coaming: 147
Aft Deckhouse Assembly: 116
Midship Deckhouse Sections: 117, 118, 119, 120, 121, 122
Fidley Top: 135
Ventilator: 136
Stack: 138
Masts and Mast Houses: 132, 139, 143, 149, 153
Kingposts: 140, 145

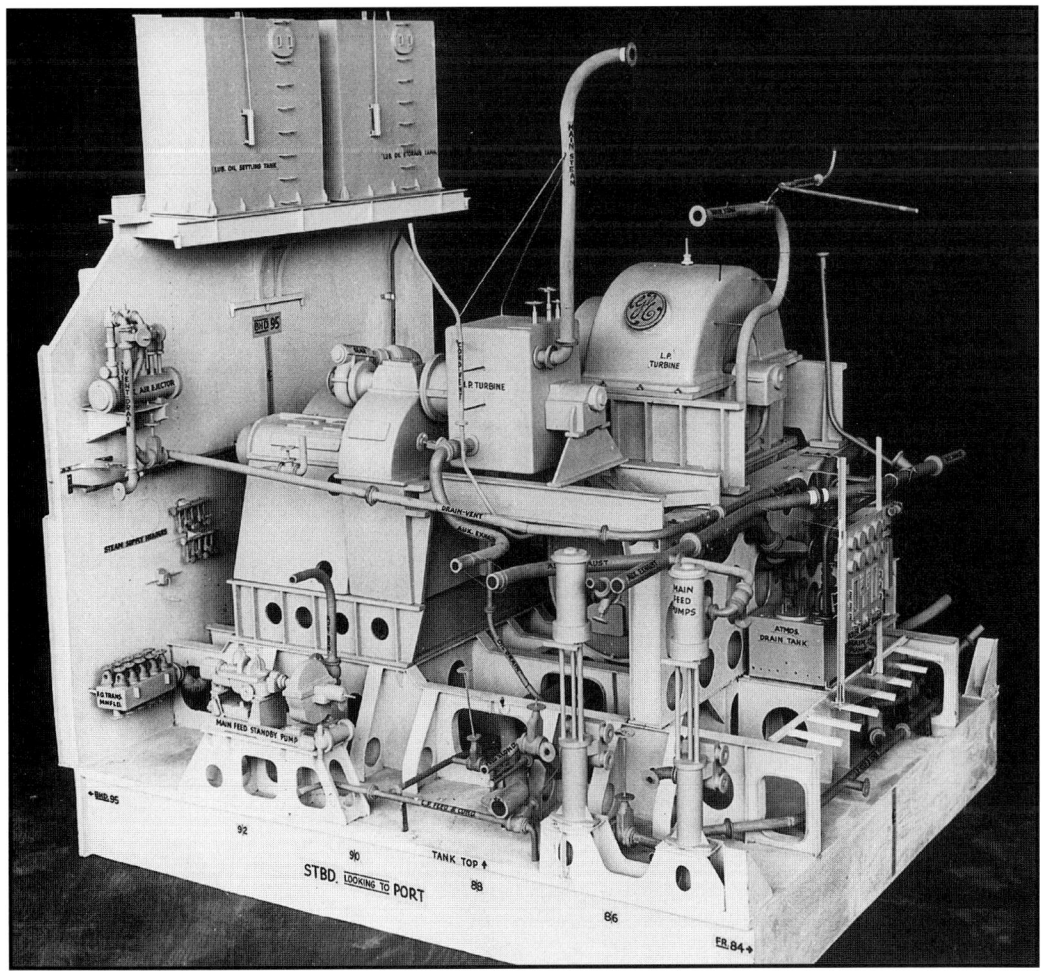

These two table-top models were among many used at the Kaiser yards to familiarize workers with the vessels they helped build. At left is a one-inch-to-one foot-scale model of a Victory ship's machinery space with geared turbine and piping in place. June 1, 1944. Each yard provided a manual of shipyard terms, procedures, signals and symbols for workers to memorize. Each worker's hard hat carried an emblem designating the worker's classification, making it easier for foremen to keep track of their crews.

THE LIBERTY SHIP

Bay Area yards for the most part built standard types of vessels designed for simplified construction and, therefore, speed of production. The best known cargo ship to emerge from World War II was the Liberty ship. Built in greater numbers than any other type, Liberties epitomized American ingenuity and became the symbol of overcoming the enemy by sheer weight of industrial production. Over 2,700 Liberties were built in American shipyards, 450 in the San Francisco Bay Area. The Liberty ship, EC2-S-C1 in official nomenclature, was called an ugly duckling and criticized for being too slow, even obsolete, by freighter standards of the time. It was a product of compromise, bringing together readily available machinery and proven design. Used in a variety of roles and carrying every conceivable cargo, Liberties operated world-wide; they were relentless and reliable and forever hold a special place, not always favorable, with the men who served on them.

The Liberty ship derived from a British type of 10,000-ton tramp steamer common in the 1930s. When Britain ordered emergency freighters from Kaiser, the design was a modified version of the British tramp. Modified further to American specifications, the Liberty prototype emerged. It was a simple layout, designed for simplicity of construction, durability, maximum cargo and optimum speed under the circumstances. Original specifications written before America's entry into the war called for a black hull with buff-cream upper works and little defensive armament. Production models were painted medium grey with dark grey decks, and bristled with life rafts, antiaircraft guns, and bow and stern gun platforms that did little to improve its appearance.

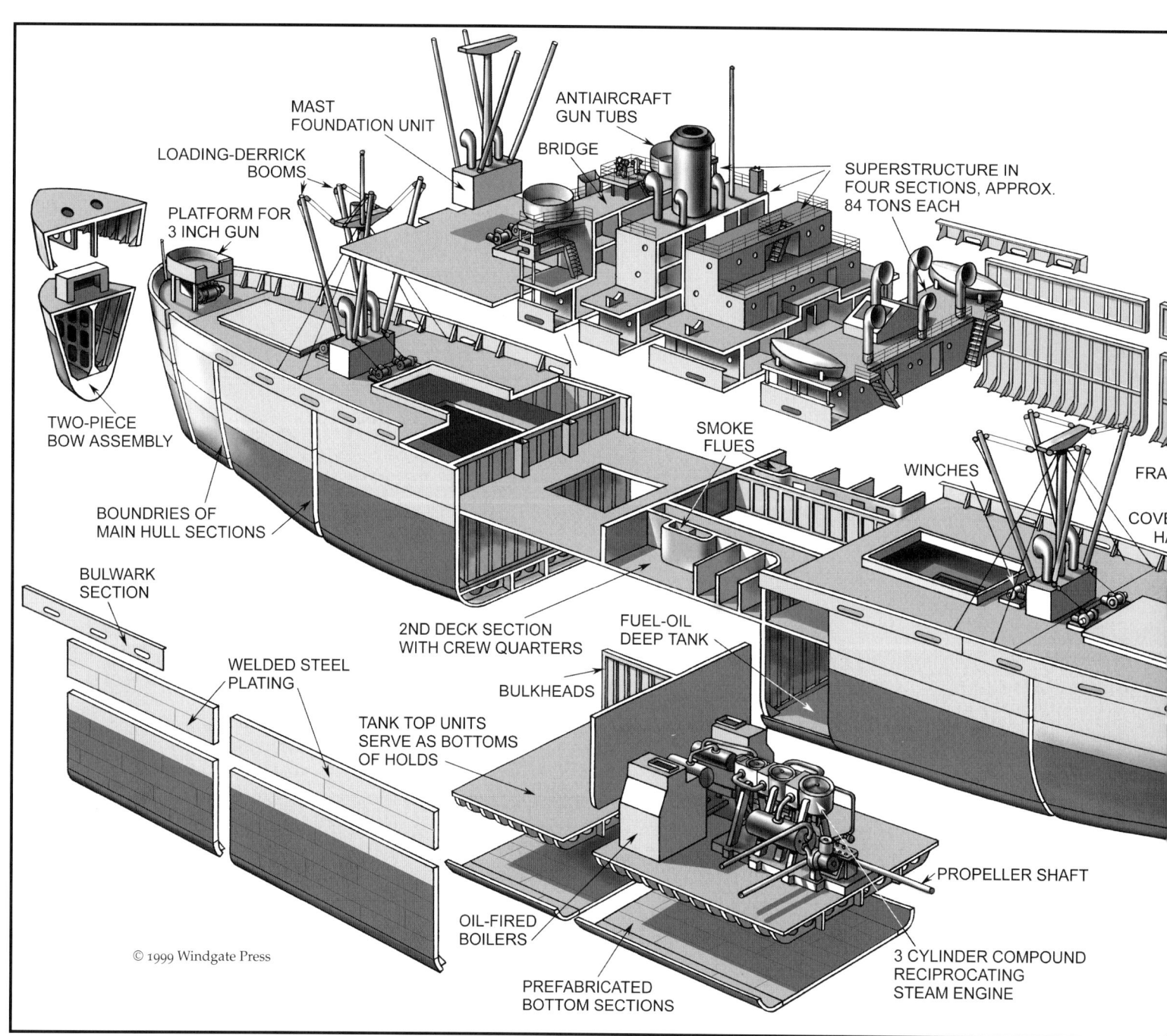

© 1999 Windgate Press

Prototype Liberty ship model in pre-war colors. Note the absence of defensive armament.

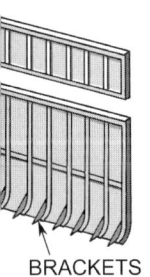

EC2-S-C1 LIBERTY SHIP EXPLODED VIEW

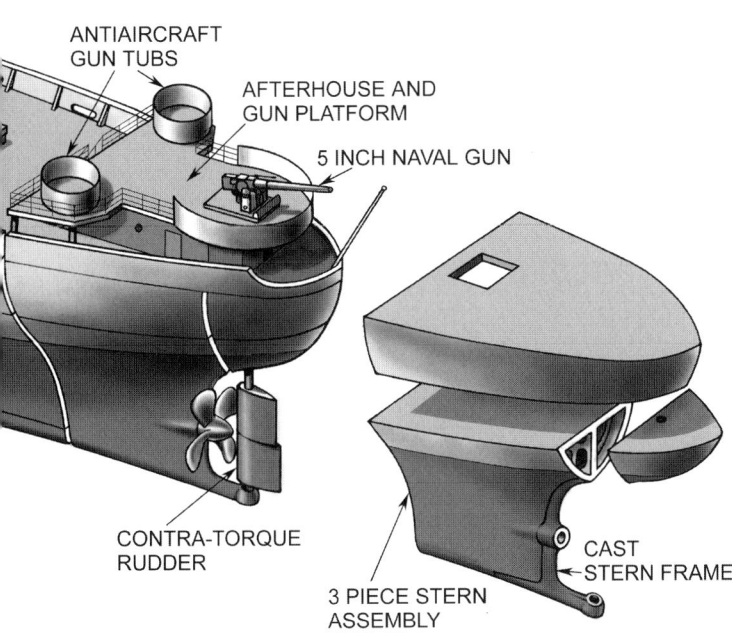

A feature that made Liberty ships so successful was a hull that lent itself to all-welded pre-assembly. It was mainly slab-sided with compound curves only at the bow and stern. The superstructure consisted of one main boxy deckhouse and standardized masts and booms. As Liberties were built, the design continued to evolve to accommodate additional pre-assembly wherever possible.

The simplified drawing at left shows a Liberty broken apart into its main components, each assembled in the shipyards and hoisted by crane into position on the launching way. With experience, builders made the pre-assembled sections larger and more complete, limited in size only by the cranes' capacity.

The main deckhouse shown here consists of four pre-assembled vertical slices. As time went by the pieces were consolidated into three, then two parts. Eventually entire deckhouses as single units were lifted aboard. The after deckhouse was built with gun platform in place and hoisted as one unit. Hull bottom sections that required extensive welding were built upside down, making welding easier and faster, then inverted for installation. Internal piping and wiring was pre-assembled whenever possible in each section.

Despite the popular assumption at the time that Liberty ships would serve little purpose after the war, they provided the postwar world with low-cost merchant marine workhorses that continued in service in ever-dwindling numbers into the 1970s.

The term "liberty ship" first was used during World War I. On July 4, 1918, three Wykes Class destroyers were launched simultaneously at Newport News Shipyard under a sign proclaiming "Liberty Launching Day — Three Destroyers, Three Cheers." The press, in reporting the triple launching, referred to the vessels as "Liberty Ships," a catch phrase that seemed appropriate. Twenty three years later as the first emergency freighter slid down the ways, the ship was called part of a "Liberty Fleet," and the occasion, September 27, 1941, was "Liberty Fleet Day." The slow, ungainly vessels were henceforth "Liberty" ships.

Liberty ships made the most of critical shortages. The Maritime Commission wanted all emergency vessels to be powered by modern steam turbine engines, the type used in C2 and C3 freighters. After the war, they reasoned, ships so powered would have useful, competitive lives with the American merchant marine. Factories making steam turbine engines, however, were already at capacity with orders for naval vessels and fast cargo types. Reluctantly, the Maritime Commission turned to an older type of engine, the triple-expansion reciprocating steam engine. Considered obsolescent by 1940, the reciprocal steam engine nevertheless was selected to power the emergency fleet. It was not the first choice, it was for all practical purposes the only choice. That is not to say the design was inferior; it was indeed one of the soundest engines ever to push a ship across the sea and the product of a long evolution.

Factories making or capable of making reciprocating steam engines and appropriate boilers were numerous and could supply machinery to shipbuilders in the quantities

WINDGATE

Two triple-expansion reciprocating steam engines built by Moore Dry Dock for installation in the lighthouse tenders *Walnut* and *Fir*. These examples are smaller than the ones used in Liberty ships but follow the same basic design. 1940.

needed. The triple expansion engine was cheaper to make and could be made far faster than a turbine engine with its complex reduction gears. A set of reduction gears for a steam turbine engine had teeth machined to ten-thousandths of an inch, cut in a special shop with a constantly maintained interior temperature of 72 degrees. Any defects or distortions in the gear teeth would cause vibration that would magnify in the turning propellor shaft. Temperature control, including that of the cutting machine lubricating oil, was maintained over the 285 hours necessary to cut a single gear.

Another point mitigating in favor of the reciprocating engine was that ships limited to ten knots by the old steam engines could keep pace with other older ships, also limited to ten knots, that would be in convoys. An unpleasant reality was that a convoy could travel safely no faster than its slowest vessel. Faster turbine-powered vessels would have to reduce speed to maintain position, thus wasting precious fuel. When the time came to choose an engine for the new emergency fleet, planners of necessity fell back on the tried and true. Modifications were made, fuel switched from coal to oil, and production began. The triple expansion reciprocating engine got a new lease on life and continued in use for another two decades as Liberty ships in the postwar world filled out the merchant fleets of many nations.

Preparing a Liberty smoke stack for installation, 1944.

The finished product: Launch of the first of eighteen Liberties built at Marinship, September 26, 1942. Construction on the Marinship yard began only six months earlier, March 28, 1942.

YARD LAYOUT

New Maritime Commission shipyards were designed to take full advantage of all that had been learned about mass production of ships. Older yards were modified wherever possible to accommodate new methods. This meant not only emphasis on welding and pre-assembly but also reliance on private industry to manage operations. World War II shipyards were perhaps the most successful collaboration between government and private enterprise in American history.

New shipyards were designed ideally either with straight-line work flow or turning flow. Straight-line flow required a site with inland depth so that materials could enter the yard, be processed and fabricated in a linear flow and arrive at the shoreline for final assembly at the shipways. If the site had limited space inland but a lengthy shoreline, the turning flow design was used; materials entered parallel to the shoreline as shown below, processed in a straight flow, then turned at right angles to be assembled on the shipways. Actual geographic conditions at shipyard sites resulted in modifications and variations to these two systems. As the war progressed, sub-assemblies and machinery often were built far from the shipyard and trucked to the site.

Marinship in Sausalito, shown below, was a typical turning-flow emergency yard designed for rapid ship production. From the air it appears a jumble of clutter but was in fact well planned and efficiently run. The ghost view at right locates the key facilities within the yard. Raw steel and pre-assembled machinery enters by rail at the top (1) and is held in storage yards until needed. Steel is formed in the plate shop (8) and joined into sub-assemblies (9). Cranes carry the sub-assemblies from the sub-assembly shop to the pre-hull skids (10) where the parts are joined into even larger sections, such as deck houses and bow and stern assemblies. Complete section are then lifted by crane to the building ways (often called "slipways," "shipways" or just "ways").

SAN FRANCISCO MARITIME NHP P79-141.0147pl

Marinship, looking northwest, Marin City in background, c. 1944.

After ships are launched, they are towed to the outfitting docks for completion. Hardware and other essential parts have arrived a the shipyard by rail or truck and are stored in the huge warehouse (14) adjacent to the outfitting docks and shops. From the docks, the completed vessels (T-2 Tankers in the photo) proceed to sea trials and delivery to their new owners.

Although most emergency shipyards were completely dismantled after the war and their sites put to other uses, several of Marinship's building remain. The warehouse (14) is today the U.S. Army Corps of Engineer's Bay Model and also houses the Marinship Exhibit, a museum of artifacts and photographs of World War II shipbuilding. Both facilities are open to the public. The Mold Loft (7), where full-size ship patterns were made from drawings, today houses artists' studios and workshops. The outfitting piers are used by commercial fishing boats and the Army Engineers for their debris-collecting vessels. The Administration Building (2) and the General Shop (16) are today occupied by private offices and studios.

MARINSHIP:
1. Railroad into shipyard
2. Administration Building
3. Storage Area (later, site of barge program)
4. North Steel Yard
5. Shipwright's Mill & Yard Maintenance
6. Northwest Storage Yard, Cafeteria and Training Classrooms
7. Mold Loft
8. Plate Shop
9. Sub-assembly
10. Pre-hull Skids
11. Building ways
12. Outfitting Docks
13. Outfitting Shop
14. Warehouse
15. Machine Shop
16. General Shop
17. Ferry Slip
18. Emergency Housing (Marin City)
19. Distillery (not part of shipyard)

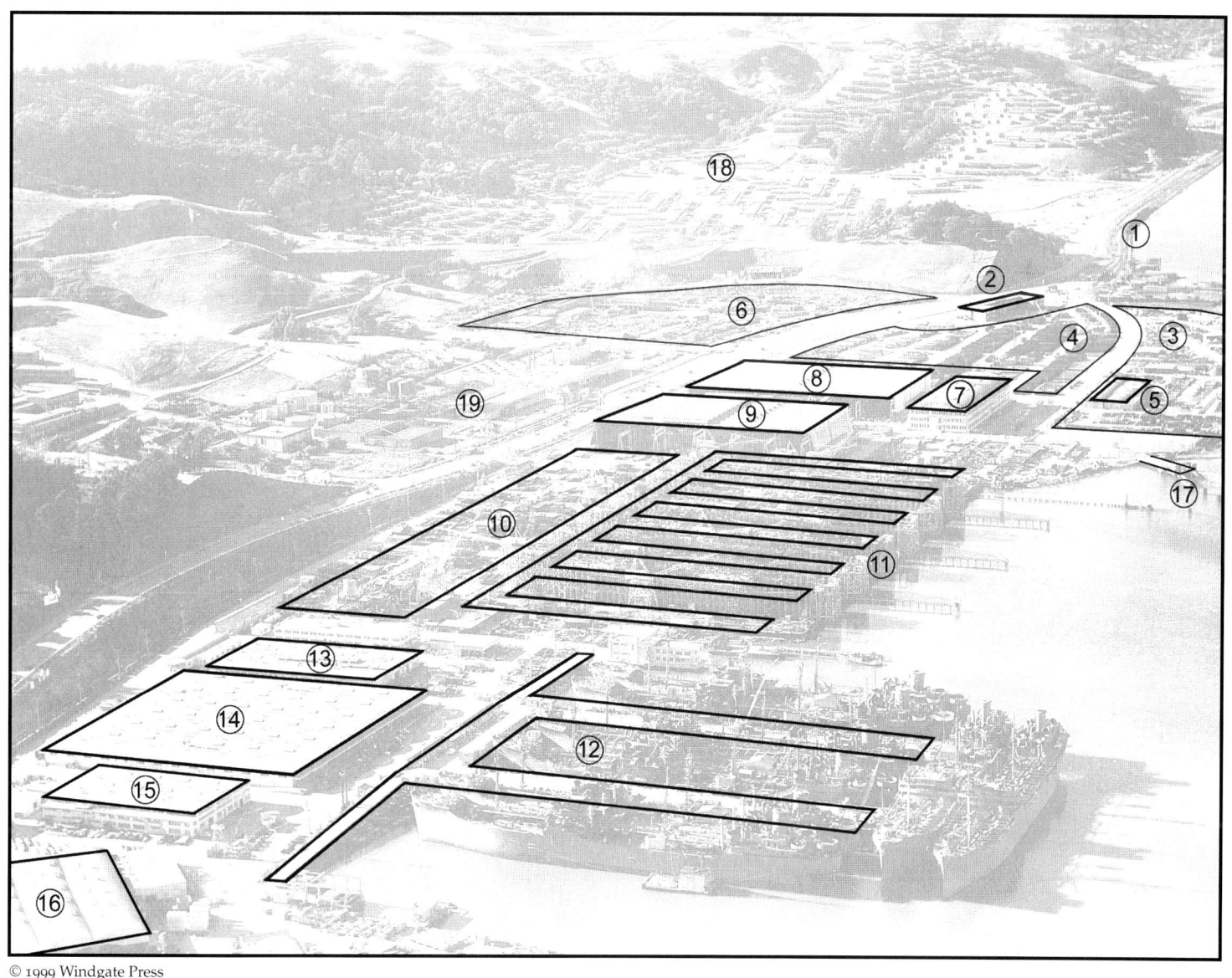

© 1999 Windgate Press

THE HAGGIN MUSEUM

SAN FRANCISCO MARITIME NHP P83-119.00075pl

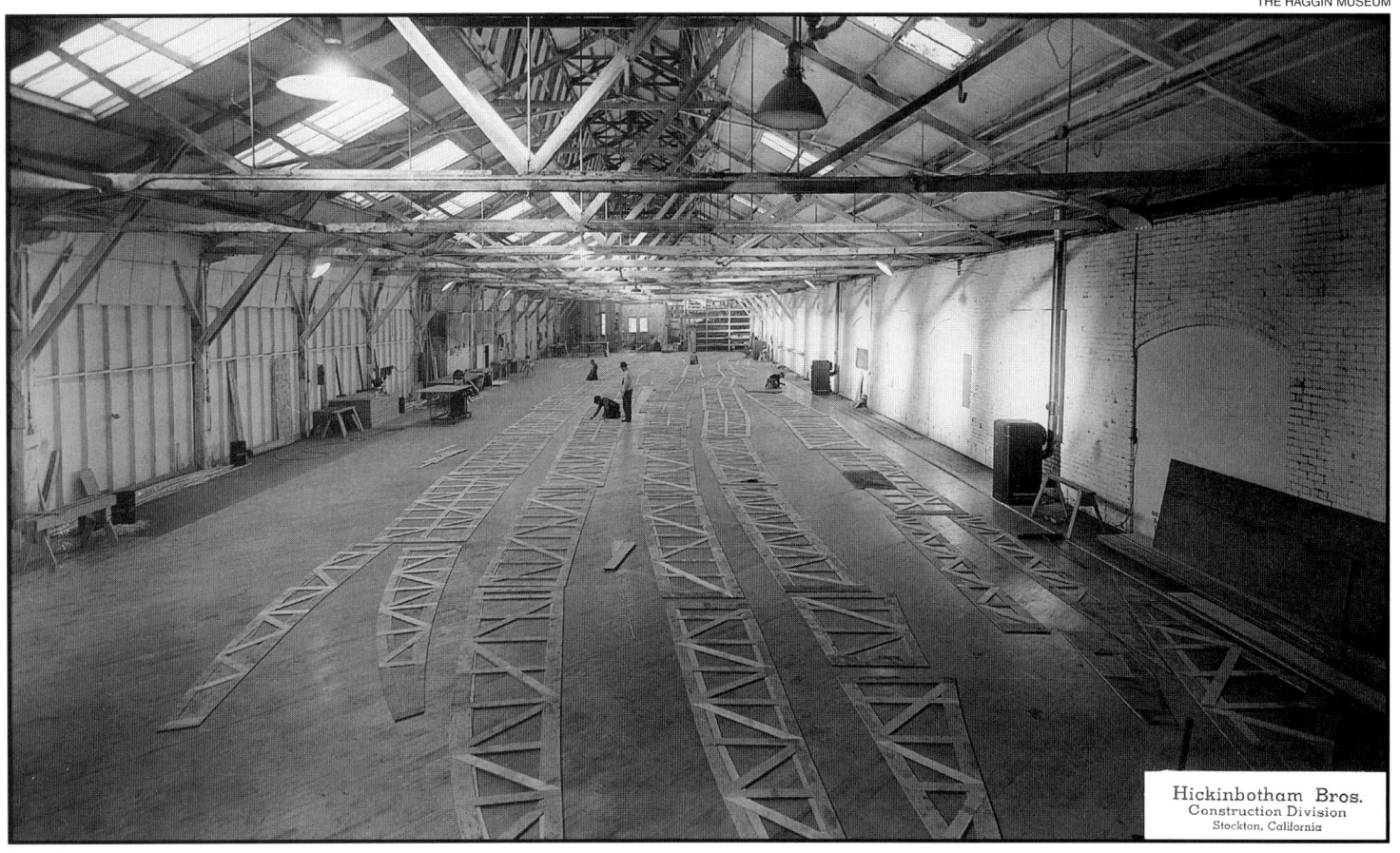

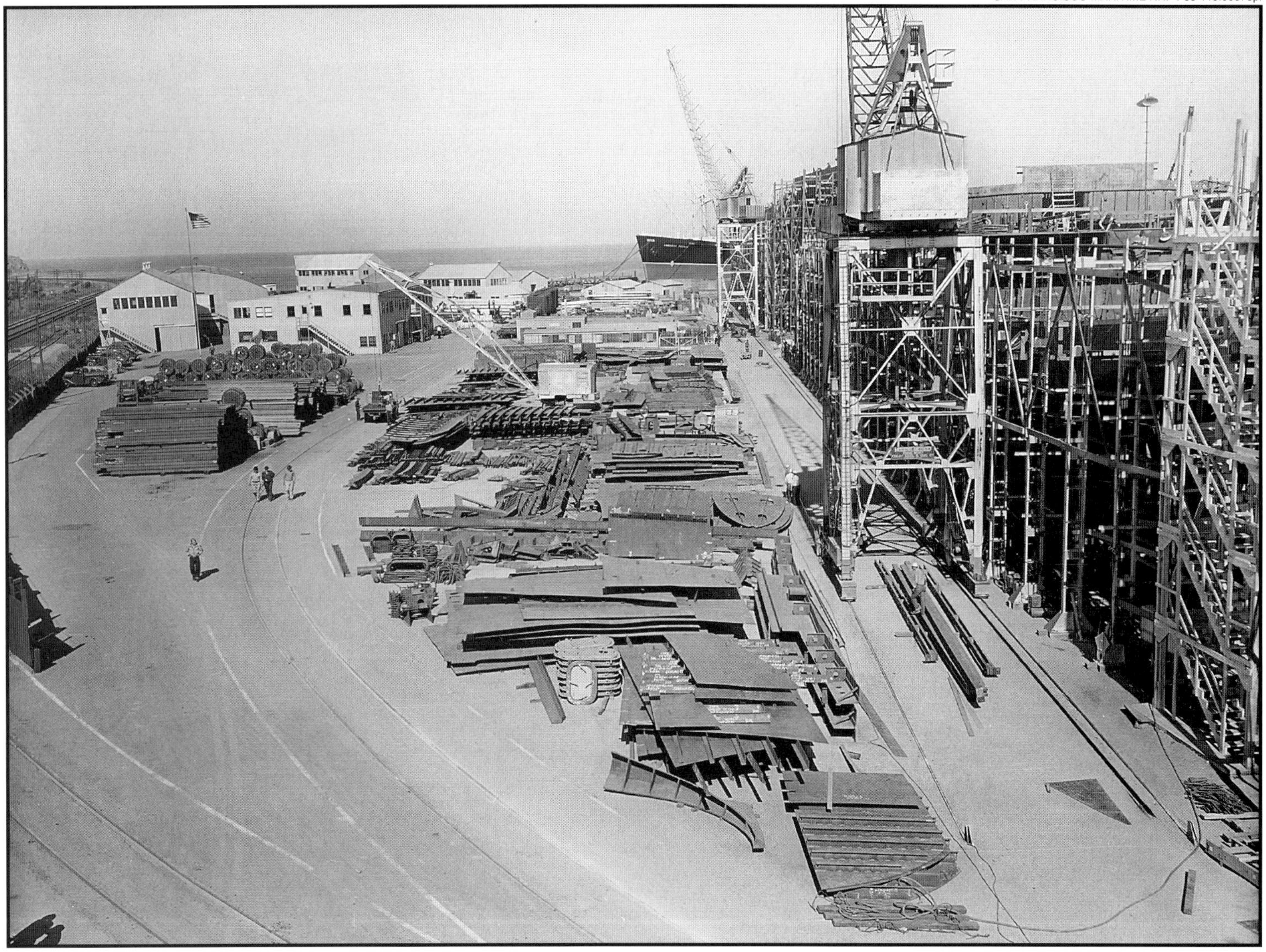

Side-launch shipway, right side of photo, at Western Pipe and Steel shows a C3 hull being erected as gantry cranes stand ready to lift pre-shaped parts stacked neatly by the shipway, September 24, 1941.

Above left: Second-story mold loft at Hickinbotham Brothers, January 26, 1944.

Above: Bending steel channels for a C3 hull at Moore Dry dock Company, April 5, 1939.

While innovation marked World War II shipbuilding, nobody tried to reinvent the wheel. Many methods of steel ship construction used for decades were retained and adapted, wherever possible, to prefabrication and pre-assembly. Each big yard, for example, had a mold loft, a large enclosed space where full-size hull drawings were transferred to wooden patterns. Mold lofts such as the one at top left had been an integral part of shipyards for at least a century by the time World War II began. In that pre-computer age, working full size was the surest way to create accurate and fair shapes. The wood patterns were sent to the fabrication shops and replicated in steel. In prewar days, ships were often one of a kind or made in pairs. World War II shipyards produced the same basic hull designs repeatedly so loft patterns need not be made for each vessel. As hull designs were modified, however, the mold loft would produce new patterns reflecting the changes.

Another procedure, shown above, unchanged from World War I was bending steel channels by heating and forcing the piece to proper shape on cast iron bending blocks. These 12-inch channels are heated in the gas furnace at rear, right then dogged down to the bending block to match a precut pattern (seen at center lying next to the bent channel) from the molding loft.

SAN FRANCISCO MARITIME NHP P79-071a Scr55:d pl.1138

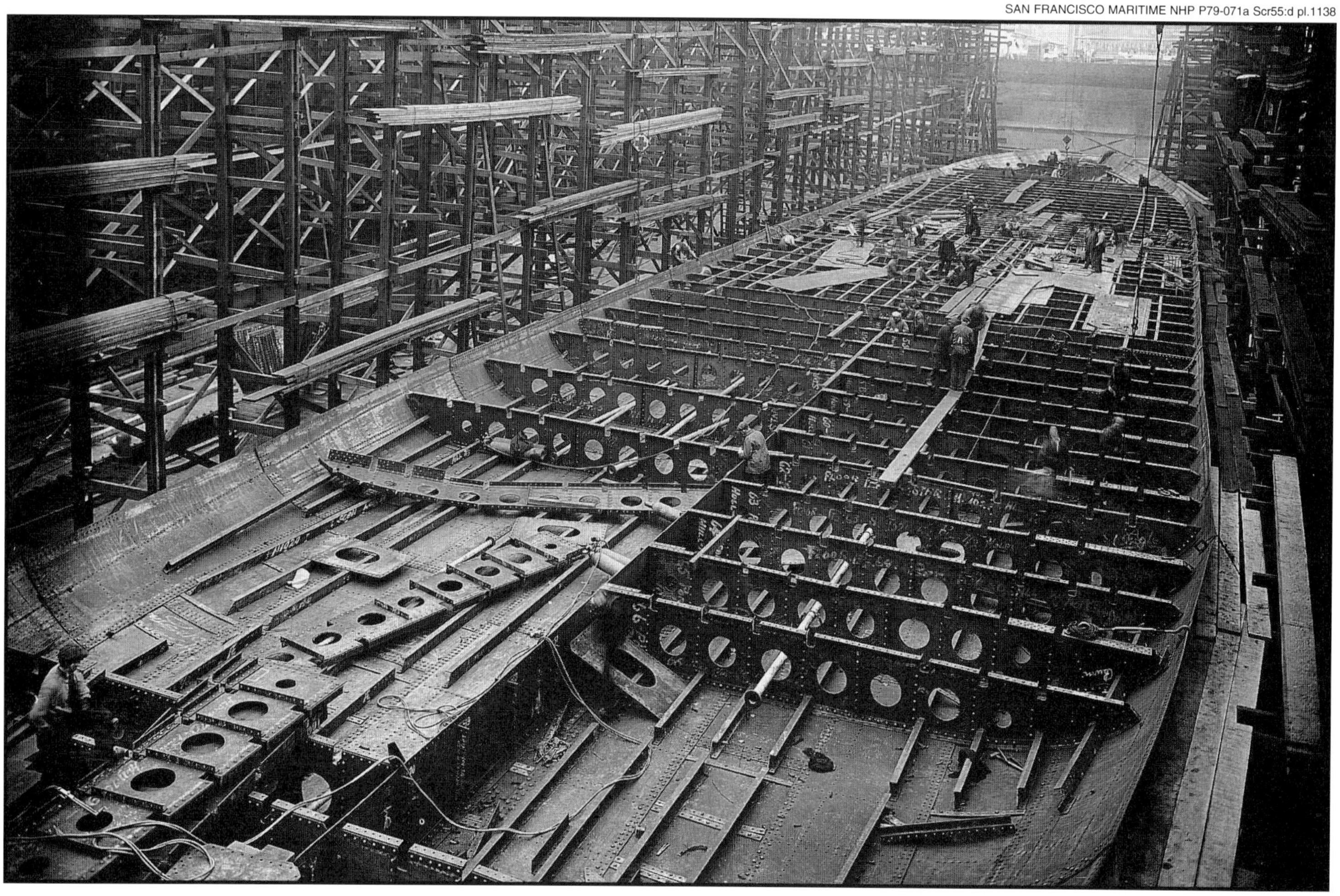

Above: Looking aft, SS *Nokatay*, Moore & Scott, January 15, 1919.

SAN FRANCISCO MARITIME NHP P79-071a Scr55:b pl.580

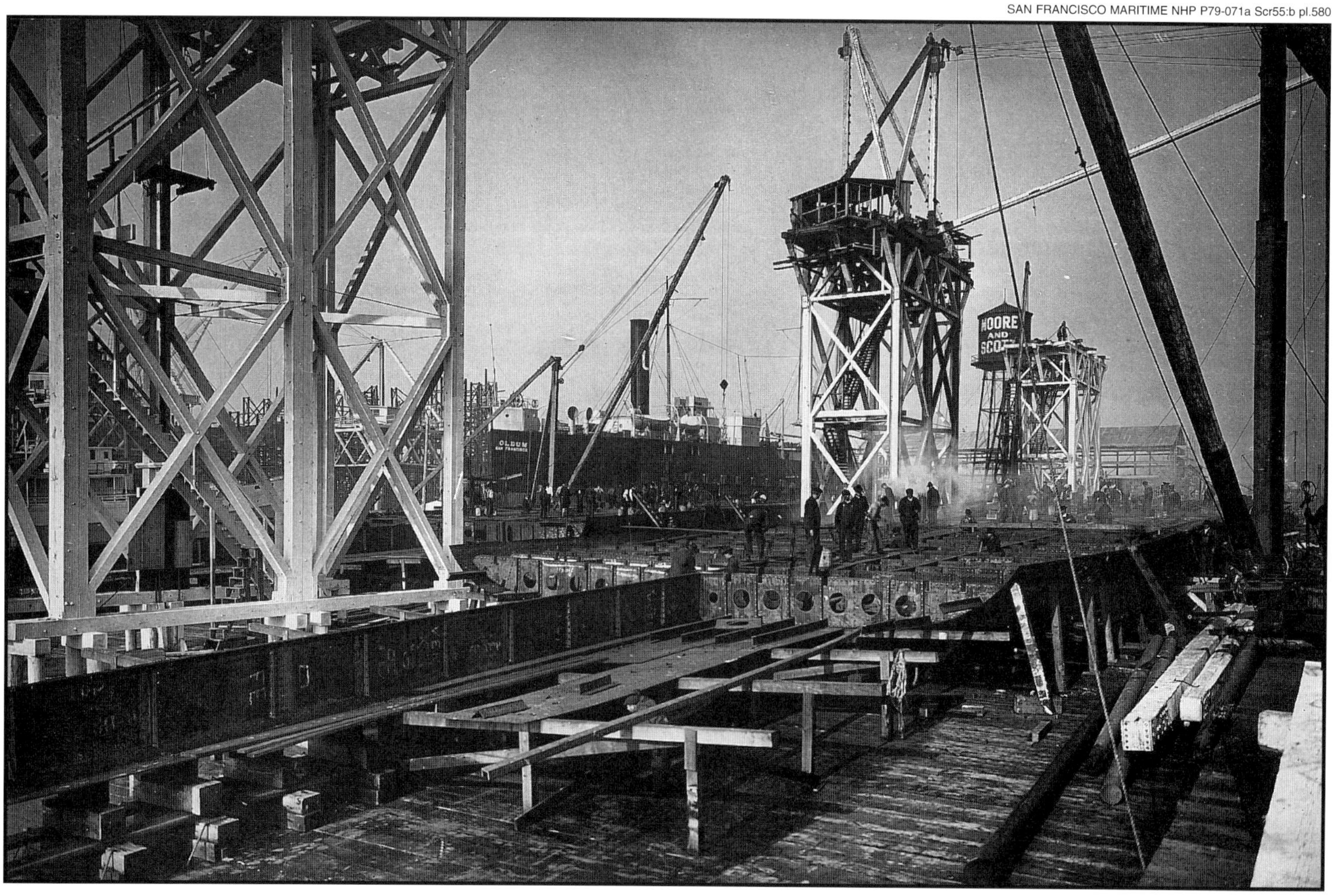

Hull of SS *Alloway* under construction, Moore & Scott, December 19, 1917.

A 47-ton inverted section of welded double bottom, Moore Dry Dock Company, July 25, 1942.

Both prefabrication of steel and pre-assembly of parts were used to speed ship production during World War I but not nearly to the extent as in World War II. At the World War I Hog Island shipyard near Philadelphia, ships were built with parts pre-assembled elsewhere and shipped by rail to the yard. Between the wars, with so few ships being made, pre-assembly was not necessary and offered no cost savings. By 1940, as shipyards geared up to meet rapidly increasing demand for ships, extensive pre-assembly was recognized as the only way production goals could be met. These three photographs contrast World War I construction and World War II methods. On the left-hand page are two shots of typical hull floor construction in 1917 and 1919. Each piece of the floors making up the double bottom is positioned on the shipway and riveted to the keel. Piping is threaded through pre-punched holes as work progresses. Riveters had to work in the cramped space beneath the hull to fasten the plates. Above, a double bottom section is pre-assembled during World War II showing the all-welded construction that had replaced riveting. The section is built inverted for ease of welding, then flipped by gantry crane for installation in the hull. Piping will be pre-installed. This procedure for building double bottoms saved weeks, enabling the yard to greatly shorten the overall time a hull under construction would occupy the way. Obviously, the sooner a hull could clear the shipway, the sooner another hull could be started.

SAN FRANCISCO MARITIME NHP P79-071a Scr55:a pl.273

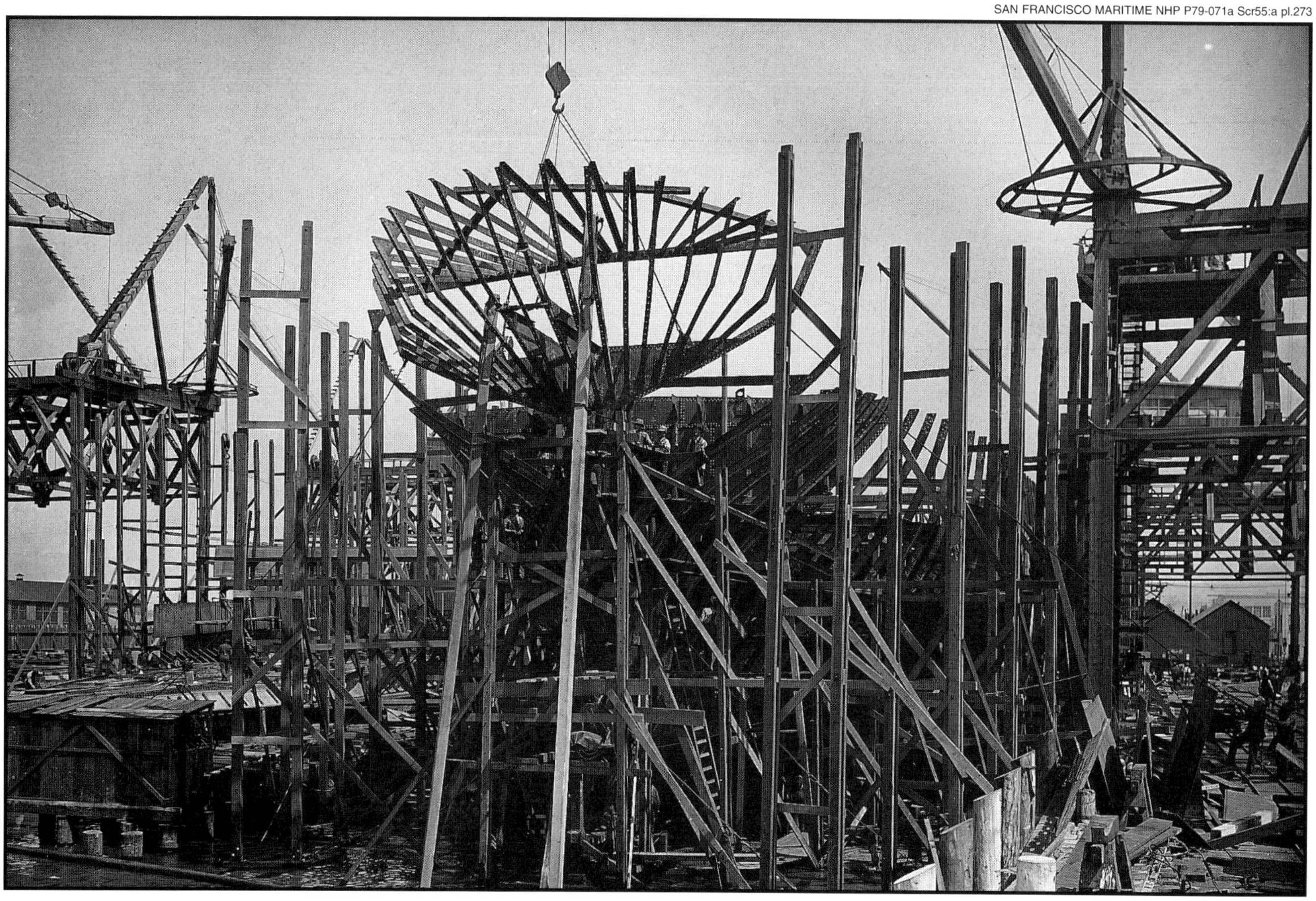

Above: Typical World War I stern construction shows riveted stern framing being lifted by stiff-legged derrick aboard the SS *Capto*. Plating will be riveted piece-by-piece to the pre-punched frames. Moore & Scott, 1916.

WINDGATE

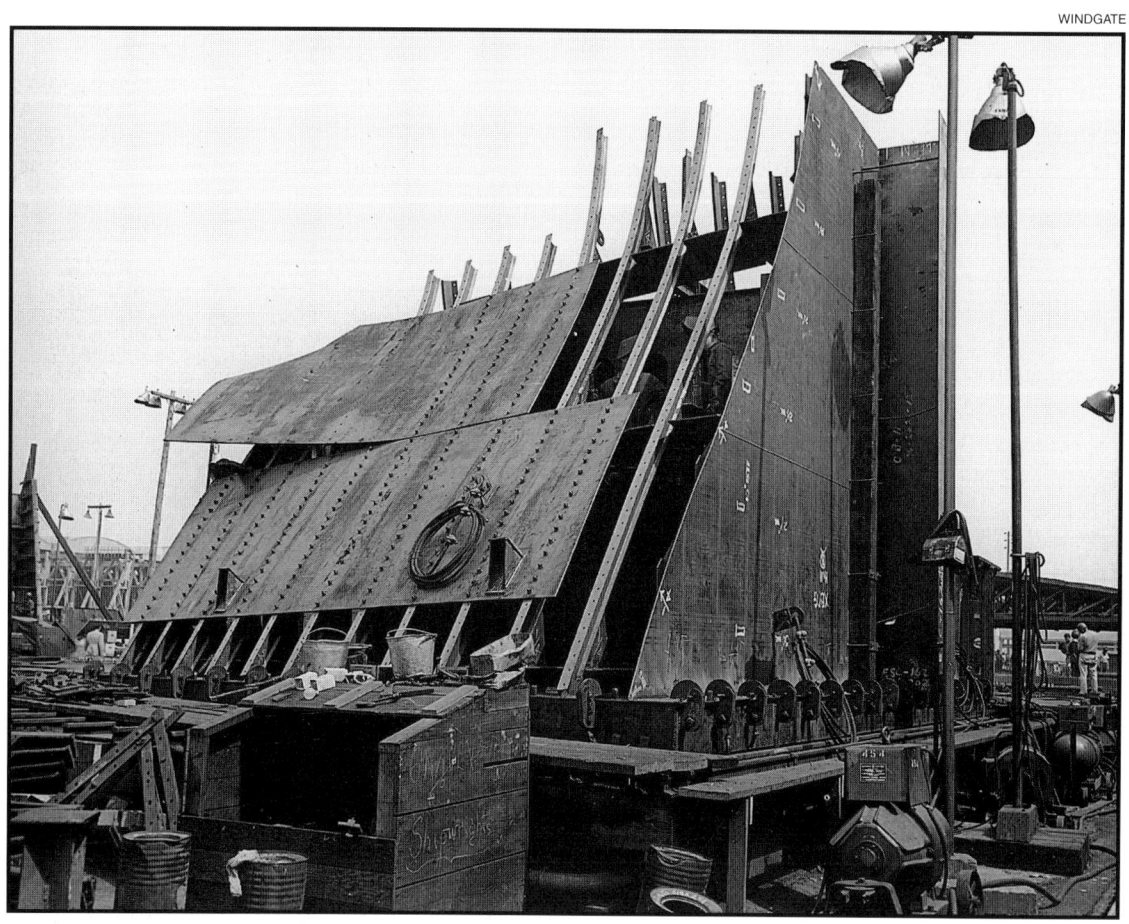

A Liberty ship bow section prior to welding. What appear to be rivets are bolts holding steel plates in position. After welding the seams, workers will remove the bolts and fill the holes by welding. Calship, 1944.

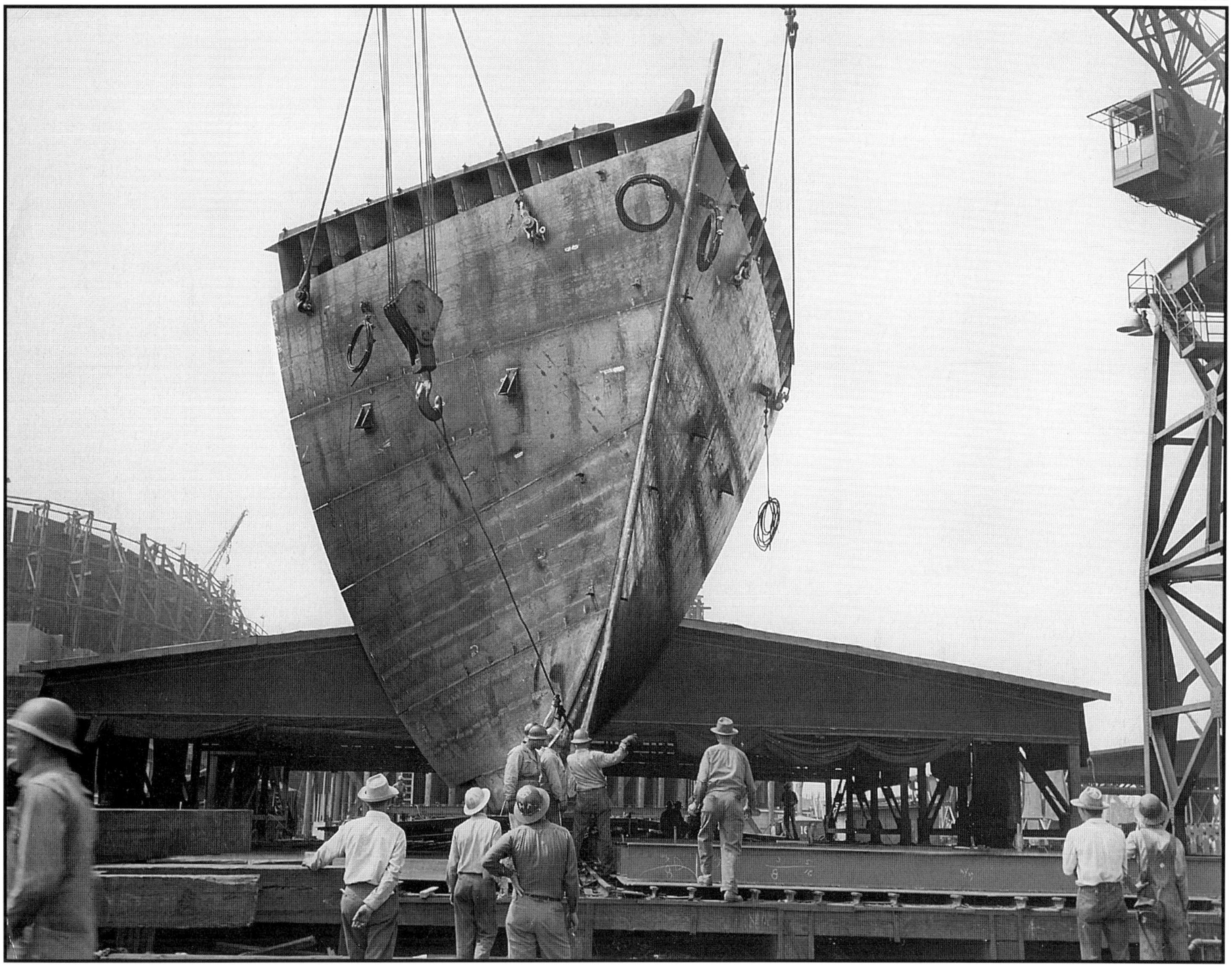

Above: A welded lower bow section of a Liberty ship ready for installation, Calship, 1944.

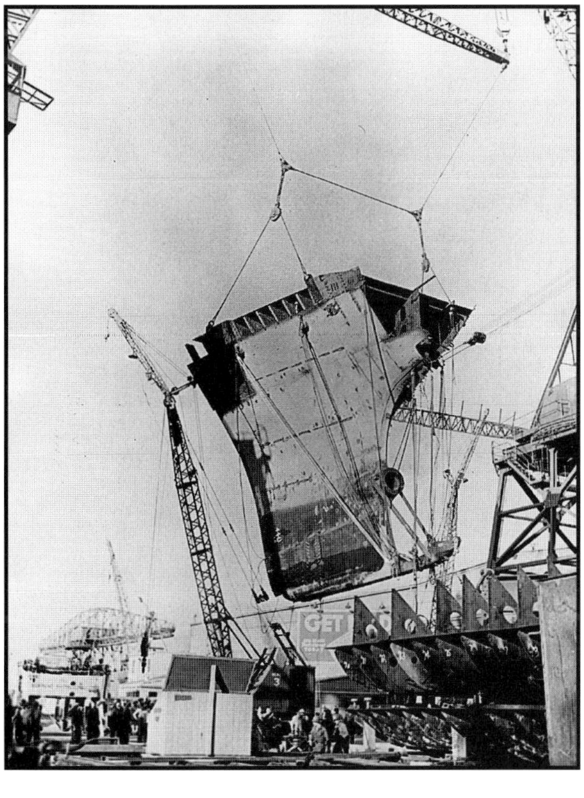

Welding of hull sections was essential to speedy pre-assembly. Estimates of time saved by welding over riveting ranged from weeks to months depending on the type of vessel. In addition to time saving, welding subtracted the weight of 150,000 rivets, over 300 tons, needed to fasten hull and deck plates. Bow and stern sections were the most complicated part of hull erection because of the compound curves involved.

Left: A Liberty ship stern pre-assembly is lifted into position at Kaiser #2. This is part of the record-setting *Robert E. Peary*, built from keel laying to launch in 4 days, 15 hours and 26 minutes.

SAUSALITO HISTORICAL SOCIETY

A special from the east pulls into Marinship, April 8, 1943. The train left Schenectady, New York seven days earlier and rolled through Ohio, Indiana, Iowa, Nebraska, across Wyoming, Utah and Nevada, through Sacramento to Suisun. From that junction it headed north around San Pablo Bay to Shellville, Sonoma County, then down to San Rafael and on to Sausalito.

SAUSALITO HISTORICAL SOCIETY

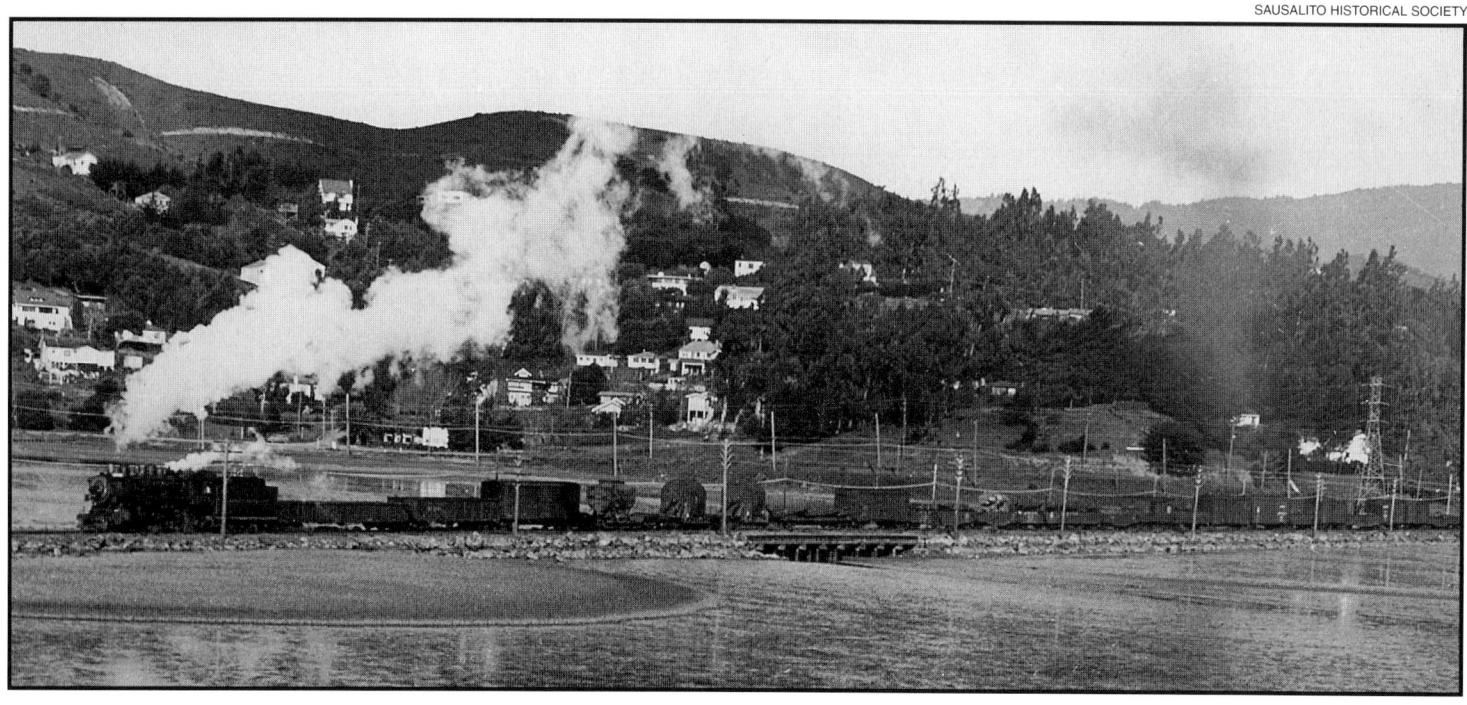

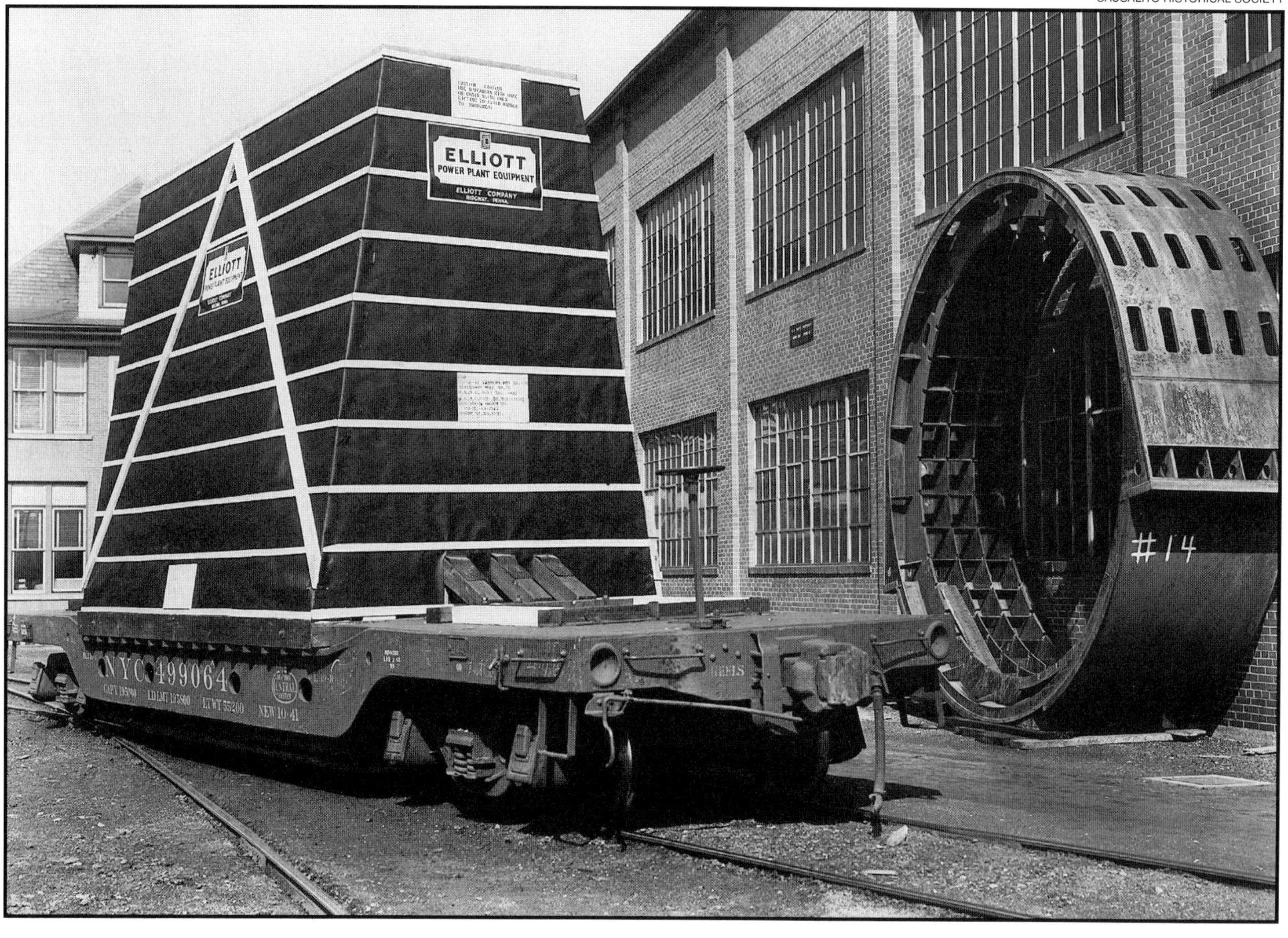

Shipment destined for Marinship being loaded at the factory in Ridgway, Pennsylvania. Number 14 is chalked on a huge stator for the main propulsion motor of a steam turbine. On the flatcar a stator is packed for transit.

Isolated geographically from eastern industrial centers, Bay Area shipyards had efficient direct rail links without which there would have been no shipyards. Not only did America's railroads provide the primary means of moving troops and supplies throughout the country, they supplied war industries with raw material and machinery and delivered finished goods for shipment overseas. Rails made it possible to create a continuous, endless flow of steel, the lifeblood of shipbuilding. By 1941, America's railroads had declined from 1918 levels with less trackage, 20,000 fewer locomotives and 600,000 fewer freight cars. Yet in 1942, railroads moved two thirds more ton-miles of freight than in 1918. In 1943 the amount of freight carried by America's railroads doubled over that of 1942. This miracle came about through railroad and government cooperation, masterful scheduling so that no rail car sat idle and every train heading east, west, north or south carried a full load. The achievement is even more remarkable considering that the Panama Canal was closed to merchant trade and everything previously carried coast to coast by ship had to be carried by rail overland.

SAUSALITO HISTORICAL SOCIETY

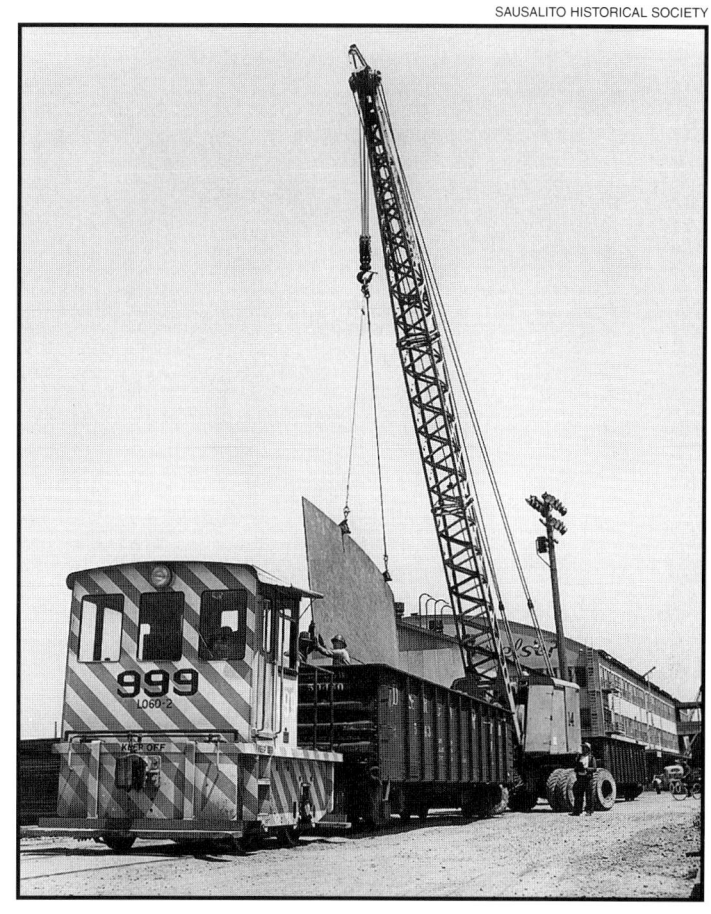

Right: Once inside the yard, the cars were shunted off to diesel electric yard locomotives. Here, steel plates are offloaded in Marinship's north storage yard. A single tanker required a trainload of steel and another trainload of parts and machinery. Yard locomotives often were manned by volunteer retired railroad engineers.

SAUSALITO HISTORICAL SOCIETY

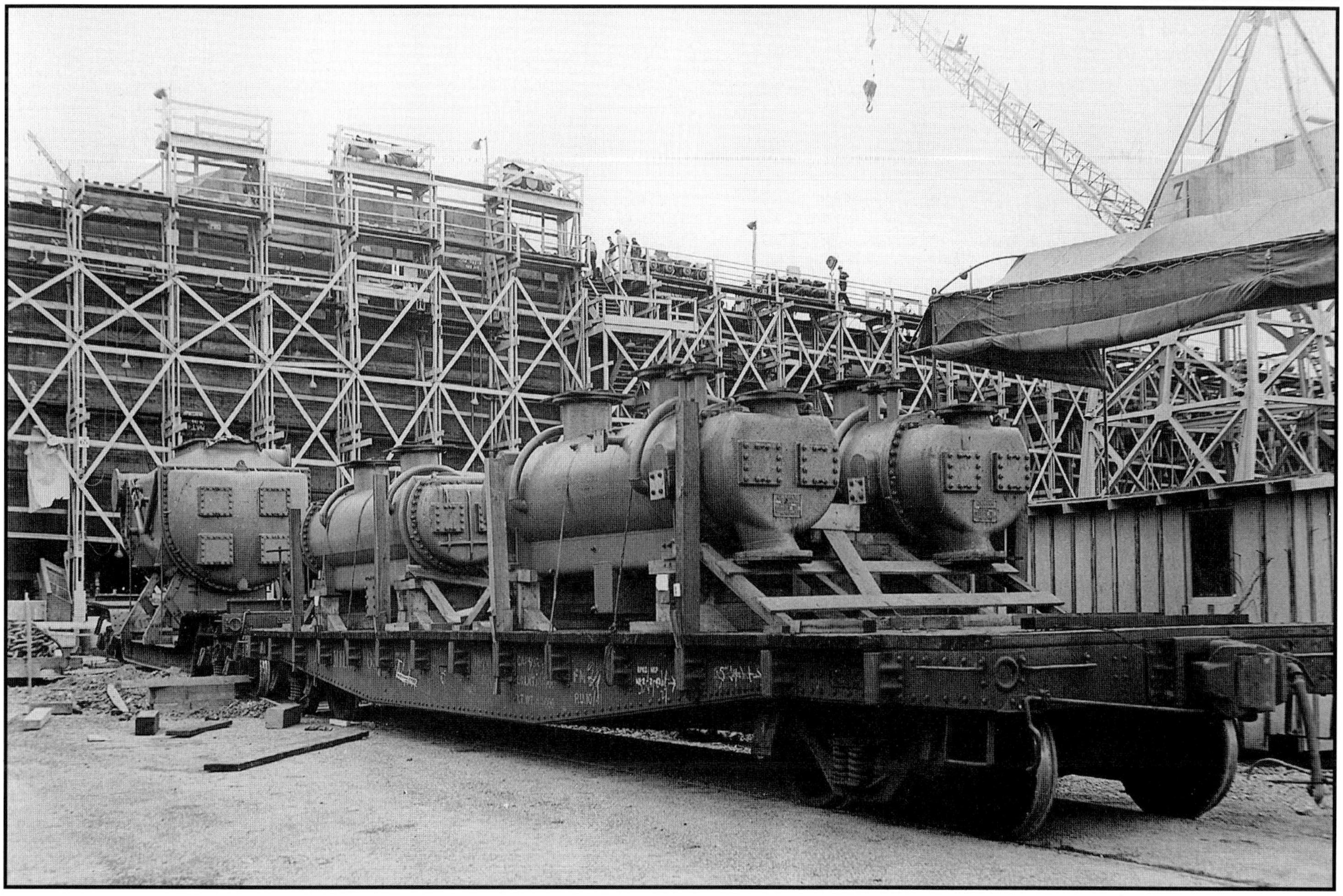

These auxiliary condensers for the main boilers are rolled right to the head of the shipway, ready to be landed in tanker hulls.

Above: This tanker boiler, trucked north across the Golden Gate Bridge from Pacific Erecting Company in San Francisco, will just clear the top of the tunnel on Waldo Grade. The highway system in Bay Area proved an additional asset to wartime shipbuilding. Although railroads carried the bulk of war materials, trucks provided speedy links between suppliers. Established shipyards such as Bethlehem and Moore Dry Dock could manufacture almost all needed machinery on site but new yards and eventually older ones were overwhelmed. By 1943, the need for boilers at Marinship and other yards, for example, exceeded on-site construction capacity, so assembled boilers were delivered from other Bay Area manufacturers. Boilers for Liberties and tankers arrived at the yard both by rail and truck.

Above: Marinship with tankers on the ways, 1944.

Above: A trucked-in boiler ready to be landed aboard a tanker hull at Marinship, supported by a strongback that balances the load between two gantry cranes. Marinship boilers weighed sixty to seventy-five tons and had to be fitted with a special foundation, shown here, for the lifting operation.

Left: The main shipyard thoroughfare at Marinship had to accommodate gantry cranes, trucks, Hysters, and workers on foot. Shipyards employed every type of truck available, flatbeds, semi-trailers, pickups, and a number of specialized vehicles unfamiliar to most workers before the war. These went by a variety of names including jeeps, chug-chugs and scooters. The Buda Chore Boy was an electric runabout; the Clarket, a three-wheeled gas-powered tow vehicle, and the Atlas Carloader was an early forklift pallet carrier. Shipyard traffic cops kept order. c.1944.

A whirley crane at Moore Dry Dock lands triple-expansion engine on the lighthouse tender *Walnut*, April 18, 1939. Sister ship *Fir*, launched the same day, lies alongside.

SHIPYARD CRANES

One of the outstanding tools of World War II shipyards was the traveling, high-capacity gantry crane. Commonly called the "whirling" or "whirley" crane, it was a self-propelled machine that could rotate its boom 360 degrees and move parallel to the shipways at speeds up to 200 feet per minute. Developed before the war, the whirley crane became almost universal in new shipyards and replaced older immobile cranes in older yards. The 50-ton capacity model was most common although larger and smaller capacity versions also were built. The flexibility and mobility of whirley cranes helped boost shipyard output in the Bay Area and across the county.

Power to the cranes was supplied either through an electric collector arm on the wheels or through a diesel-powered generator installed in the cab. The rails running lengthwise of the shipways were heavier than ordinary railroad tracks and set 32 feet apart to provide wide, stable bases for the cranes.

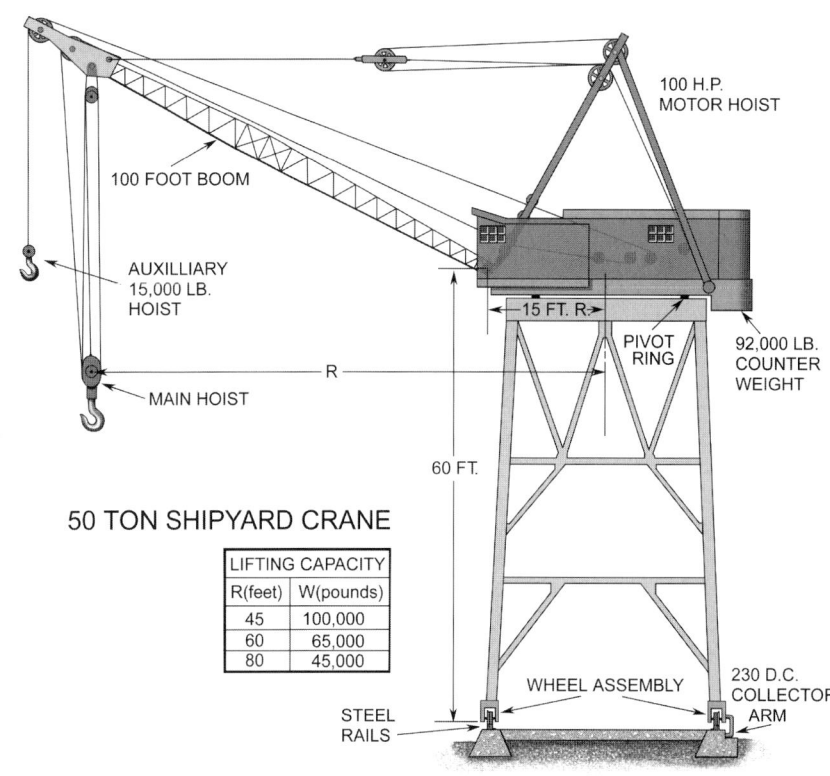

50 TON SHIPYARD CRANE

LIFTING CAPACITY	
R(feet)	W(pounds)
45	100,000
60	65,000
80	45,000

Above: Each of these Moore Dry Dock cranes differs in construction details but all get the job done: lifting in unison a section of double bottom for a C3 freighter, April 21, 1939. The crane machinery was built by Clyde Iron Works of Duluth, Minnesota, and shipped to Moore by rail. The traveling gantries were built by Moore.

Cranes lifting a 97-ton tanker deckhouse, Marinship, 1945.

Left: Four gantry cranes at Marinship orchestrated in a graceful but complicated lift; two cranes carry a tanker deck house from the pre-assembly skid to the shipway, then pass the house off to two other shipway cranes which will land it on the hull. Needless to say, this was a delicate operation fraught with potential dangers. The maximum lift performed by these cranes at Marinship was 116 tons, consisting of a section of inner bottom with shell plating, tank top with foundations and machinery installed. On rare occasions when a crane was not busy, it might be used to carry photographers aloft to shoot shipyard panoramas.

Each shipway in the big yards had a port and starboard gantry crane that ran the length of the way. In the first eight days after keel laying at Marinship, a tanker hull required over 1,500 crane lifts. The Colby gantry cranes were operated by riggers, whose duties also included handling machinery, large pipe, rudders, and propellers. Crane riggers developed their own hand signals to identify each part of the type of vessel under construction.

Above: Even in smaller scale, crane lifts required careful planning and execution. This deckhouse being lifted aboard refrigerated supply ship *YP646* has steel piping inserted through portholes to evenly distribute the weight and provide attachment points for the lifting cables. Large sub-assemblies had to be stabilized with wood or steel stiffeners prior to the lift to prevent distortion and cracking of welded seams. Colberg Boat Works, March 19, 1945.

In addition to the gantry cranes prevalent in most big yards, every type of crane and hoist available, old and new, was pressed into service. Almost every part of ship construction involved lifting or moving weights exceeding a man's capacity; the crane was essential. Older yards such as Mare Island and Bethlehem had older steam-powered cranes that were converted to electricity. Interior cranes were usually overhead traveling types that had changed little since World War I.

The illustration at right shows most of the major types of cranes used in World War II shipyards. Many smaller types and variants were incorporated in shop interior operations, anywhere something heavy had to be lifted. Older shipyards used shear-leg derricks, often mounted on barges, and large stiff-leg railway mounted or immobile derricks (Figure 1). Many older shipyards, such as at Mare Island, had overhead traveling bridge cranes that straddled the shipways (Figure 7). The huge structures rolled on rails into position over the vessel under construction to lower parts and machinery into place. To handle lighter loads, smaller mobile cranes were fitted to the same rails and used in conjunction with the overhead bridge cranes. In addition, even smaller cranes were mounted on ordinary railway flatcars for use on tracks within the shipyard. Some yards also had locomotive-type cranes (Figure 6) and one-legged gantry cranes. In the smaller shipyards at Stockton, mobile yard cranes, often called crawler cranes, (Figure 5) were indispensable and handled a wide variety of tasks. Every yard had some sort of floating crane (Figure 3). This profusion of crane types led to difficulties in scheduling the movement of cranes to keep them from getting in one another's way.

THE HAGGIN MUSEUM

A crane operator riding an overhead crane deftly positions a steel engine room assembly. Overhead cranes moved loads along two planes; were less flexible but better balanced than gantry cranes.

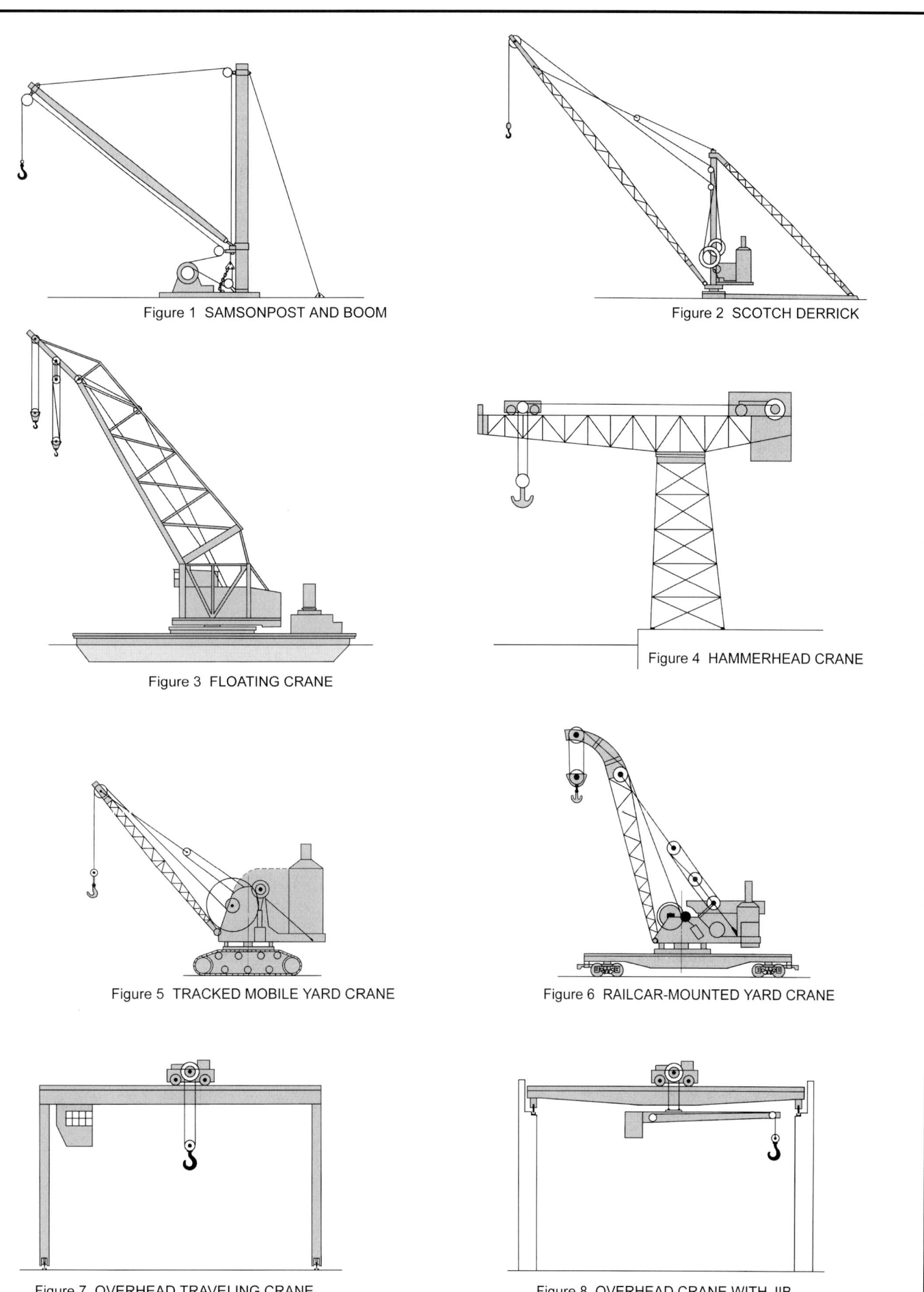

Figure 1 SAMSONPOST AND BOOM
Figure 2 SCOTCH DERRICK
Figure 3 FLOATING CRANE
Figure 4 HAMMERHEAD CRANE
Figure 5 TRACKED MOBILE YARD CRANE
Figure 6 RAILCAR-MOUNTED YARD CRANE
Figure 7 OVERHEAD TRAVELING CRANE
Figure 8 OVERHEAD CRANE WITH JIB

© 1999 Windgate Press

1. February 13, 1943

2. February 20, 1943

5. April 10, 1943

6. May 1, 1943

3. February 27, 1943

4. March 13, 1943

7. May 15, 1943

A TANKER GROWS IN SAUSALITO

Each ship in a series benefitted from lessons learned on the previous one. The first tanker built at Marinship took 140 days from keel laying to launch, the last, 28 days. This one, Hull #20, took 119 days.

1. Three days after the first keel plate was laid, eight raised keel sections are in place. Stern view.

2. Day ten, bow view, shows hull bottom plating well under way and main tank bulkheads starting amidships.

3. Day seventeen, stern view shows main tanks almost complete; curved hull plates begin to form the stern.

4. Day thirty-one, bow view, bulkheads amidship are extended to full width of hull forming bilge tanks; centerline girder for eight tanks in place. Bow flooring sections being placed.

5. Day fifty-nine, lower bow assembly taking shape, upper deck sections form midship tank tops.

6. Day eighty, outer hull complete except for bow, decking complete, machinery installed.

7. Day ninety-four, forepeak section fitted to bow, raised forecastle deck not yet in place. Pre-assembled midship house hoisted on board, hull is twenty-five days from launch. The vessel became the Navy fleet oiler U.S.S. *Ocklawaha*.

SAN FRANCISCO MARITIME NHP P79-141.0921p .0922p .0925p .0928p .0936p .0942p .0946p

Tankers were more complex than Liberty ships and less complex than most warships. Therefore, even though competition was strong in every yard, direct comparisons of speed in construction were inherently unfair. Yards such as Kaiser #1, which stuck to one type, the Liberty ship, had an advantage over Kaiser #4, or Marinship which had to change vessel type in mid production. Moore Dry Dock was a jack-of-all-trades during the war, handling difficult assignments of production, repair and conversion that slowed overall output.

Above: Truck arrives at Marinship after a nonstop run from Portland, Oregon with anchor windlass for *Huntington Hills*, June 11, 1945. Date set for launch: June 11, 1945.

Right: The driver hurries directly to the shipway, where a gantry crane is waiting.

Left: The windlass is lifted aboard just hours from launch ceremonies. *Huntington Hills* set a national record for tanker construction, 28 days from keel laying to launch and just 33 days from keel laying to delivery. The ship's main condenser, last piece of internal machinery to be installed, was flown at the last moment from the manufacturer in Newark, New Jersey, to Hamilton Field in Marin County and trucked to the shipyard.

Below: Mission Purisima, sister to *Huntington Hills,* on trial run, November, 1943.

Big yards and small yards used similar techniques where possible. Shipyard representatives visited other yards to learn the most advanced methods that might expedite operations. Even though most yards were in competition with one another, they openly shared information that increased overall production.

World War II shipbuilding has been compared to an automobile assembly line but the analogy is not entirely accurate. On an automobile assembly line, the chassis moves down the line as parts are attached to it until a finished car emerges at the end. Moving assembly lines were applied to small landing craft production in some parts of the country. In 1944 alone over 25,000 landing craft of less than 50 tons each were built on assembly lines for the Navy in various yards nationwide. Based on that experience, some yards were able to apply assembly lines to larger vessel construction. But for large cargo ships, moving the bulky hull along a line was impractical. Shipyards assembled hulls in one place, on the shipway, as pre-assembled sections and parts were brought to it. In some yards, such as Hickinbotham Brothers in Stockton, vessels were built in ranks parallel to the shoreline (see Page 137). After one completed hull was launched, the others under construction were skidded forward one rank and a new keel laid in the empty slot at the rear.

Moving assembly lines were successfully used in the steel fabrication shops within the shipyard. As steel plates and channels moved through the shop, they were worked to final shape in repeat operations and taken to the shipways for installation. The main subassemblies were deposited at the head of the shipway in an area called a "skid" or "platen" until a crane lifted them to the hull.

SAUSALITO HISTORICAL SOCIETY

A tanker forepeak subassembly moves out of the assembly shop at Marinship in 1944 on its way to the assembly skids.

THE HAGGIN MUSEUM

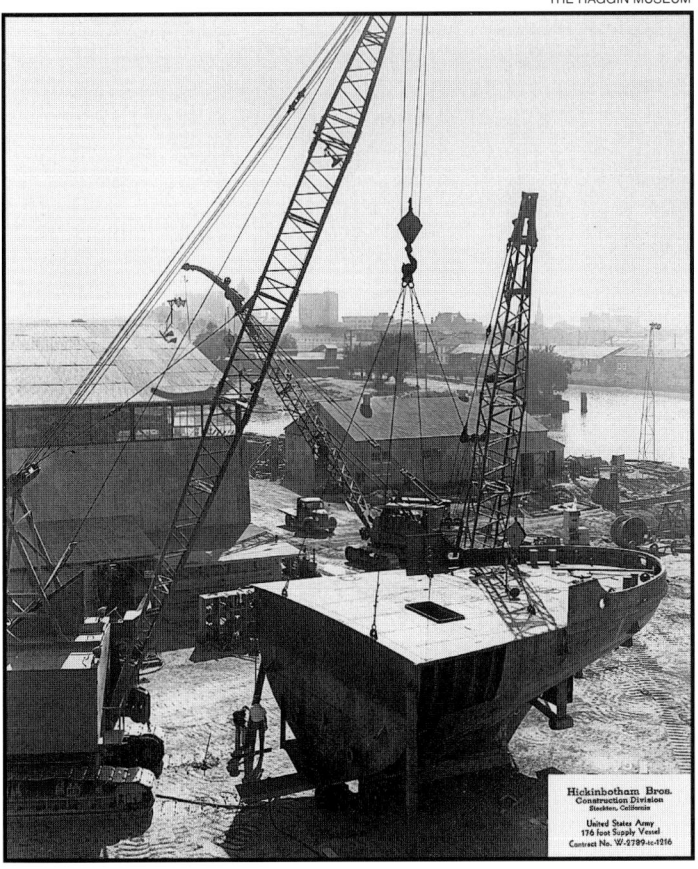

Left: The stern piece has been welded to a larger section and is about to be lifted into position on the shipway.

Below: At Hickinbotham Brothers in Stockton, a stern section is compact enough to be handled by medium-sized truck. 1944.

THE HAGGIN MUSEUM

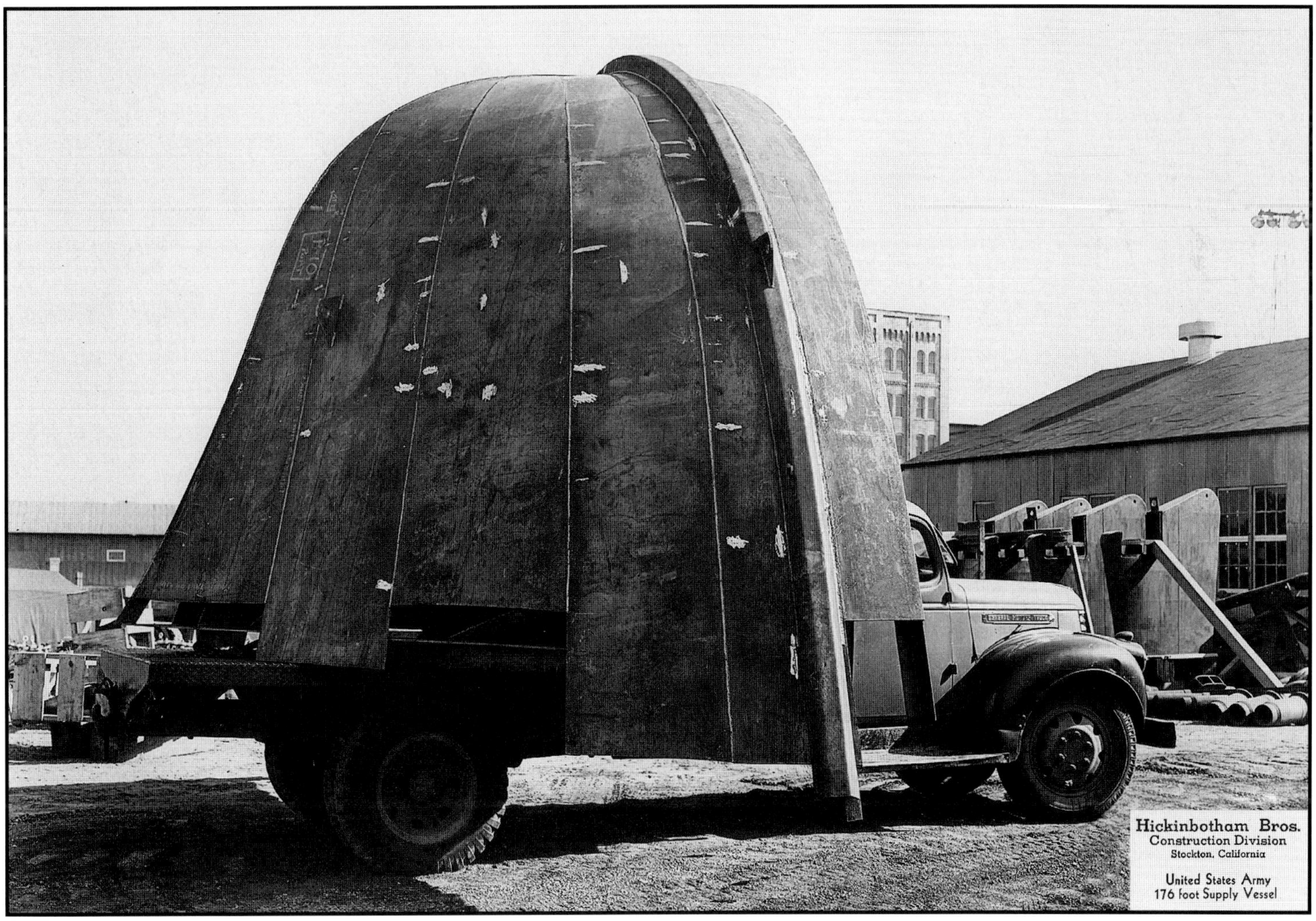

Welding was the key to pre-assembly during World War II. Although welding had been used in shipyards ever since iron and steel were introduced in the mid-1800s, riveting remained as the major means of joining plates until the 1930s. The first use of welding in shipyards was no different than in any blacksmith shop. Molten metal was applied to two heated edges and the joint held fast until the metal cooled akin to joining wooden parts with glue. The resulting welded joints were weak and suitable only on masts, small hatch coamings, bilge keels and other non-stressed joints. Arc welding commonly used in modern shipbuilding creates a far stronger bond, fastening structural members by using an electric arc to melt steel at the joint, creating a molecular bond between two pieces. Arc welding was demonstrated around 1890 and first applied in shipbuilding during World War I. It was used mainly to fill holes and repair flaws in castings and steel plates. Arc welding gradually replaced blacksmith welding and its use spread to structural assemblies. By the late 1920s arc welding was used in oil barge construction and for tank top seams in larger cargo vessels. Advantages of arc welding—low cost compared to riveting, speed of application and strength— became apparent.

In spite of these advantages, welding was slow to supplant riveting. Sun Shipbuilding & Dry Dock Company built the first all-welded tanker in 1931. Not until World War II created demand for rapid ship construction did welding replace riveting as the principal means of joining steel.

A skilled welder can make a good solid seam almost anywhere, horizontal, vertical, overhead or angled. A novice welder, as most shipyard workers were, had neither the skill or experience to match an old hand. Welding seams on flat deck plates with gravity helping the flow was simple enough but overhead welding was much more difficult. One solution was to position seams so that the welder could work in a "down-hand" position, that is, with the electrodes held at waist level or below. To accomplish that, large vertical parts to be welded were turned horizontal. Ceilings and overhead structures were inverted for welding then reversed when completed.

Automatic seam-welding machines and new alloys and welding methods added even greater speed to the process but also revealed some disadvantages. Welded steel plates tended to buckle and warp more than riveted ones. Uneven heating could result in stress fractures. Use of improperly-sized electrodes could produce weak joints. Instances of welded ships breaking apart in heavy seas, or of welded joints failing under even mild stress, were usually due to improper welding or design weaknesses created by insufficient reinforcement of welded joints.

Below: Oxygen-acetylene welding equipment also was used for "burning" or cutting steel shapes. Here, a jig is cutting steel pipe, Marinship, 1944.

SAUSALITO HISTORICAL SOCIETY

SAUSALITO HISTORICAL SOCIETY

Above: Cutting steel strips from plate with a multiple-head jig at Marinship, 1944.

SAN FRANCISCO MARITIME NHP P79-071a Scr55:q pl.4618

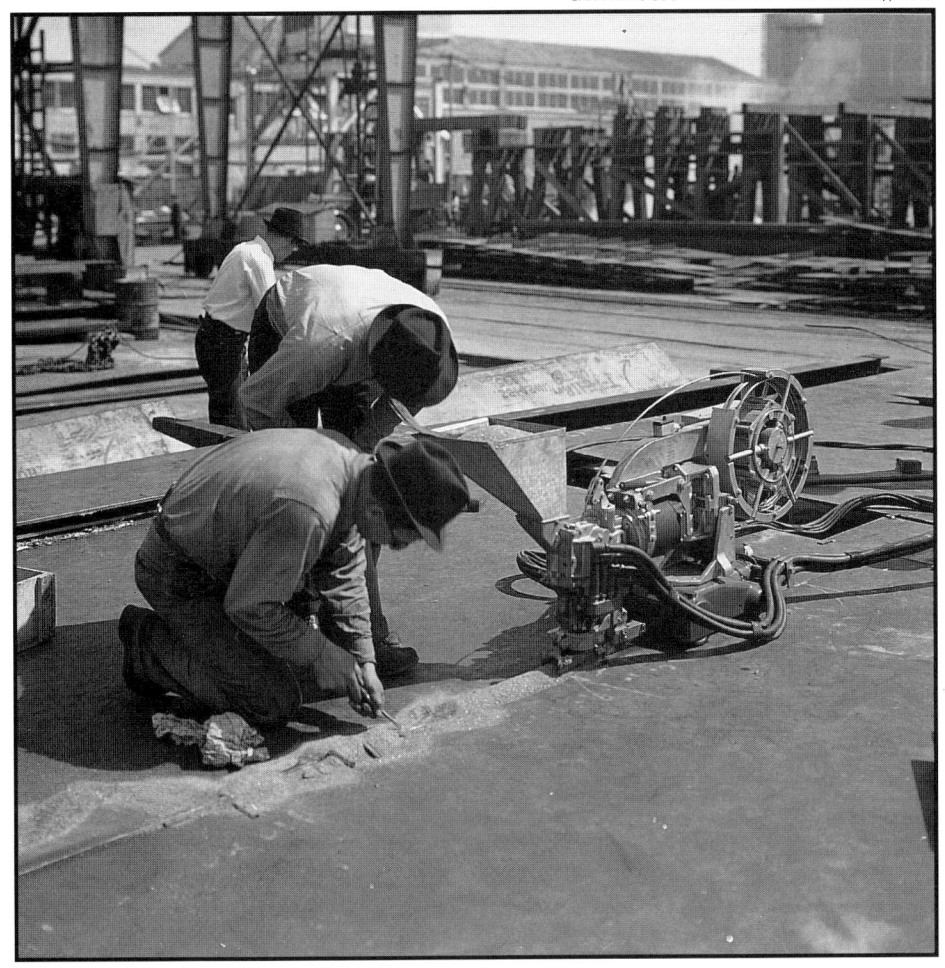

Left: Workers welding tank-top plating using a "submerged arc" Unionmelt automatic welding machine, Moore Dry Dock Company, April 7, 1939.

Below: Burning machine at Colberg's Steel Fabrication Shop. The device "burned" or cut two opposing bevels in abutting steel plates prior to welding.

THE HAGGIN MUSEUM

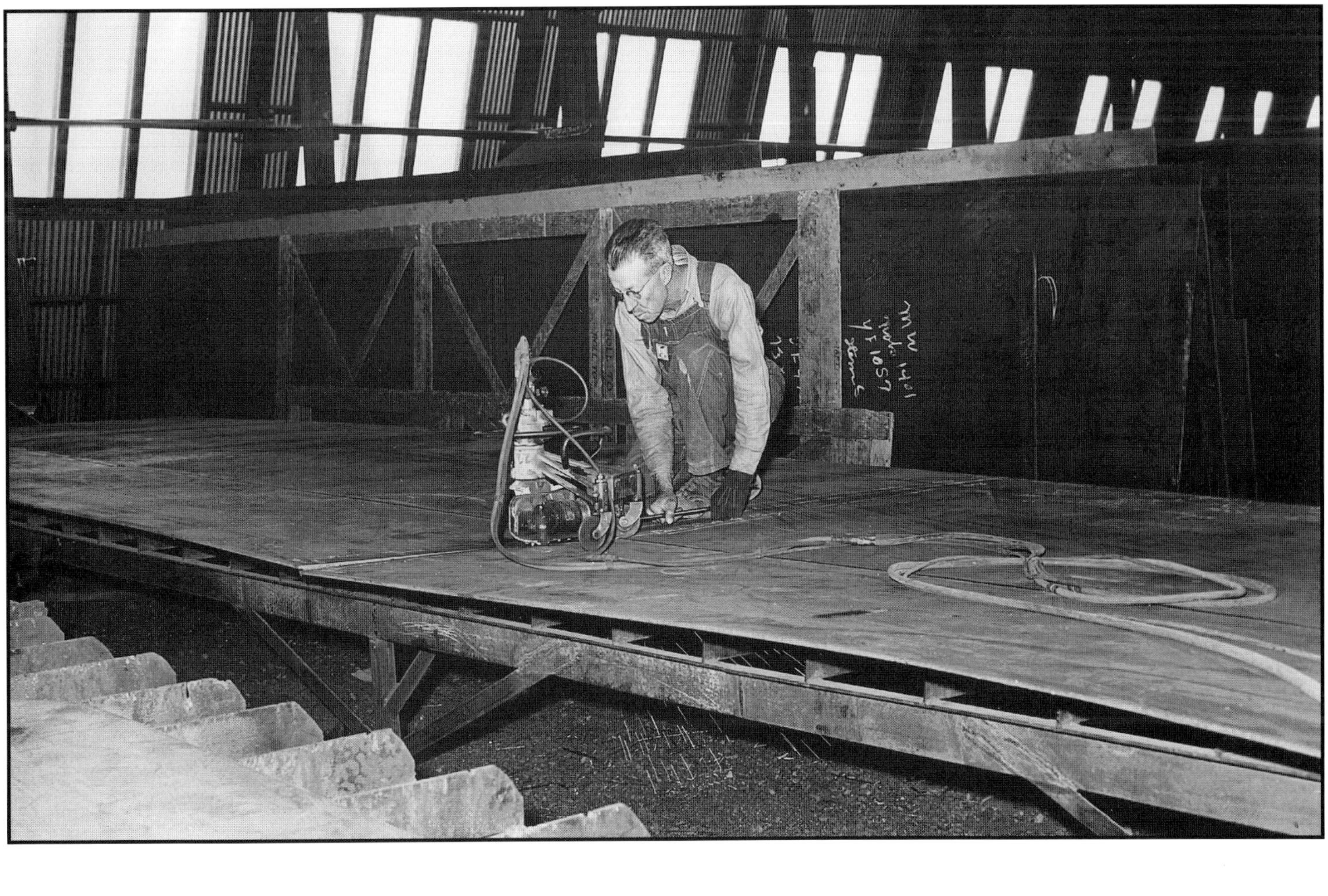

THE HAGGIN MUSEUM

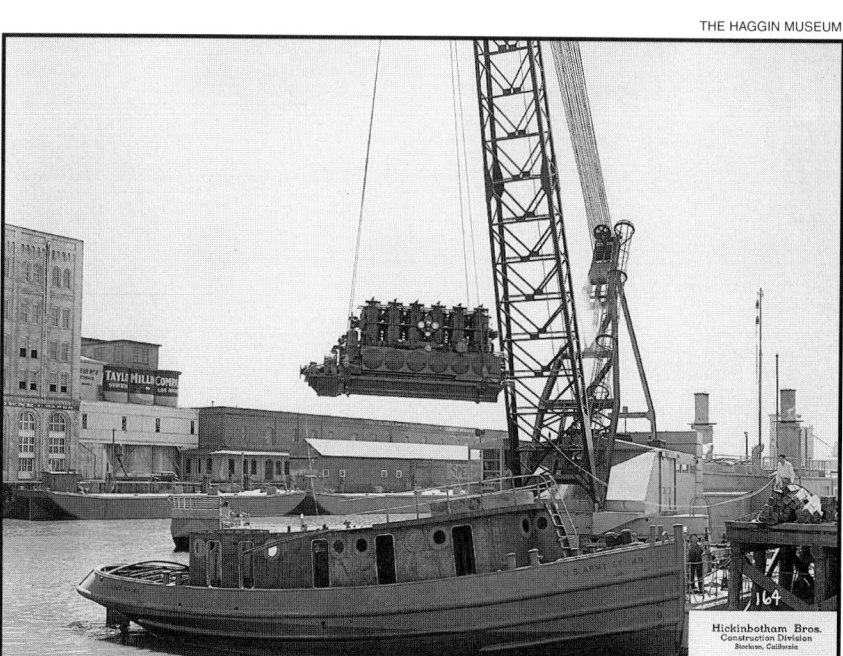

Right: Welded steel hulls proved highly effective for small, powerful craft destined for heavy work such as this 74-foot Army tug, shown receiving its power plant, Hickinbotham Brothers, August 7, 1943.

THE HAGGIN MUSEUM

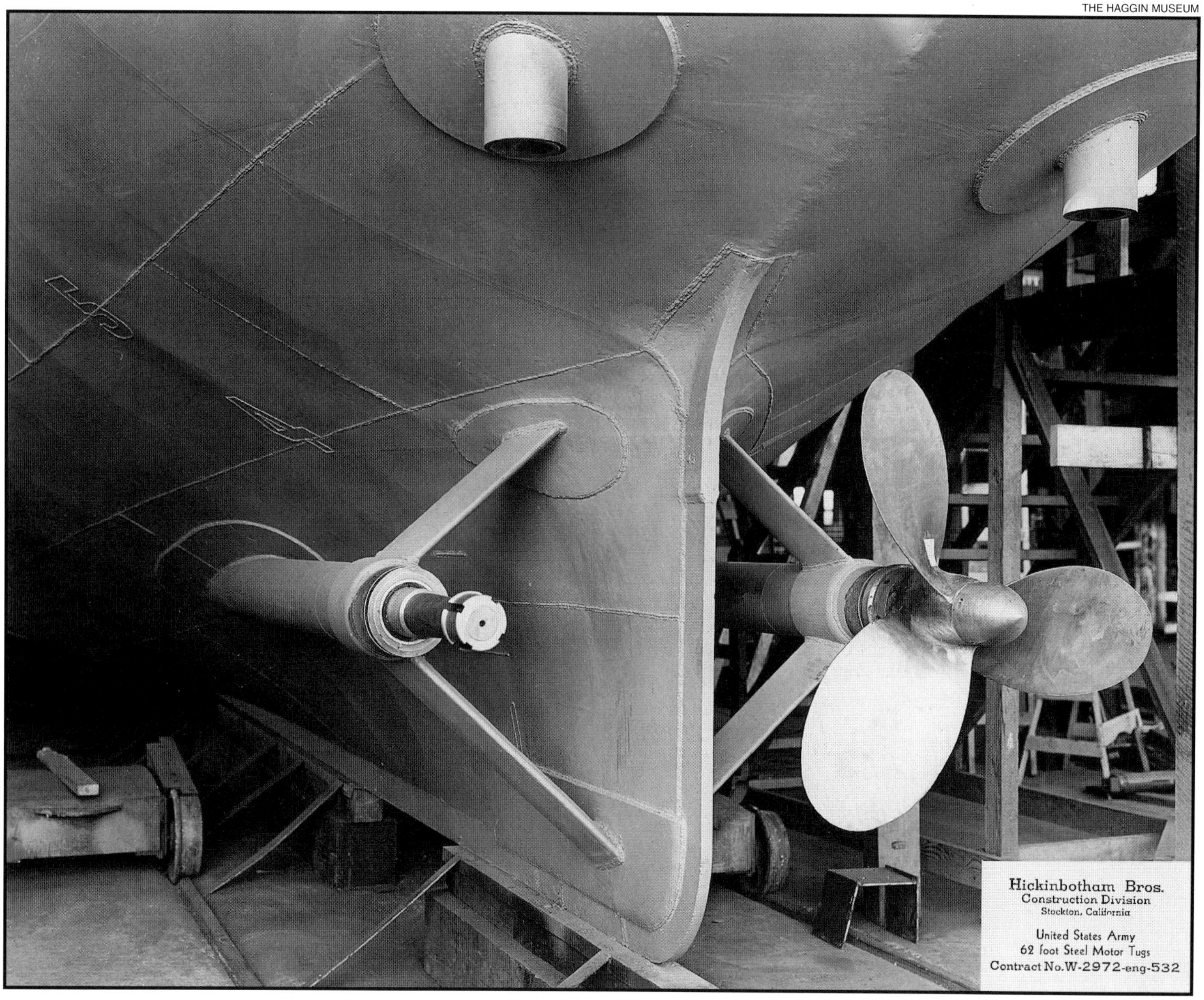

Close up of welded stern, steel tug, December 14, 1943.

THE HAGGIN MUSEUM

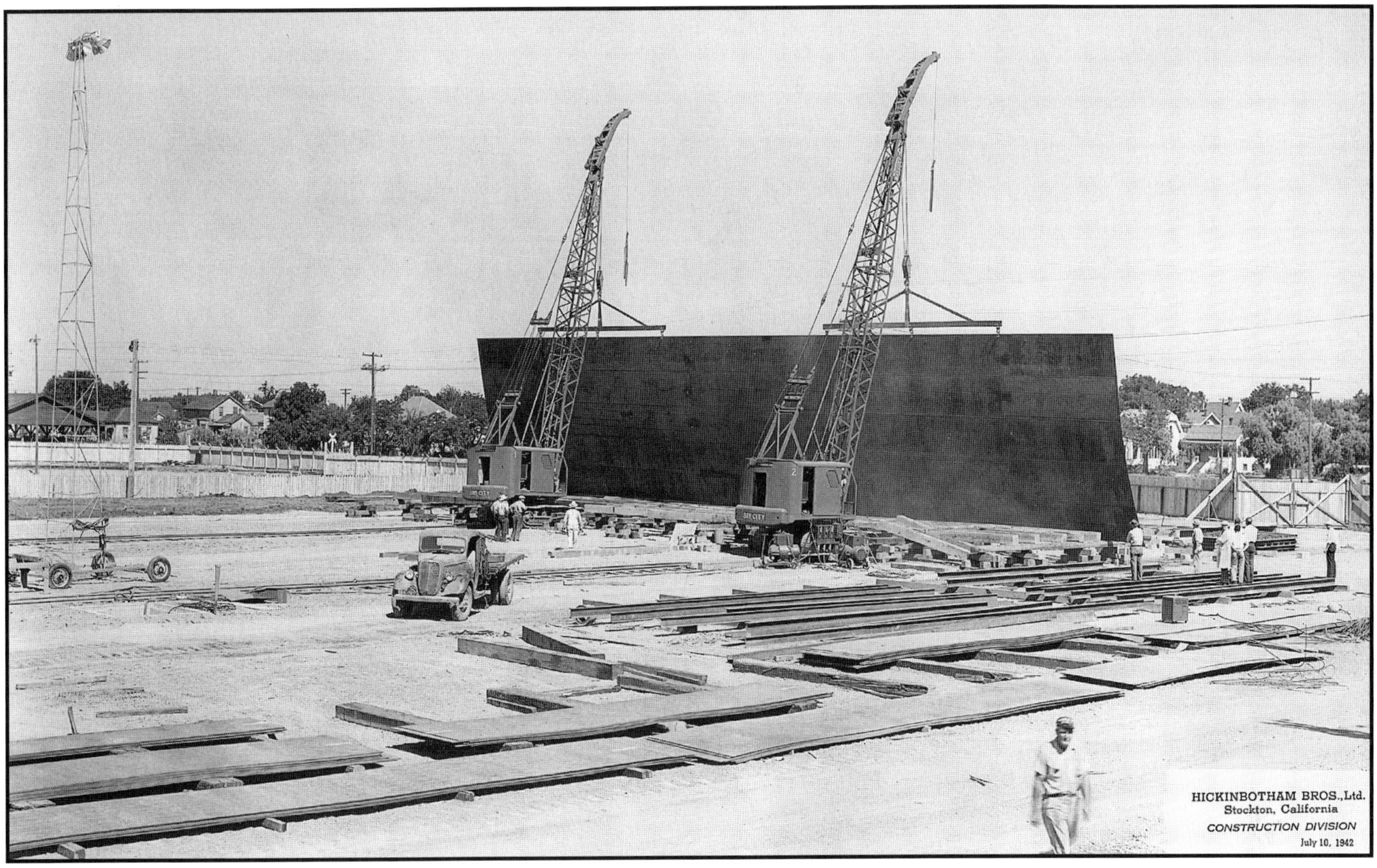

Welding became the basic glue of steel shipbuilding, allowing for fabrication of almost any shape in any size. Here, welded plates form a bottom for a large crane pontoon.

THE HAGGIN MUSEUM

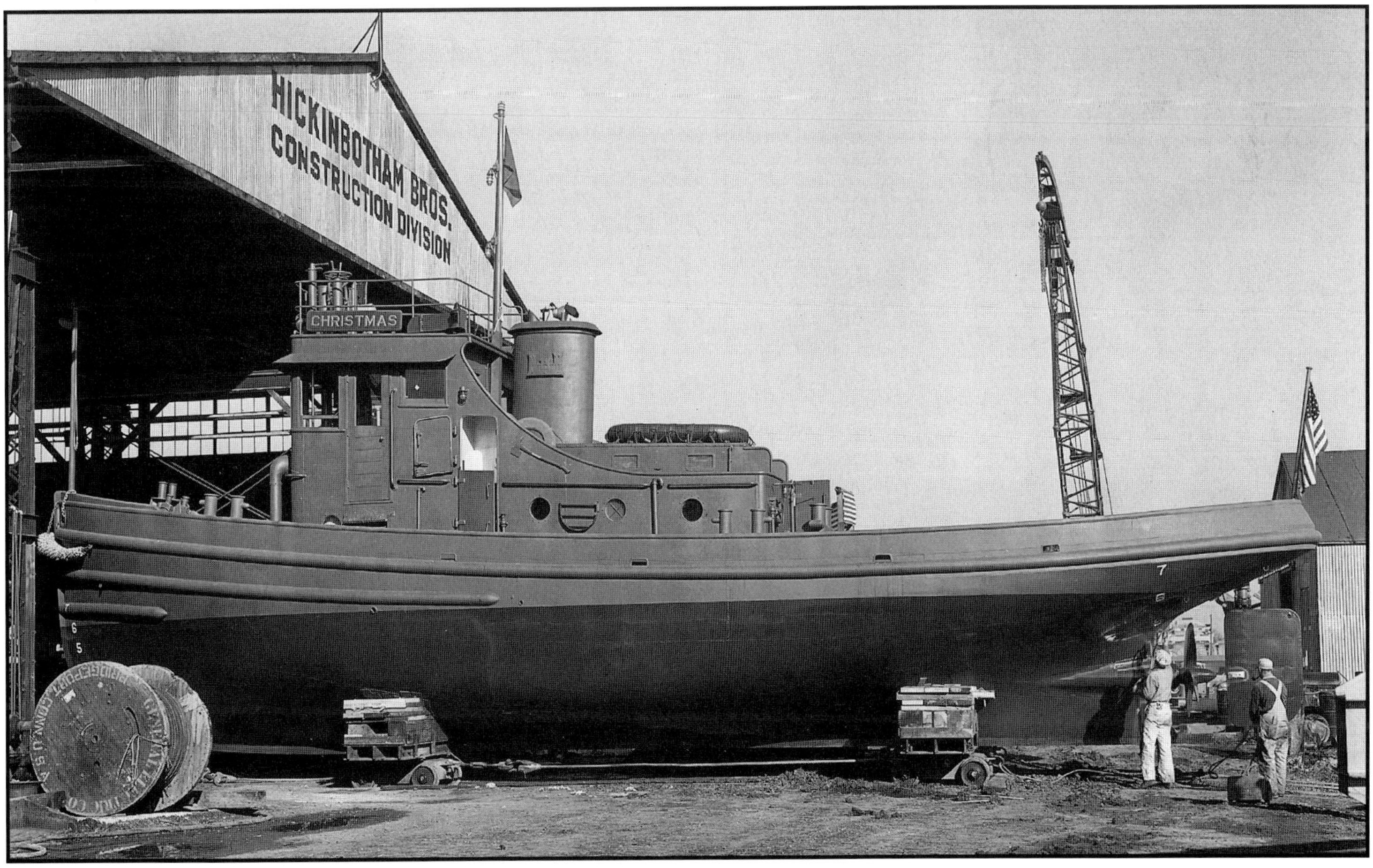

Skilled welders could duplicate in steel the subtle compound curves of finely crafted wooden hulls. Steel tug for the U.S. Army Corps of Engineers, December 14, 1943.

SAUSALITO HISTORICAL SOCIETY

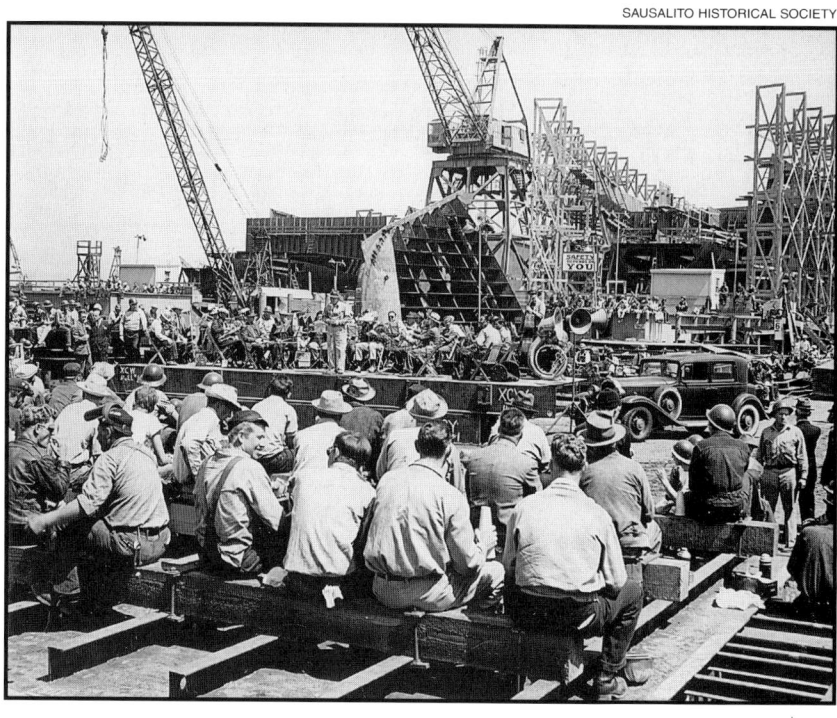

Band performance at lunch break, Marinship, 1944. Bay Area shipyards worked around the clock in three shifts, day shift, 8 A.M. to 4 P.M.; swing shift, 4 P.M. to midnight; and graveyard shift, midnight to 8 A.M.

THE HAGGIN MUSEUM

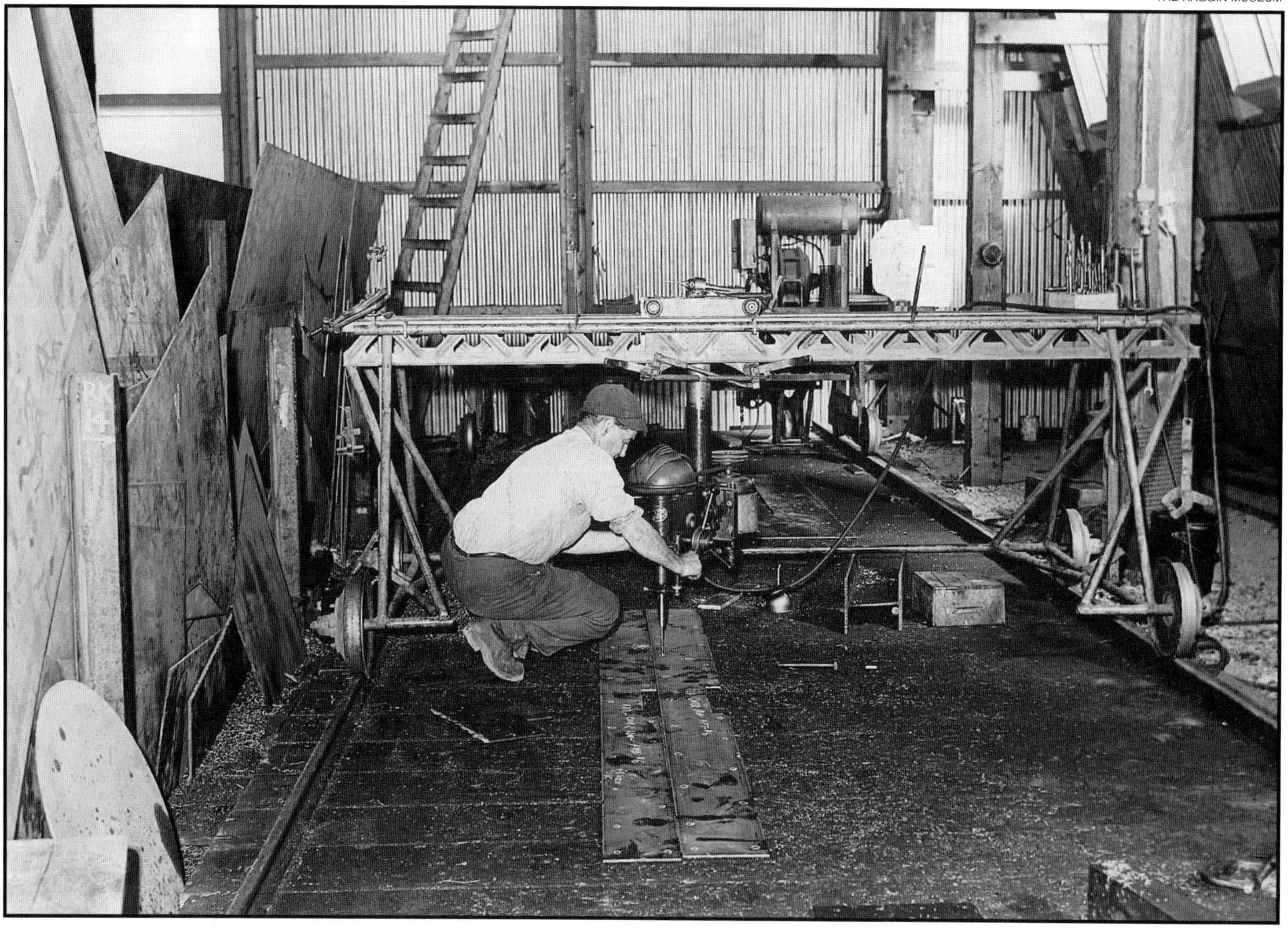

At Colberg Boat Works, workers built this rail-mounted plate drilling rig. Many ideas to shave minutes and seconds off repetitive tasks came from people with little engineering experience.

SAUSALITO HISTORICAL SOCIETY

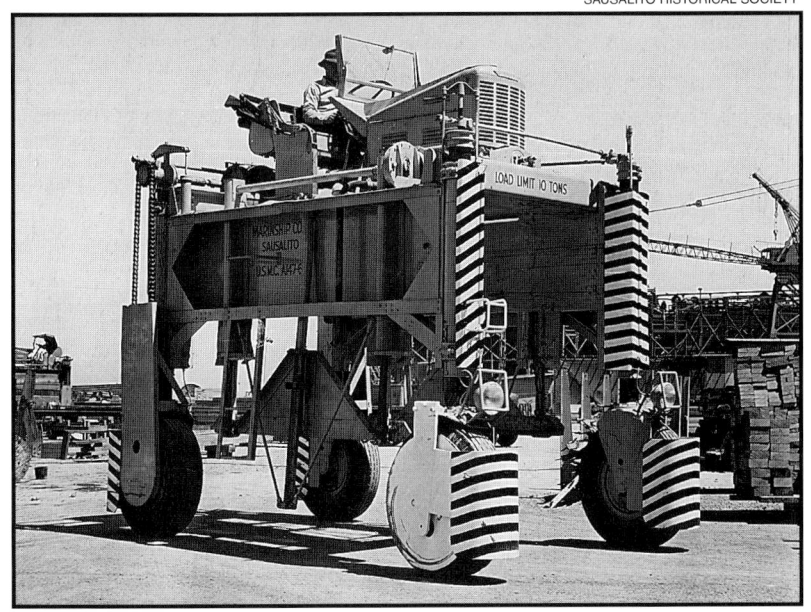

A most useful shipyard tool was this long-legged Hyster crane on wheels, able to drive over a load, hoist it, and deliver it quickly to any part of the yard. Poor forward visibility, however, led to several fatal accidents at Marinship. Guards were installed over the wheels and the operator position was moved forward to eliminate the blind spot.

SAUSALITO HISTORICAL SOCIETY

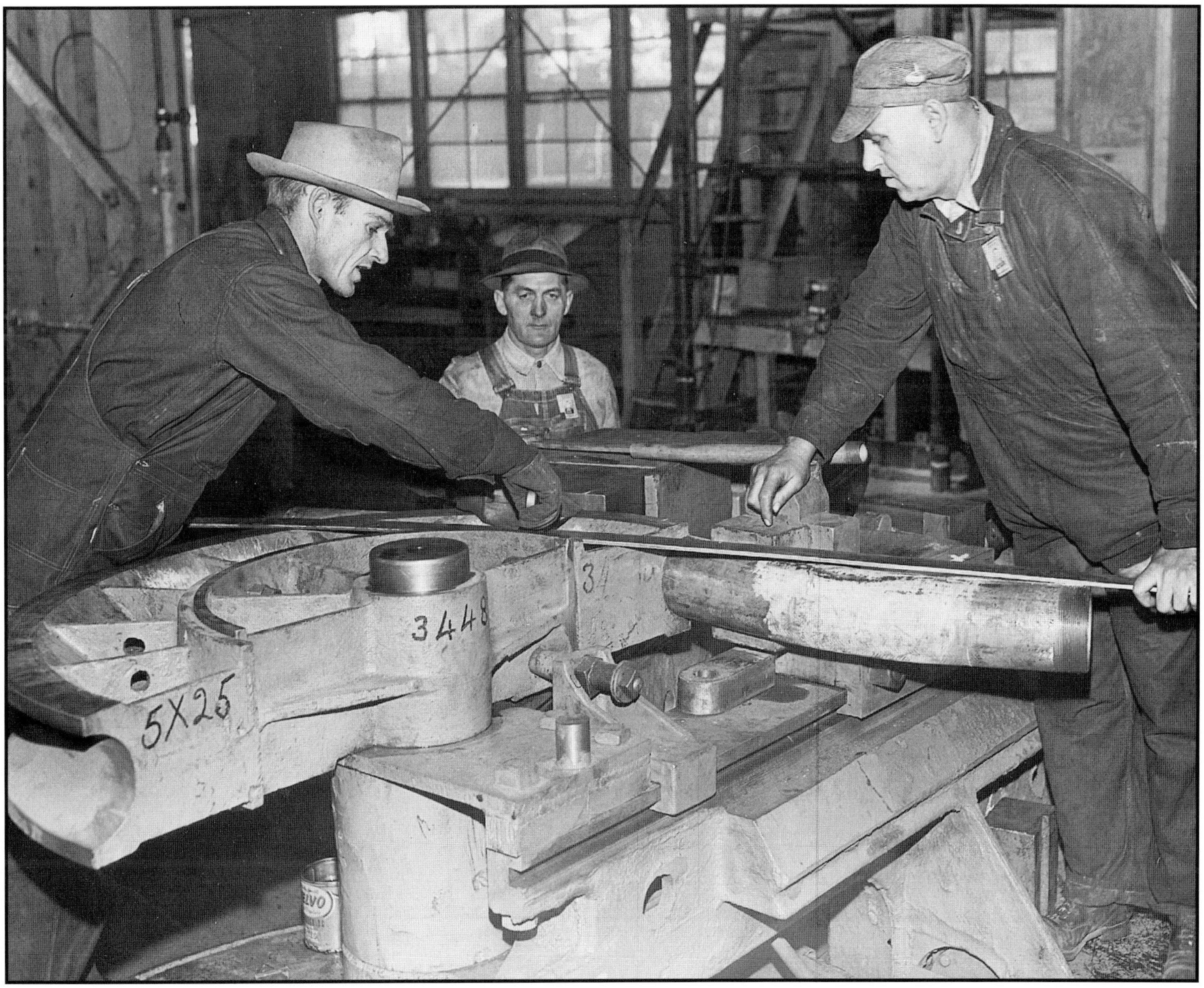

Pipefitters at Marinship in 1943 working a five-inch pipe around a bending jig in the Pipe Shop. A built-in protractor, designed by Marinship workers, enabled pipefitters to reach a high degree of accuracy.

Right: SS *War Hawk*, a C3 freighter built by Moore Dry Dock, is launched with her rudder and propellor in place with temporary steel stiffeners holding the rudder parallel to the keel during the launch.

Below: A-frame jig used at Marinship to set propellor shaft into cast bronze propellor before installing the whole assembly. This one went to tanker *Mission San Rafael*, 1943.

SAUSALITO HISTORICAL SOCIETY

SAN FRANCISCO MARITIME NHP P79-071a Scr55:x pl.6145

SAN FRANCISCO MARITIME NHP P79-071a Scr55:q pl.4766

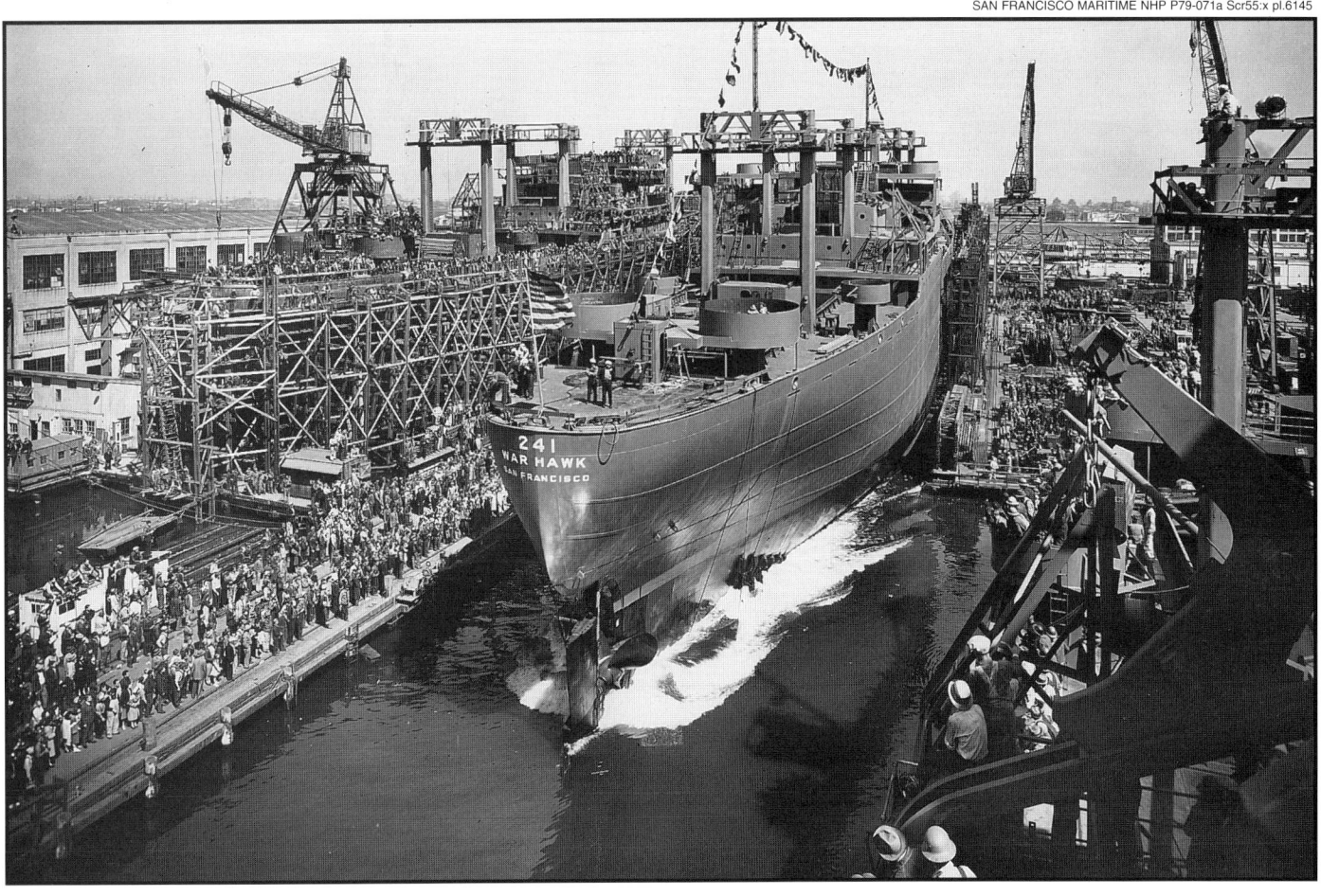

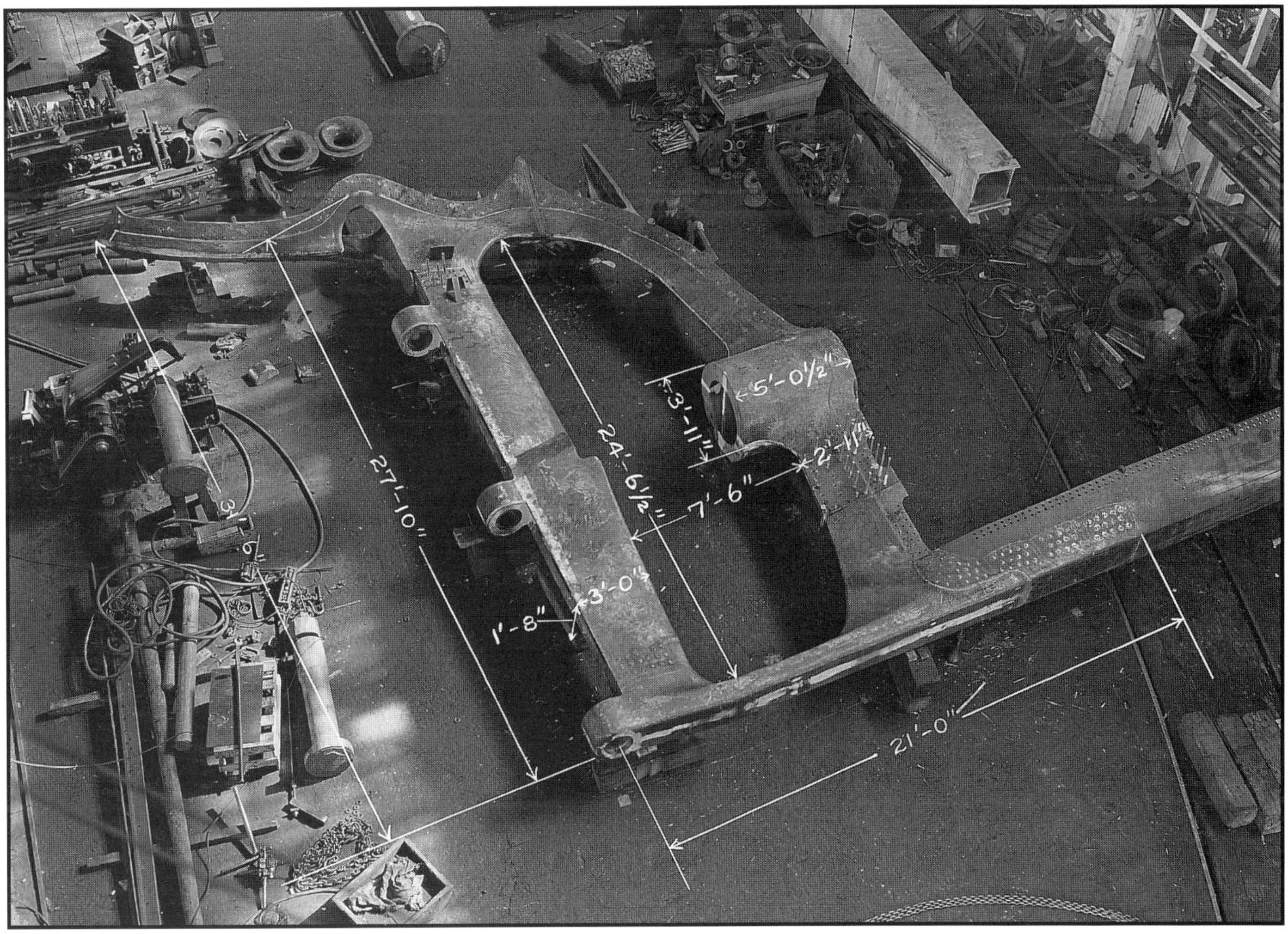

Forged stern frame for SS *Sea Star* Moore Dry Dock shows dimensions of the finished piece. After being set in position, the shaft bearing was reamed to precise alignment. October 31, 1939.

SAN FRANCISCO MARITIME NHP P82-125a.4320pl

Bethlehem's destroyer program was well under way before Pearl Harbor. First bulkheads are placed in the hull of Bensen Class destroyer USS *Coughlan*, July 2, 1941.

Most major combat vessels built in the Bay Area during World War II were delivered under Navy contract by Bethlehem, San Francisco, Mare Island, and Kaiser. Bethlehem launched 52 combat vessels; 36 destroyers, 4 light cruisers and 12 destroyer escorts.

Top right: An inverted propellor-shaft strut assembly is lifted at Bethlehem, Alameda, for delivery to San Francisco.

Bottom right: Allen M. Sumner Class destroyer USS *Lofberg*, right, a month prior to launch, July 6, 1944. The hull alongside at left is probably USS *John W. Thomason*, launched six weeks after *Lofberg*.

LAUNCHING SHIPS

Shipyards large and small measured progress and efficiency by cost effectiveness, number of man hours per vessel and total tonnage built. For the general public, however, ship launchings marked how well the ship building effort was progressing. Nothing else in a shipyard matched a launch for drama and pure exhilaration. It was the moment of truth when all the days and weeks of work culminated in a graphic display toward winning the war. Despite wartime secrecy surrounding shipyards and defense plants, it would have been impossible to hide ship launchings, so the events were made public, at least for invited guests and the press. Less generally known was how much work was yet to be done following a ship launching, the weeks of outfitting, equipment and machinery testing and, finally, the sea trials before the ship was ready for service.

Bay Area shipyards in World War II launched ships of all sizes regularly, sometimes more than one per day per yard. Yet each of the fourteen hundred vessel launchings between 1940 and 1945 was a singular event that required careful planning and skilled execution. Launching ships has changed little in principle over the centuries. The ships have gotten bigger and little improvements have sped the process but the main point remains to get the vessel into its natural element without mishap.

Most Bay Area shipyards launched ships in the time-honored tradition of sliding the completed hull fore-and-aft into the water, a feat accompanied by speeches, music, a bottle smashed against the prow, and cheering throngs of workers. The ceremony was abbreviated as the war progressed and as the time between launchings became briefer. Still, each launching was special and well-remembered by anyone who witnessed it.

The principle of ship launching looks deceptively simple; build the vessel on an incline near the water, grease the skids beneath the hull, cut her loose and let gravity take care of the rest. But the mechanics and physics involved in a launch present complex problems and potentially disastrous consequences. First, the slipway on which the vessel is built must be inclined properly so the hull slides at just the right speed to avoid stalling as it hits the water and slow enough to prevent it from striking the water with excessive strain on the hull plates and framing.

In the simplified sequence shown at right, a typical steel ship hull is launched. Figure 1 shows the slipway (from a bow view) as the keel is laid for a vessel. A heavy concrete pad has been set up with the proper slope to the water and permanent wooden ground ways have been mounted to the foundation pad. In some shipways these were removable and laid only when the ship was ready for launch. The slipway is inclined 1/2 inch to 3/4 inch per foot of length. Massive oak keel blocks have been stacked along the center line of the ship to support the keel and hull as it rises. In Figure 2 and Figure 3, as the hull is assembled, wooden shoring along the bilges supports the added weight.

Figure 4 shows the completed hull still supported by keel blocks and an array of shoring the length of the ship. Prior to launch, the ground ways are heavily greased and the sliding ways, large oak planks, are placed on top of the ground ways. The sliding ways are a series of oak planks. A pine plank called a crushing timber is placed on top of the sliding ways to absorb the irregularities of the hull and provide for continuous contact between the sliding ways and the hull. Wooden wedges are driven at intervals between the planks of the sliding ways to lift the hull from the keel blocks and transfer it to the sliding ways. In Figure 5, the wedges are in place, the keel blocks— no longer supporting the vessel— have been removed, and the shoring has been cleared away. In actual practice, supports called dog shores were added, designed to fall away as the ship slid down the ways.

Figure 6 shows the vessel underway. A trigger mechanism (shown on next page) has released the sliding ways; the weight and incline of the vessel cause it to slide toward the sea. The sliding ways, poppets and wedges enter the water with the vessel and fall away to be recovered for another launch. A 400-foot vessel, such as a Liberty ship, traveled down the ways in forty to fifty seconds.

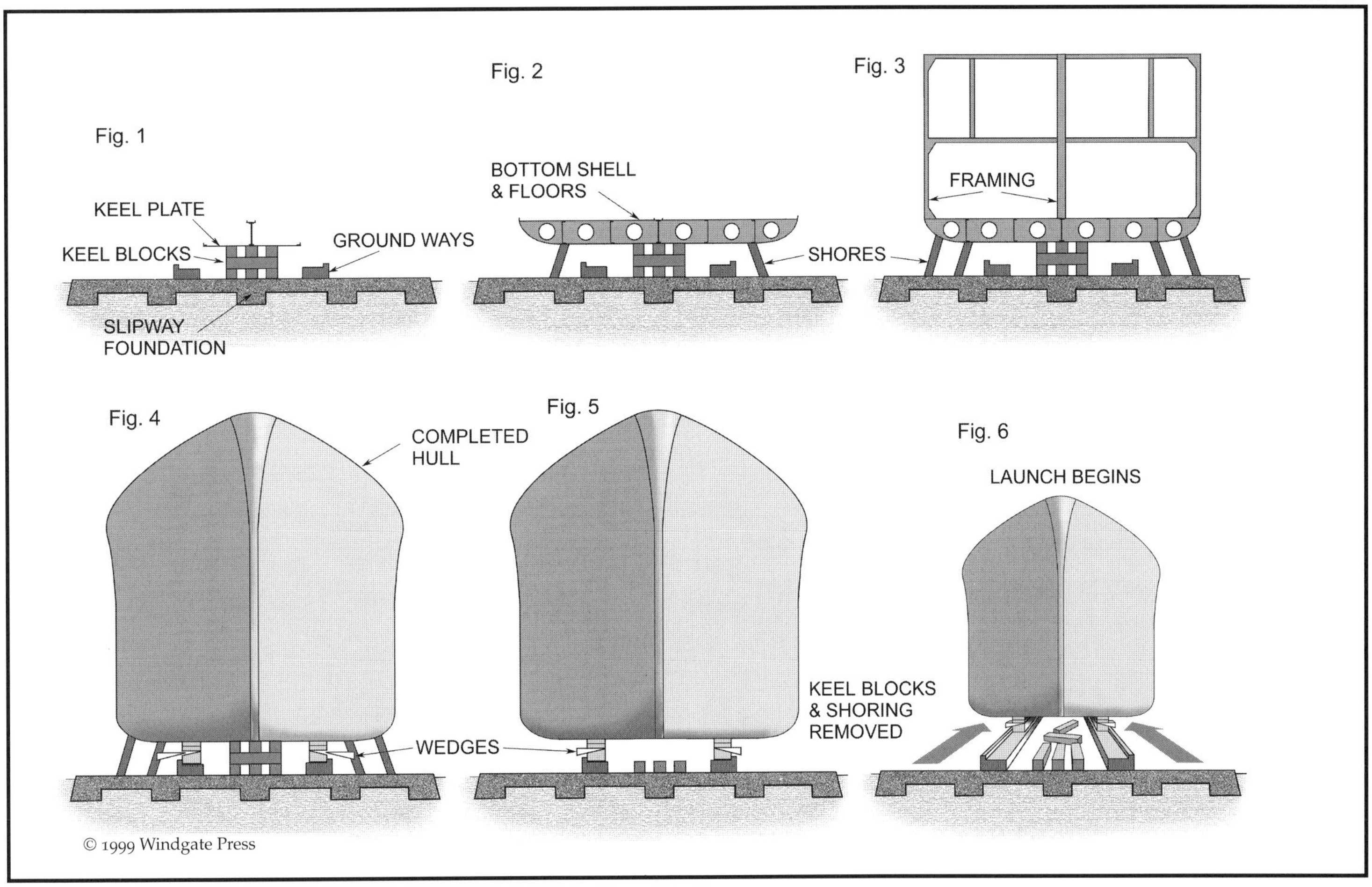

Fig. 1 — KEEL PLATE, KEEL BLOCKS, GROUND WAYS, SLIPWAY FOUNDATION

Fig. 2 — BOTTOM SHELL & FLOORS, SHORES

Fig. 3 — FRAMING

Fig. 4 — COMPLETED HULL, WEDGES

Fig. 5 — KEEL BLOCKS & SHORING REMOVED

Fig. 6 — LAUNCH BEGINS

© 1999 Windgate Press

SAN FRANCISCO MARITIME NHP P79-071a Scr55:q pl.4743

SS *Sea Arrow* after her successful launch at Moore Dry Dock, September 15, 1939. The greased ways stand out in the foreground with keel blocks stacked between them. Drag chains have slowed rearward momentum of the ship.

The unseen part of a ship launching takes place beneath the hull. This sequence taken at Marinship in 1944 shows some of the steps taken by the launch crew before the actual event. Every tanker at Marinship was launched by the same crew of 24 men and 3 women.

Above: The fixed launching ways are coated with a petroleum-base grease 3/8 inches thick, a 5,600-pound base coat and a ton of top coat. In earlier days this was done with soft soap on top of tallow. One Gulf Coast shipyard even experimented with crushed ripe bananas as a lubricant.

Above right: After measuring the curvature of the bilges, workers use adzes to shape a bilge block. Note that the hull above them has not yet received its final coat of paint.

Right: After the block is fit snugly against the hull, hundreds of wedges are driven in to lift the hull from the keel blocks, a process called "ramming up." Here the ram is a timber fitted with multiple pipe handles. Some yards used hydraulic or electric hammers, some used old-fashioned muscle power with heavy mauls.

SAUSALITO HISTORICAL SOCIETY

Left: This team is ready to release a dog shore at the signal, the last step before launch. As in other areas of shipyard operation, launch crews became more efficient with experience.

Below: An elaborate system of launching triggers at Moore Dry Dock used in launching the USS *AS18*, October 14, 1942. At the foreman's signal a weight drops operating a cam, releasing the trigger's grip on the sliding ways. Shown are a series of port-side triggers; a matching set is fixed to the starboard side. Launch triggers sometimes were used in conjunction with hydraulic rams that pushed the sliding ways insuring that the hull moved out smoothly and on time. All of the timbers used in a ship launch are recovered and reused for the next launch.

SAN FRANCISCO MARITIME NHP P79-071a Scr55:v p.136

SAN FRANCISCO MARITIME NHP P82-125a.4838pl

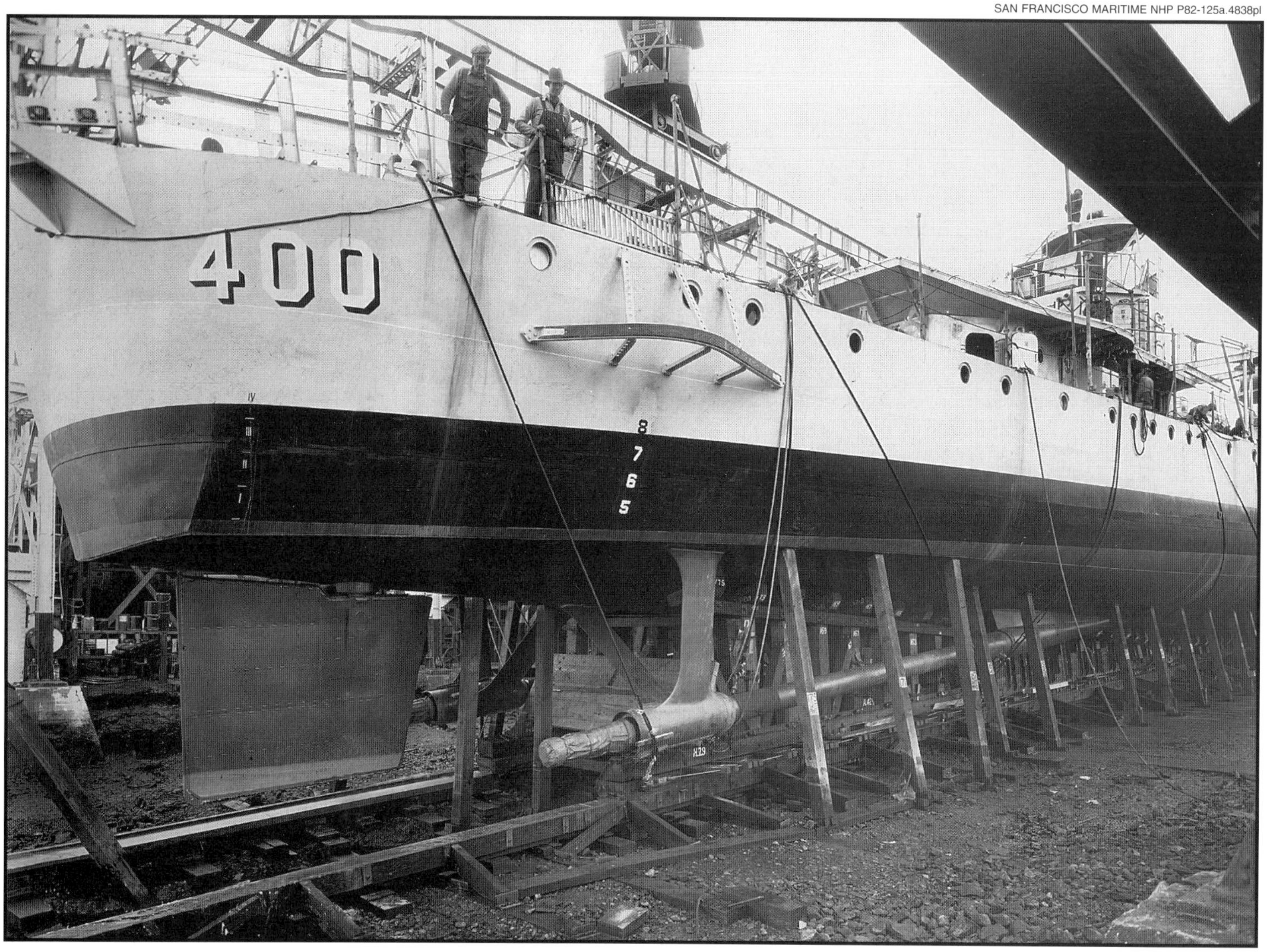

The aft poppet for a destroyer at Bethlehem consists of a wooden support sled between the propellor shafts mounted on the sliding ways. USS *McCall,* November 19, 1937.

A major concern in launching a hull is that the bow and stern of the vessel are usually narrower than the sliding ways. As the stern enters the water and becomes buoyant, the hull is unsupported momentarily and could capsize or be thrown off the ways. Seconds later, as the narrow bow enters the water, a similar danger exists as the weight of the hull is momentarily carried by the narrow structure. To reduce this danger, poppets or temporary supports are built under the bow and stern to distribute weight and mass evenly to the sliding ways. Poppets consist of shores resting on the sliding ways and support slings under the hull attached to the shores.

An efficient launch procedure used widely in Bay Area shipyards was the use of retainer plates. Steel plates were secured to the ground ways and sliding ways as the ship was built. When the time came for launch, the plates were burned through by workers and the hull began its slide.

SAN FRANCISCO MARITIME NHP P82-125a.4402pl

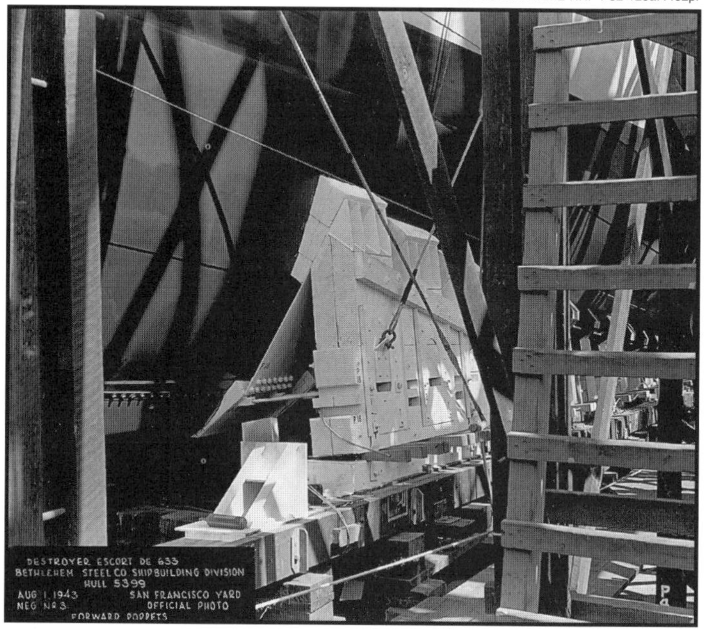

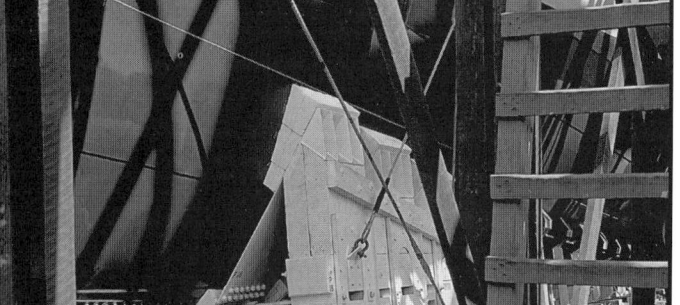

Above: A typical forward poppet clearly shows a sling reaching under the bow that distributes weight evenly to the sliding ways. Destroyer escort *Foreman*, Bethlehem, San Francisco, August 1, 1945.

SAN FRANCISCO MARITIME NHP P79-071a Scr55:v pl.5639

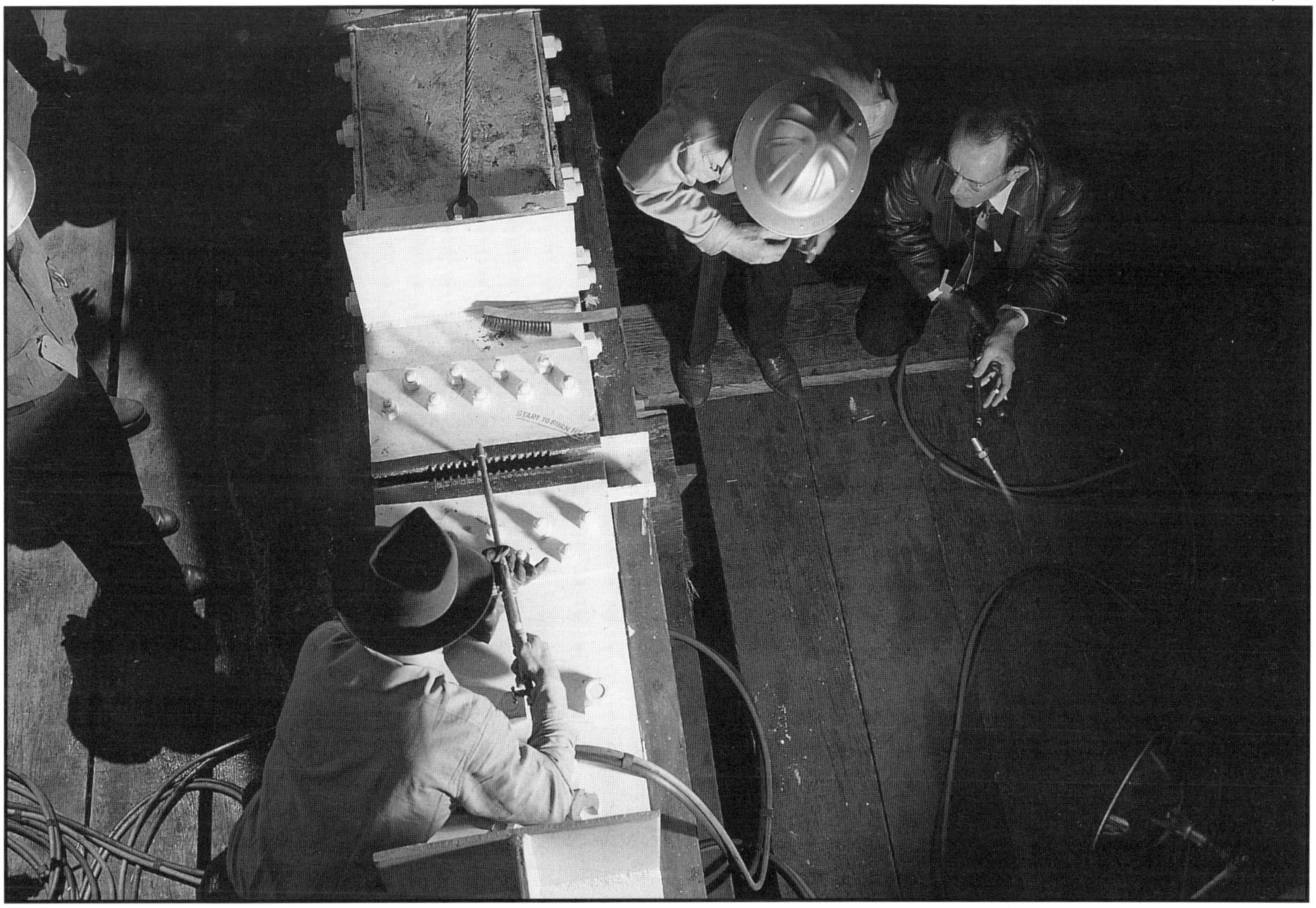

Burning retainer plates, SS *Macaw*, Moore Dry Dock, July 12, 1942.

SAN FRANCISCO MARITIME NHP Scr55:v p.35

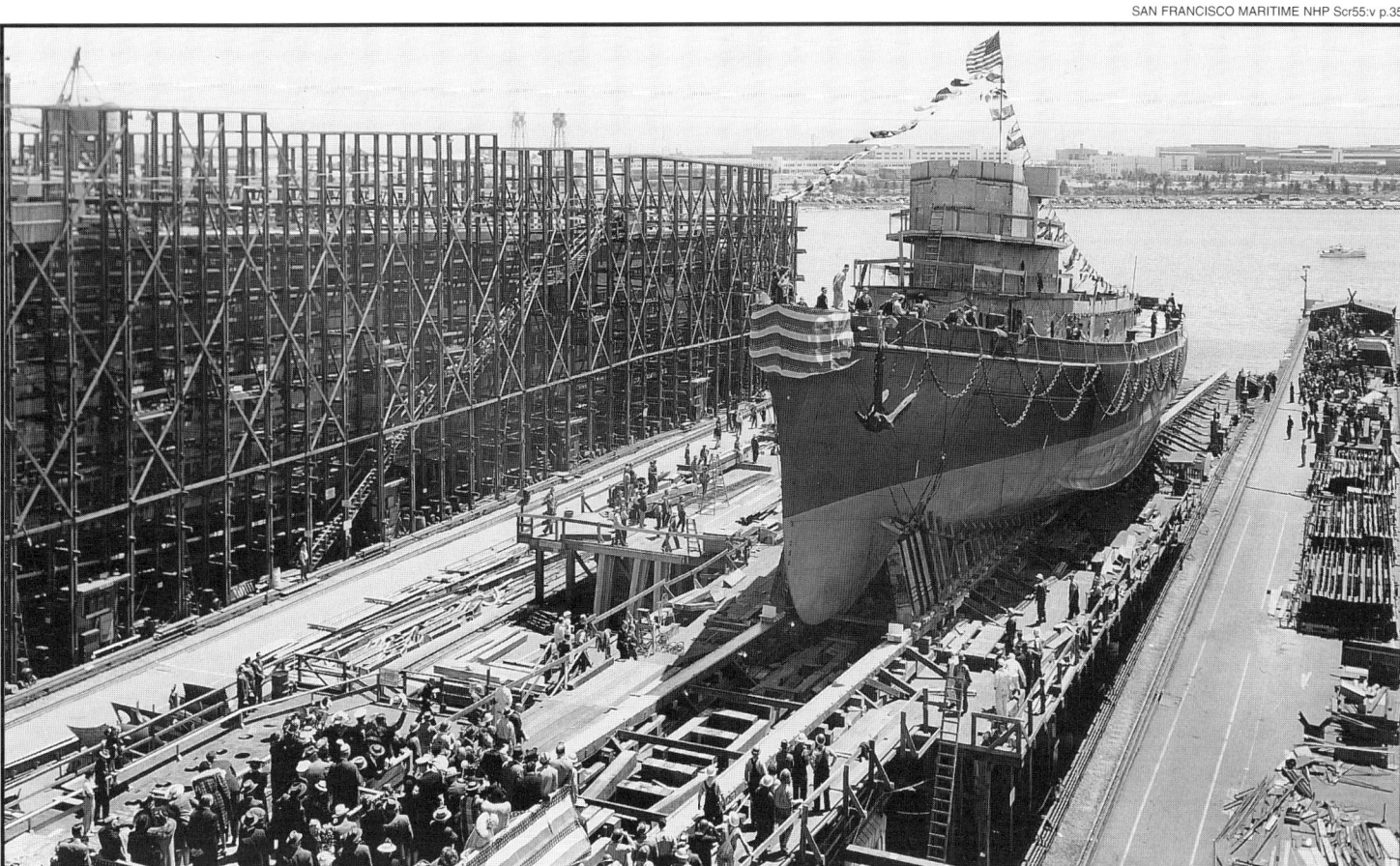

USS *Florikan* slides toward the Oakland Estuary moments after retaining plates have been cut, June 14, 1942. The burned retainer plates are visible at the bow, one on each ground way sliding with the vessel. Forward poppets supporting the narrow bow are also clearly shown. The poppets float free from the vessel after launch and are recovered for reuse.

Launching ships sideways rather than fore and aft permitted shipyards to be built on restricted waterways. The narrow San Joaquin River at Stockton and the shallows of San Francisco Bay at Western Pipe & Steel required side launching for large vessels. One advantage to side launch construction is that the vessel is laid down level without the incline necessary for a fore-and-aft launch. This allows perpendiculars and bulkheads to be installed without having to compensate for the slope. The keel is laid parallel and close to the shore on keel blocks. When the time for launch approaches, standing ways are placed beneath the hull extending from the far side of the ship and sloping down to the shoreline. The standing ways are placed passing between the keel blocks; additional blocks, called packing, are placed on the ways and the hull is wedged up onto the packing. When a trigger releases the hull packing, the planks and vessel begin a rapid slide to the water. The hull does not, however, slide into the water but tips into it from the end of the ways. If placed correctly, the ways allow the hull's bilge (the curve between the bottom and side of the hull and the surface least likely to be damaged) to strike the surface of the water first. Momentum carries the hull clear of the ways so that the reverse roll of the vessel does not cause it to strike the shore or the ends of the standing ways. Side launches were dramatic but brief events, taking ten to twelve seconds from release to water entry.

An undramatic but effective way of launching ships was to build them in flooding basins or dry docks and simply float them out when completed. This method was used at Kaiser #3 in Richmond and at Belair. Shipyards in South San Francisco. For most wartime emergency shipyards, however, construction of suitable launch basins would have taken too much time.

Wooden freighter *YP-646* enters her element, Colberg Boat Works, March 3, 1945.

SS *Sea Oriole* tips in, Western Pipe & Steel, 1942. Workers atop the bridge and gun tubs experience a brief but memorable ride.

The diagram below shows a hull before launch resting on blocks that keep the hull plumb during construction. Standing ways are inserted under the hull between the blocks after completion and the hull remains vertical as it slides until it tips into the water. After the hull is waterborne, its forward momentum is slowed by restraining cables.

WINDGATE

WINDGATE

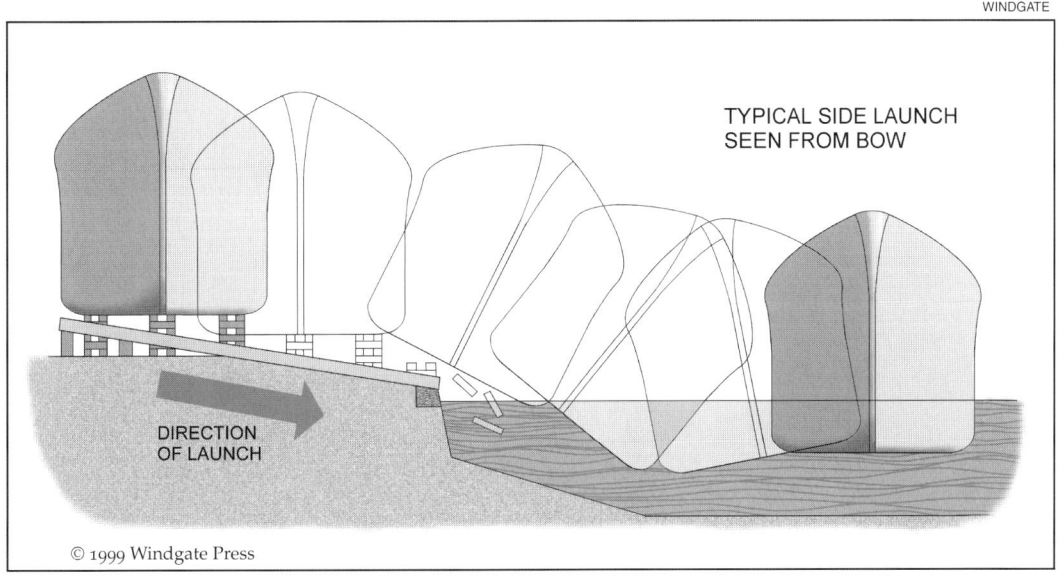

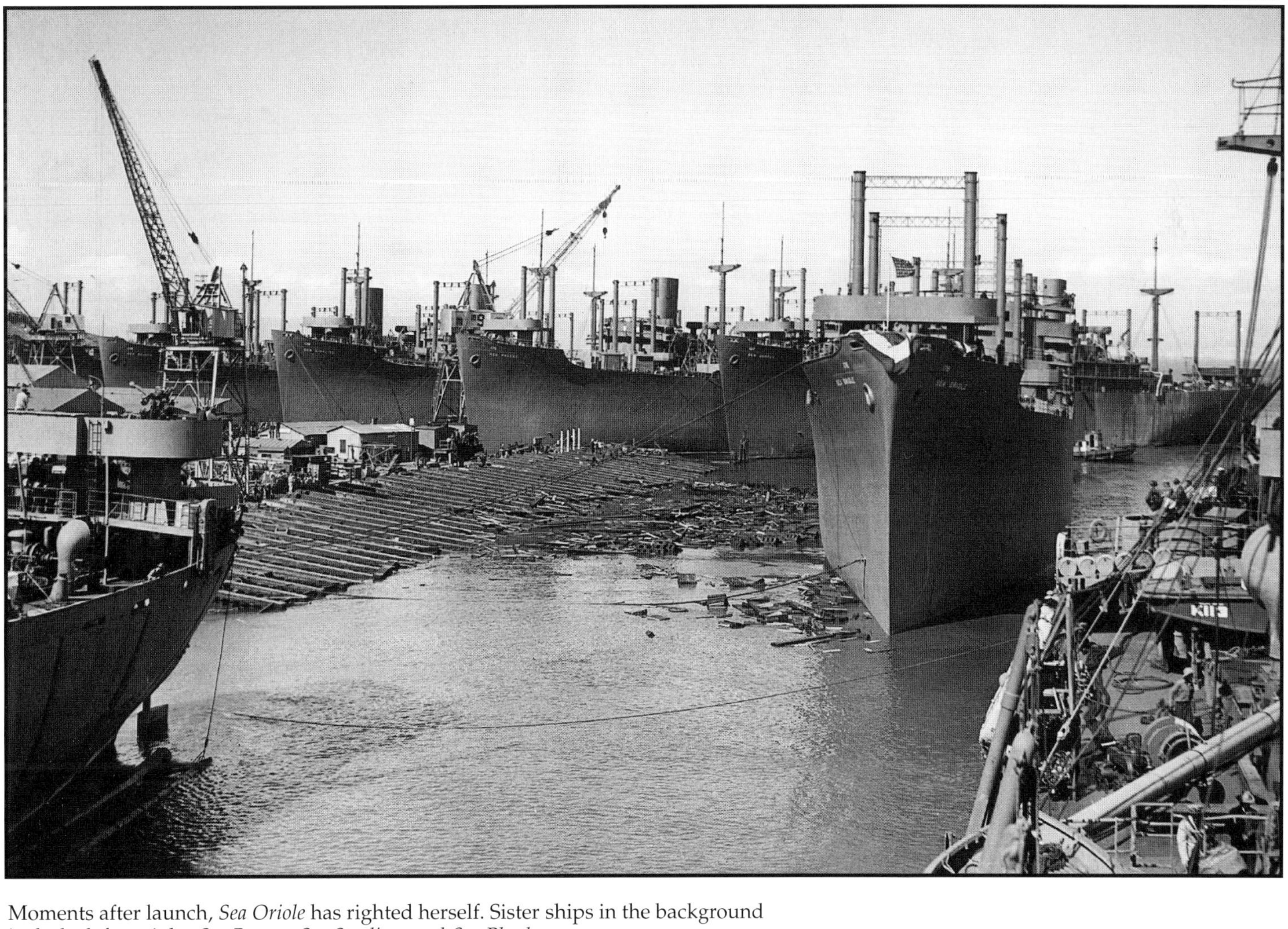

Moments after launch, *Sea Oriole* has righted herself. Sister ships in the background include, left to right, *Sea Beaver*, *Sea Starling*, and *Sea Phoebe*.

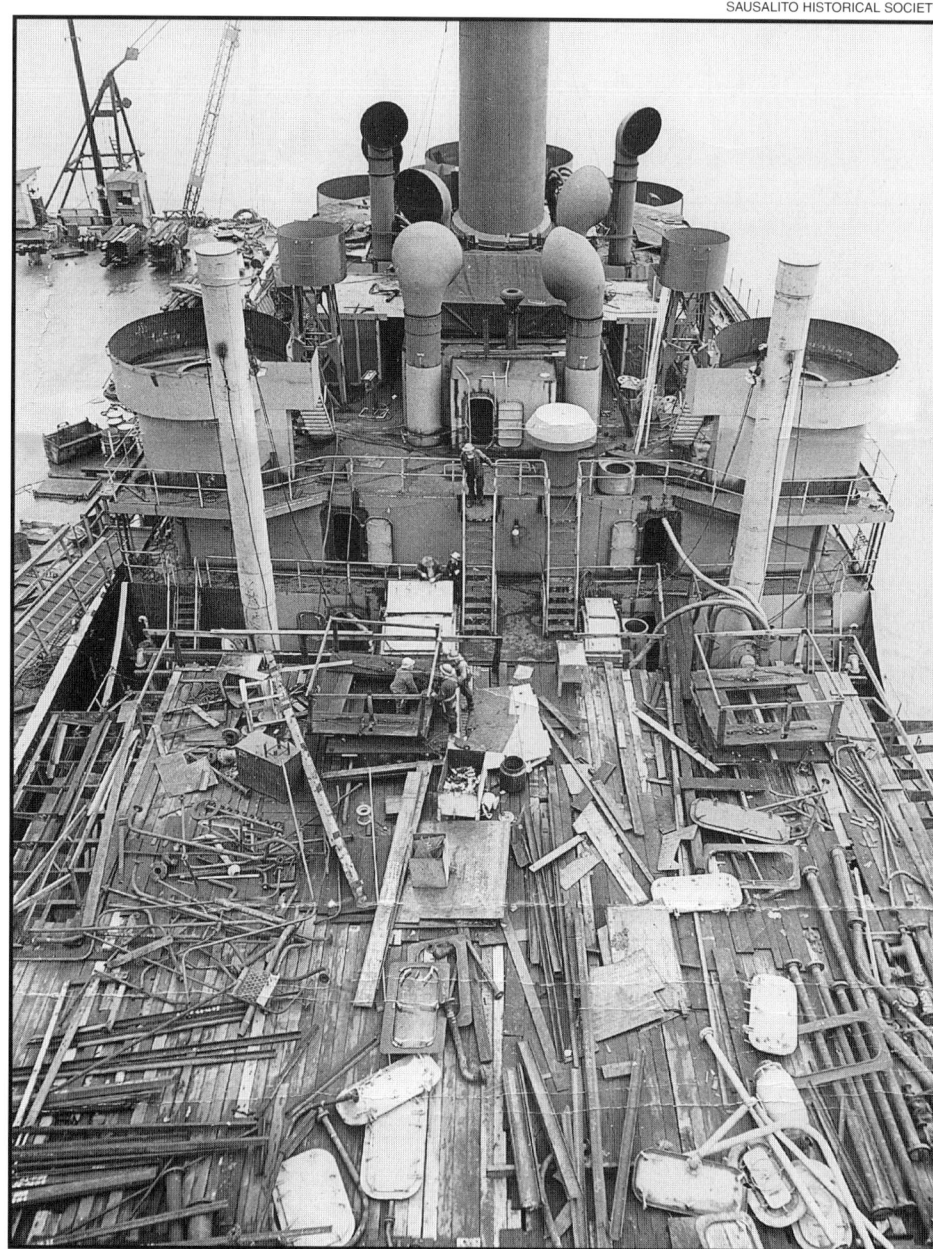

Right: This Marinship tanker at the outfitting dock in 1945 appears in total disarray but outfitting crews had an efficient system and work is proceeding in an orderly fashion. Painters, welders and installers had to work amidst the confusion of crane-loads of supplies and equipment being lifted aboard and stowed.

FITTING OUT

Immediately after launch, a vessel was towed to an outfitting berth, usually one of several alongside a pier within the perimeter of the shipyard. Outfitting transformed a hull into a ship ready for delivery, a process that began before the hull left the launching ways. The object was to clear the shipway as soon as possible for the next hull, therefore, all work necessary to make the hull watertight was done on the ways. Additional work that would not delay the launch was done; all else was completed at the outfitting dock. Outfitting involved every craft in the yard and the work of many sub-contractors; installation of electrical systems, navigation instruments, weapons, plumbing, insulation, ventilation, joinery, floor and deck coverings, rigging, and painting.

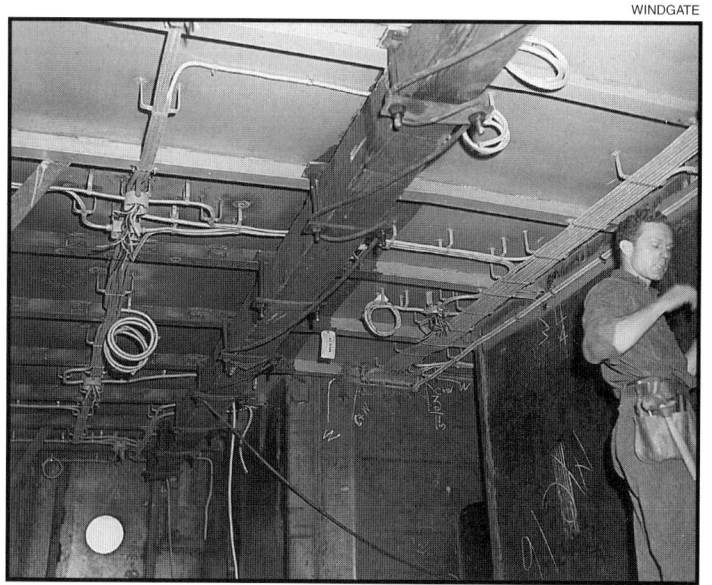

Right: An electrician at Marinship pulling cable on a tanker deck house, 1945. Early on, arguments were common among workers debating which craft had priority in a given space but with experience came greater efficiency.

SAN FRANCISCO MARITIME NHP P79-071a Scr55:v pl.5707

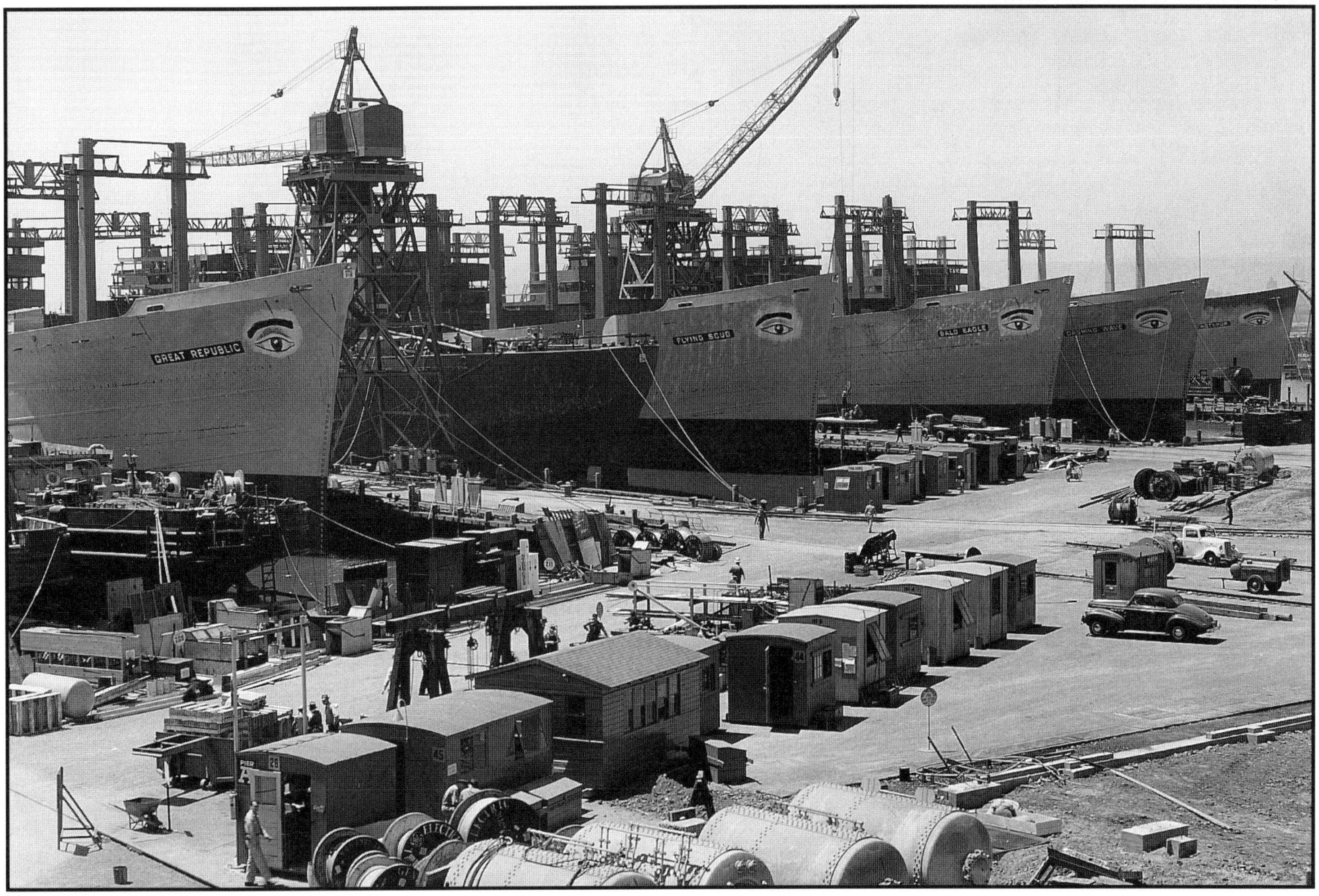

SAUSALITO HISTORICAL SOCIETY

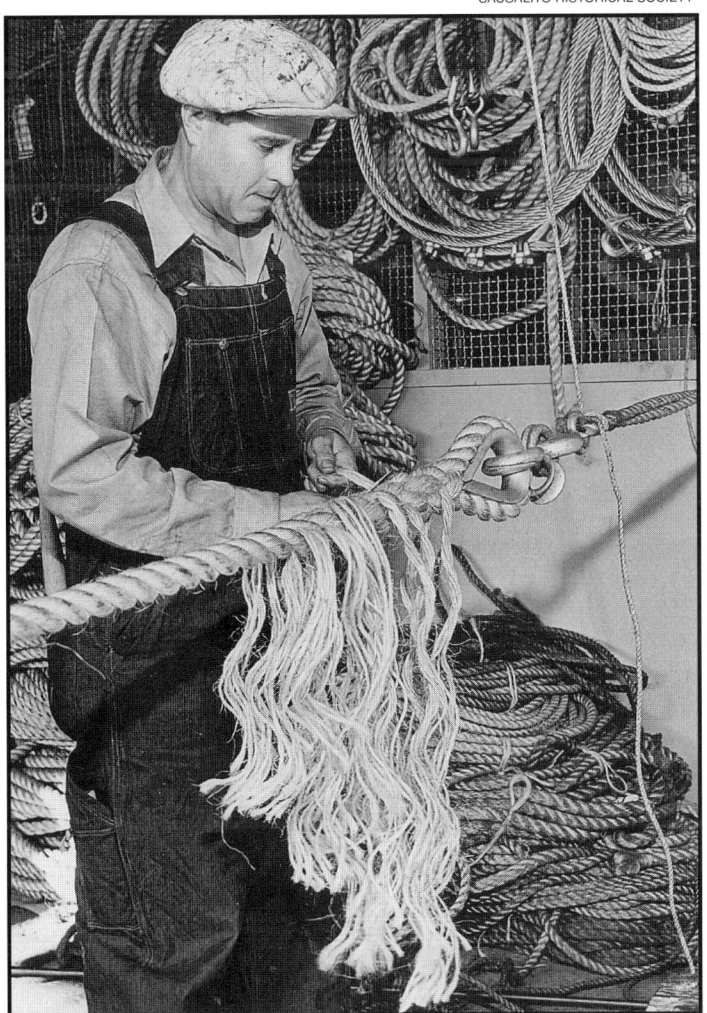

Above: At Moore Dry Dock, work progresses on six post-launch C2's, August 13, 1942. Efficient outfitting depended on timely delivery of parts and supplies to the shipyard. The eyes painted on the bows of Moore-built ships carried on the ancient Greek and Asian tradition of painting eyes on vessels to guide them through unknown seas. When the ships were delivered, the eyes and large names were painted over.

Left: A rigger at Marinship making an eye splice around a thimble. Rigging, booms, pumps, galley equipment and ventilation systems were tested at the outfitting dock before sea trials.

Two examples of transformation at the outfitting dock from newly launched hulls to finished ships ready for duty. Bethlehem, San Francisco.

Light cruiser U.S.S. *Reno*, above, moments after launching, December 23, 1942. Warships sometimes spent longer at the outfitting dock than on the shipway.

Cape San Martin, a C-1B cargo ship for the U.S. Maritime Commission in pre-war colors, shown September 24, 1940, at left, and December 24, 1940, above.

Reno's sister ship U.S.S. *Flint* nearing completion at the outfitting dock, July 6, 1944.

After the vessel was fully outfitted, inspected and her hull, piping and boiler systems tested, she was ready for sea trials before delivery from builder to new owner. The procedure called for a series of tests not only to measure actual performance against specifications but to inspect and observe the ship's components under operating conditions. Prior to World War II ship trials were conducted both dockside and at sea. During the war, the process was condensed somewhat but remained thorough. A special crew conducted the trials along with representatives of the Maritime Commission or Navy, marine surveyors, vendors' representatives and shipyard officials.

Each vessel was given two trial runs, first by the builder, then by the owner's acceptance team. Each vessel was put through her paces at full speed, reverse and tight turns and every instrument tested for accuracy. Data collected on the trials seldom had any bearing on the acceptance of a ship. If faults were found, they were corrected either before or after delivery. During the trial run, photographers made "official" portraits of the new ships from various angles, such as the broadsides following Page 154.

Right, above: The Benson Class destroyer U.S.S. *Caldwell* being outfitted for sea trails, June 12, 1942, Bethlehem, San Francisco. Alongside is an old cargo vessel taken into service by the Army. The *Caldwell* served in the Aleutian campaign and in the South Pacific in the Gilbert and Marshall Islands campaigns and the Battle of Leyte Gulf in the Philippines.

Right, below: Crewmen get familiar with equipment and armaments aboard a Mahan Class destroyer after a major refit at Mare Island. Shown is a quad torpedo launcher common to most U.S. destroyers during World War II.

Below: On the same vessel, gunners run through a non-firing practice session with one of the ship's 20 MM antiaircraft guns while other crewmen check out a searchlight.

SAN FRANCISCO MARITIME NHP P82-125a.4268pl

WINDGATE

Far left: A big day at Bethlehem, San Francisco, as the Buckley Class destroyer escort USS *Foreman* is dressed up for launching. Lying next to her is her sister USS *Whitehurst*, launched 39 days later. In the background, looking southwest, is Third Street. September 5, 1943.

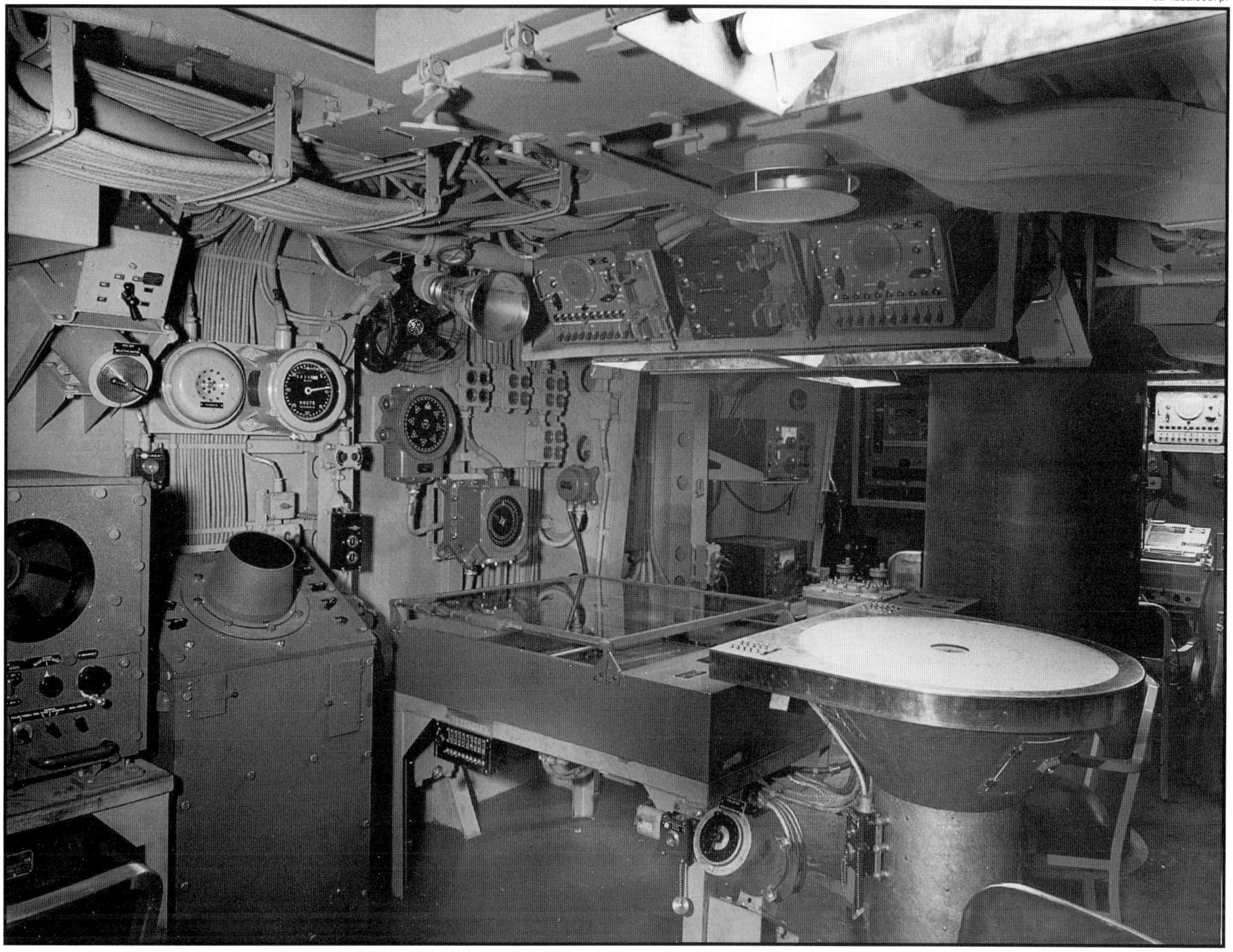

Above: Warships interiors were more complex than cargo vessels due to weapons control systems and the latest radar, sonar and position-finding gear. As a result, construction time for warships was longer. This is the Combat Information Center, starboard side, light cruiser USS *Reno*, launched at Bethlehem December 23, 1942. At left is the radar screen, at center, the DRT or Dead Reckoning Tracer. The flat disk at right is the Tactical Plotter.

Left: Continuing a World War II tradition, a keel plate for the next vessel is lowered into place as soon as the previous ship clears the launching way. The Fletcher Class destroyer USS *McCord* has just entered the water at Bethlehem as workers begin on the USS *Wedderburn*, launched August 1, 1943.

SAN FRANCISCO MARITIME NHP P79-071a Scr55:w pl.6113

SAN FRANCISCO MARITIME NHP P79-071a Scr55:w pl.6111

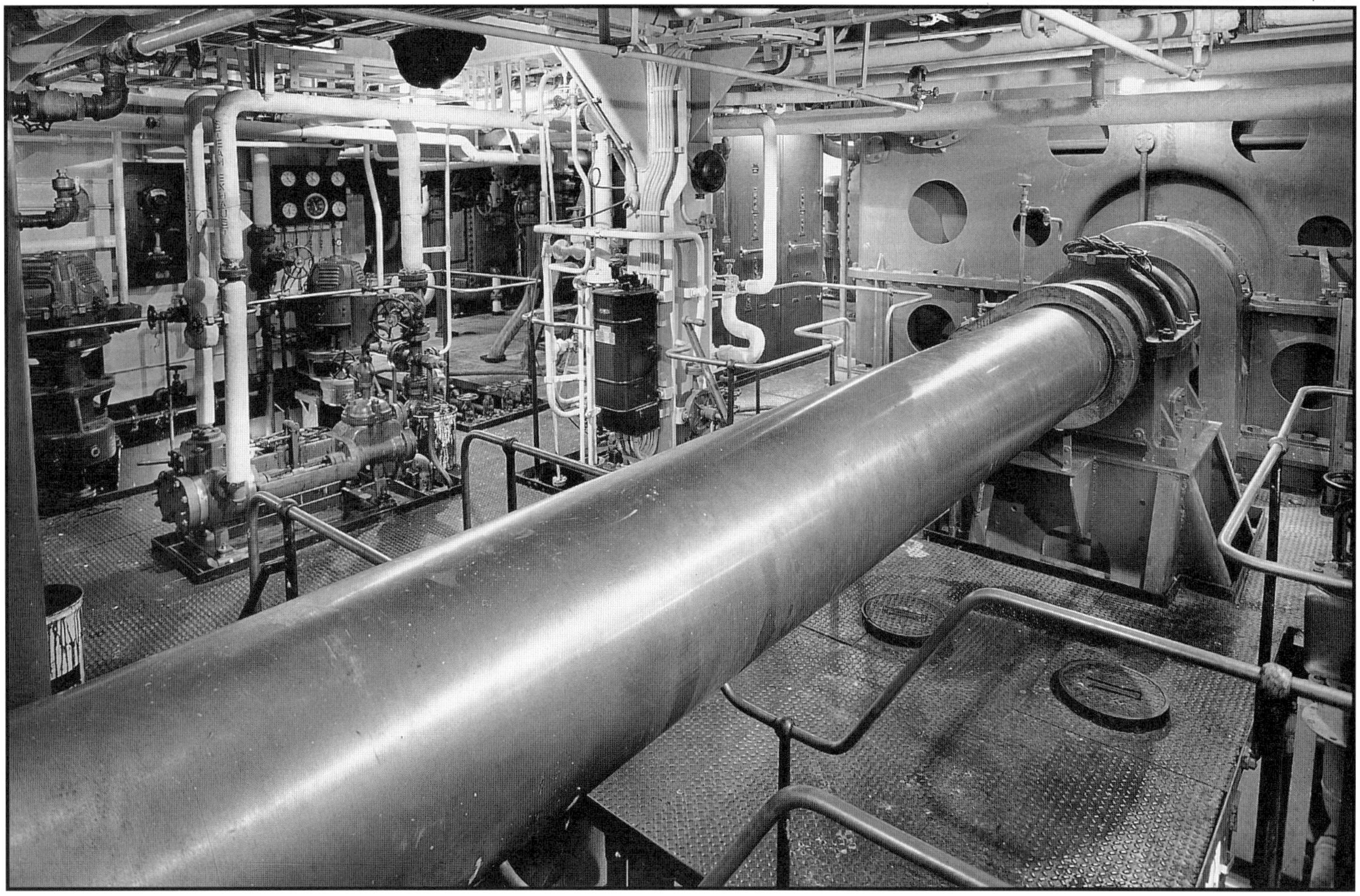

Above: Two views of C2 freighter *Young America*, built in 1943 by Moore Dry Dock. Above is looking forward in the engine room, below looks aft to port. Moore built a full-size mock up of an engine room on land to enable pipefitters to prefabricate piping for the vessels.

Internal machinery was standardized and prefabricated wherever possible. While shipyards were points of final assembly for ships, they depended on components from factories and shops in every state in the Union. The list of materials needed for a completed vessel is lengthy; steel, obviously, iron, brass, lead, bronze, zinc, and rubber, glass, and wood. Manufactured products incorporated into the vessel include miles of wire, tons of paint, canvas, lubricants, linoleum, insulation and plastic. Some parts such as screws and bolts, valves, hardware, and furniture were standard industrial products not specific to maritime use. Others such as navigational instruments, life rafts, windlasses and pumps were specifically nautical. Purchasing agents for the shipyards had to maintain a complex array of contacts throughout the country to insure a steady flow of parts and materials.

In addition to materials procurement, shipyard managers had to deal almost daily with one or more of a dizzying array of federal agencies. Among them were all branches of the military services, the National War Labor Board, National Labor Relations Board, Office of Price Administration, Office of Defense Transportation, Office of War Information, Production Executive Committee, Regional Air Priority Control, Selective Service System, General Accounting Office, Metals Reserve Company, Interstate Commerce Commission, Defense Plants Corporation, Defense Supplies Corporation, Civil Service Commission, American Bureau of Shipping, Office of War Mobilization and Reconversion, National Bureau of Standards, War Shipping Administration, and the many departments of the War Production Board.

Bay Area shipbuilders from the giant Kaiser yards to the small boatyards around the Bay had to overcome obstacles to productivity such as training inexperienced workers, housing and feeding emigrant workers and their families, dealing with labor unions and sub-contractors, crime in shipyard boomtowns, racial and gender conflicts. Problems naturally arose, breakdowns and accidents occurred, mistakes were made. When negatives are weighed against positives, however, the result is remarkable. The ultimate measure of success is that ultimate victory was achieved. By war's end, the many thousands of men and women who took part in building ships could feel justifiable pride in their accomplishment.

SAN FRANCISCO MARITIME NHP P79-071a Scr55:v pl.5917

Marine switchboards constructed by Moore in their electrical shop. These six sets will be installed in C2 vessels and used for degaussing equipment and electrical control of lifeboats. December 11, 1942.

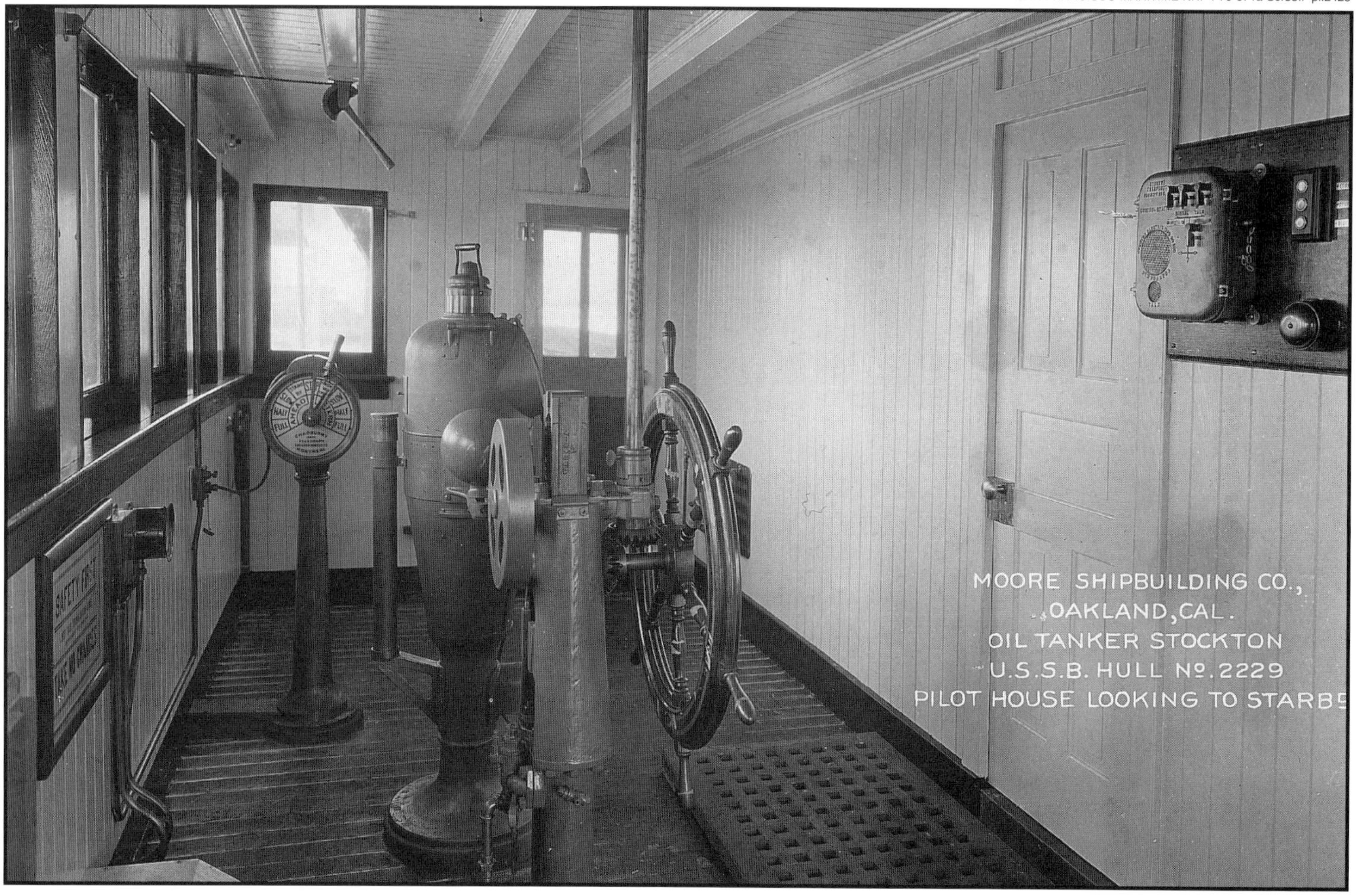

MOORE SHIPBUILDING CO.,
OAKLAND, CAL.
OIL TANKER STOCKTON
U.S.S.B. HULL No. 2229
PILOT HOUSE LOOKING TO STARB⁵

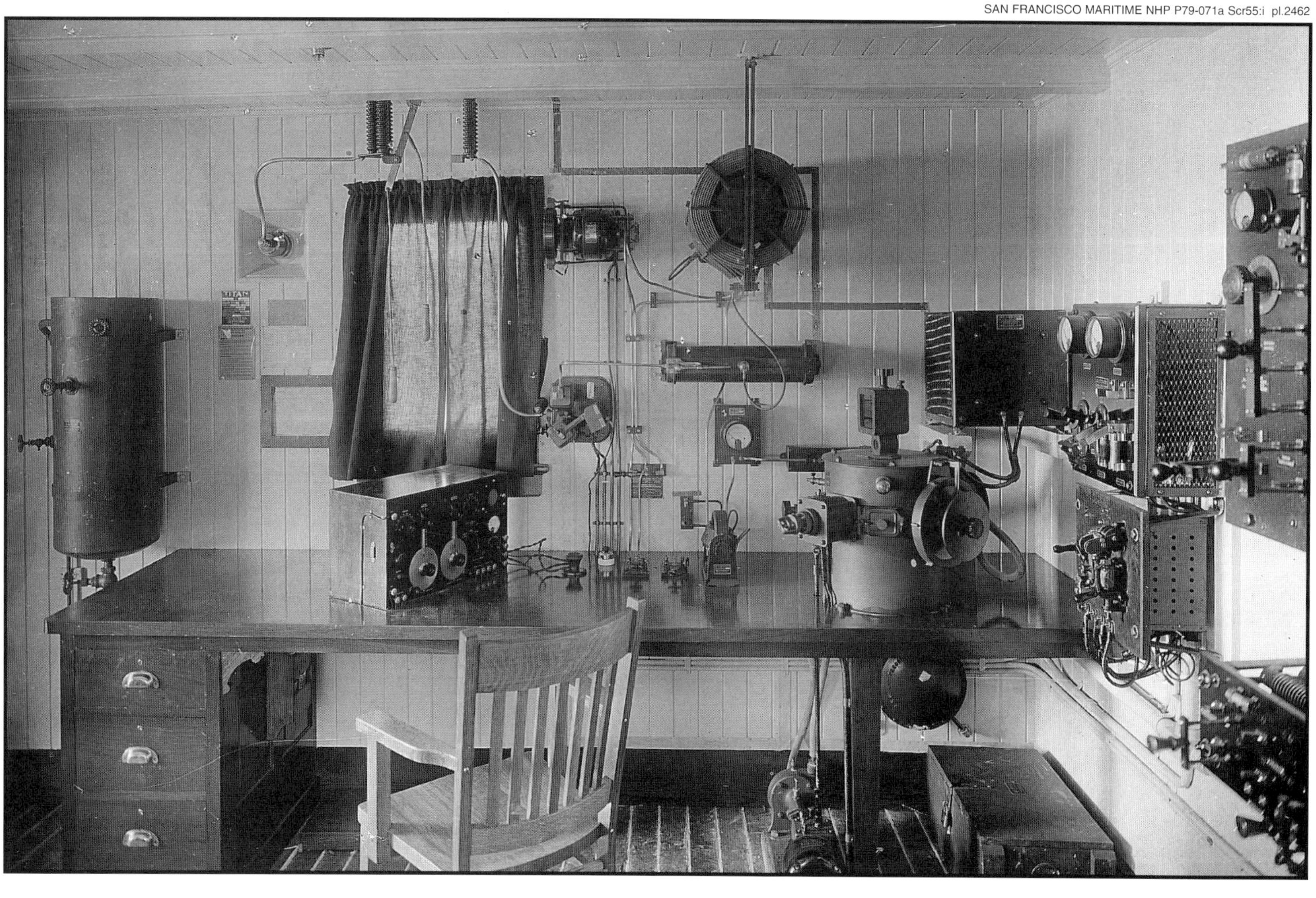

Twenty years apart, yet the functions remain the same. Above are the wheel house and wireless room of the oil tanker *Stockton* built by Moore Shipbuilding Company. October, 1920.

WINDGATE

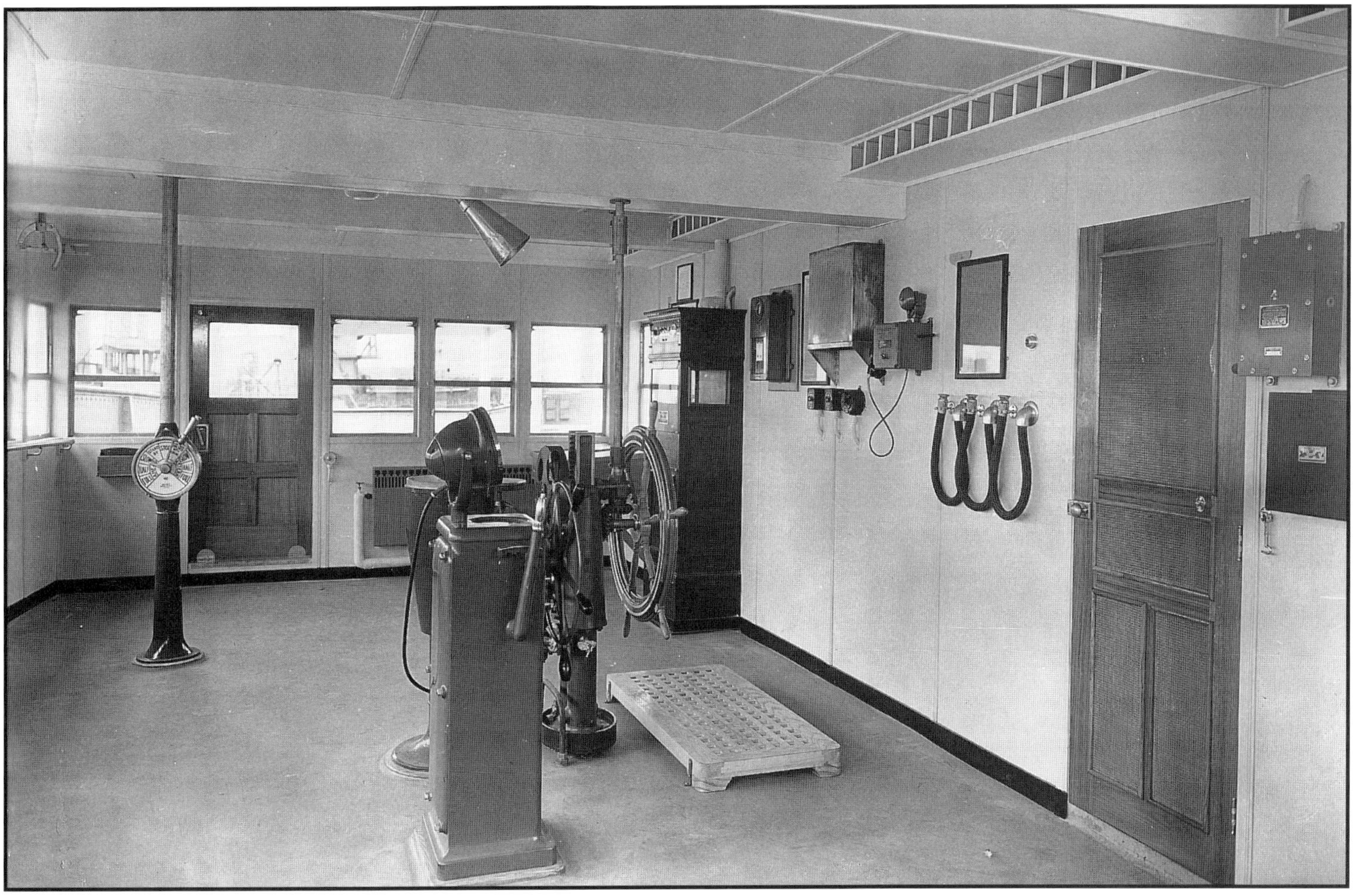

WINDGATE

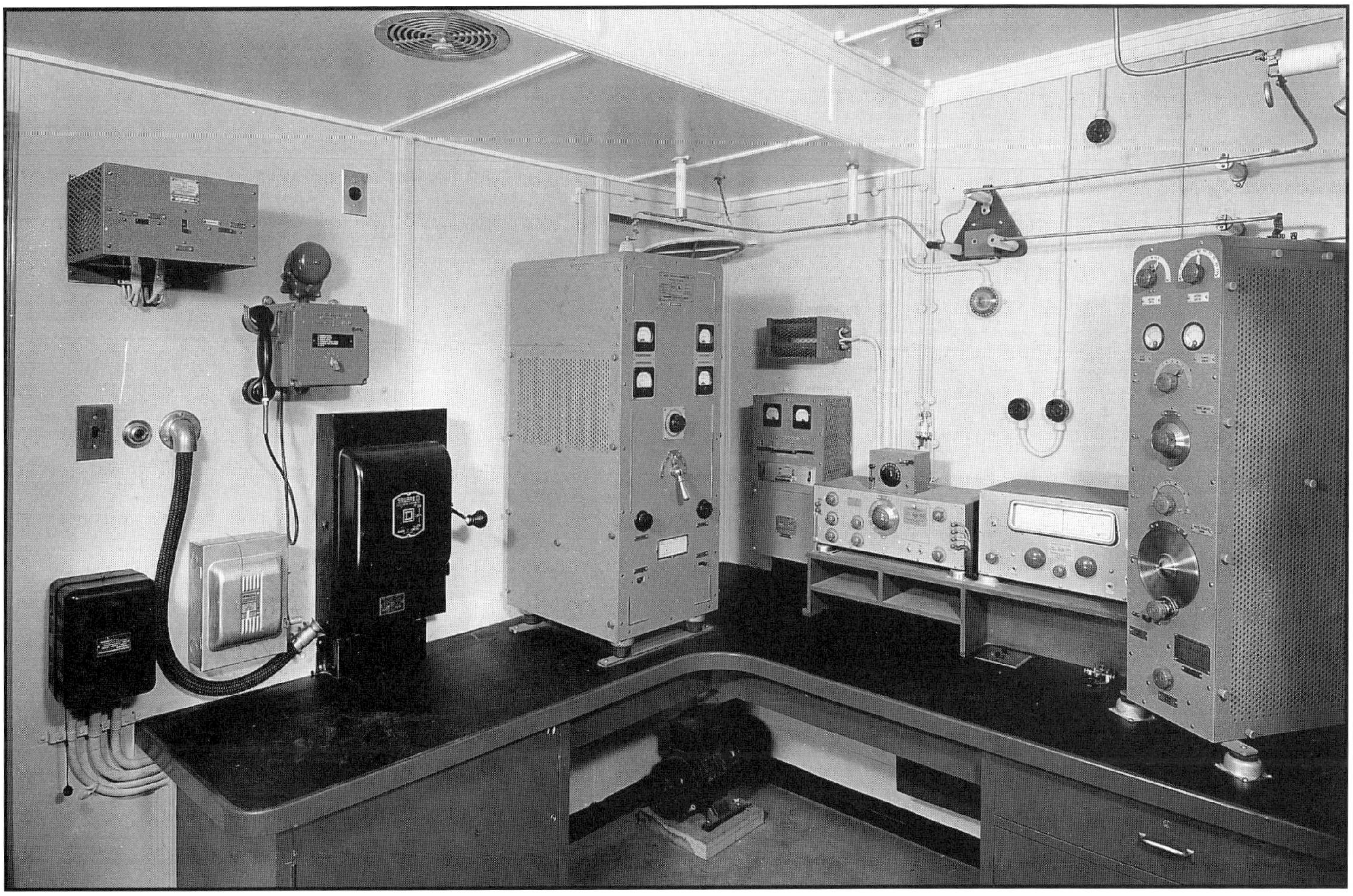

Above: The wheel house and radio room on the C3 freighter *Sea Arrow*, also built by the same shipyard, now Moore Dry Dock Company, June 26, 1940.

SMALL YARDS AND SUPPLIERS

As the war progressed and new types of ships emerged, small yards such as those in Stockton responded quickly as orders came in from both the Navy and Army. The pacific island-hopping campaign called for small inter-island tankers and freighters that could get in and out of small makeshift ports. Kyle and Company, a small Stockton shipyard, built more than twenty 162-foot tankers in 1943 and 1944. The framing system shown below is similar to the Isherwood System used in World War I tanker construction. Kyle and Company also had a small yard in Fresno where barges were built. In addition to the diesel-powered tankers shown here, Kyle and Company assembled 100-ton crane barges prefabricated by the St. Louis Steel Company and by the Dravo Corporation in Pittsburgh, Pennsylvania. Kyle also built other types of steel and wooden barges and 176-foot supply vessels.

Many small companies around San Francisco Bay contributed important services and products to wartime shipbuilding efforts. Most of these had been in business before the war in maritime trades and either continued their work under contract to the Navy or Maritime Commission or converted their peacetime product line to wartime needs.

The Pacific Coast Division of L.A. Young Spring and Wire Corporation in Oakland specialized in wire products before the war. The mainstay products were automobile springs, bed springs and inner spring mattresses. Immediately after Pearl Harbor the company switched from non-essential consumer products to essential war materials. Their first job was to fabricate 15,000 crew berths for troop ships bound for Australia. The berths consisted of special pipe frames in tiers with canvas bottoms lashed to the frames. The ships were due to leave port in seventeen days. The pipe frames presented no special problems but the 60,000 rope knots required to fasten the canvas bottoms called for expert splicers, not available on the local labor market. So the company recruited Sea Scouts from Oakland schools and the completed job was delivered on time. L.A. Young Corporation became a reliable, versatile supplier of specialty products to the Army and Navy including life rafts and floats with self-contained compartments for food and emergency supplies, chain and steel debarkation nets,

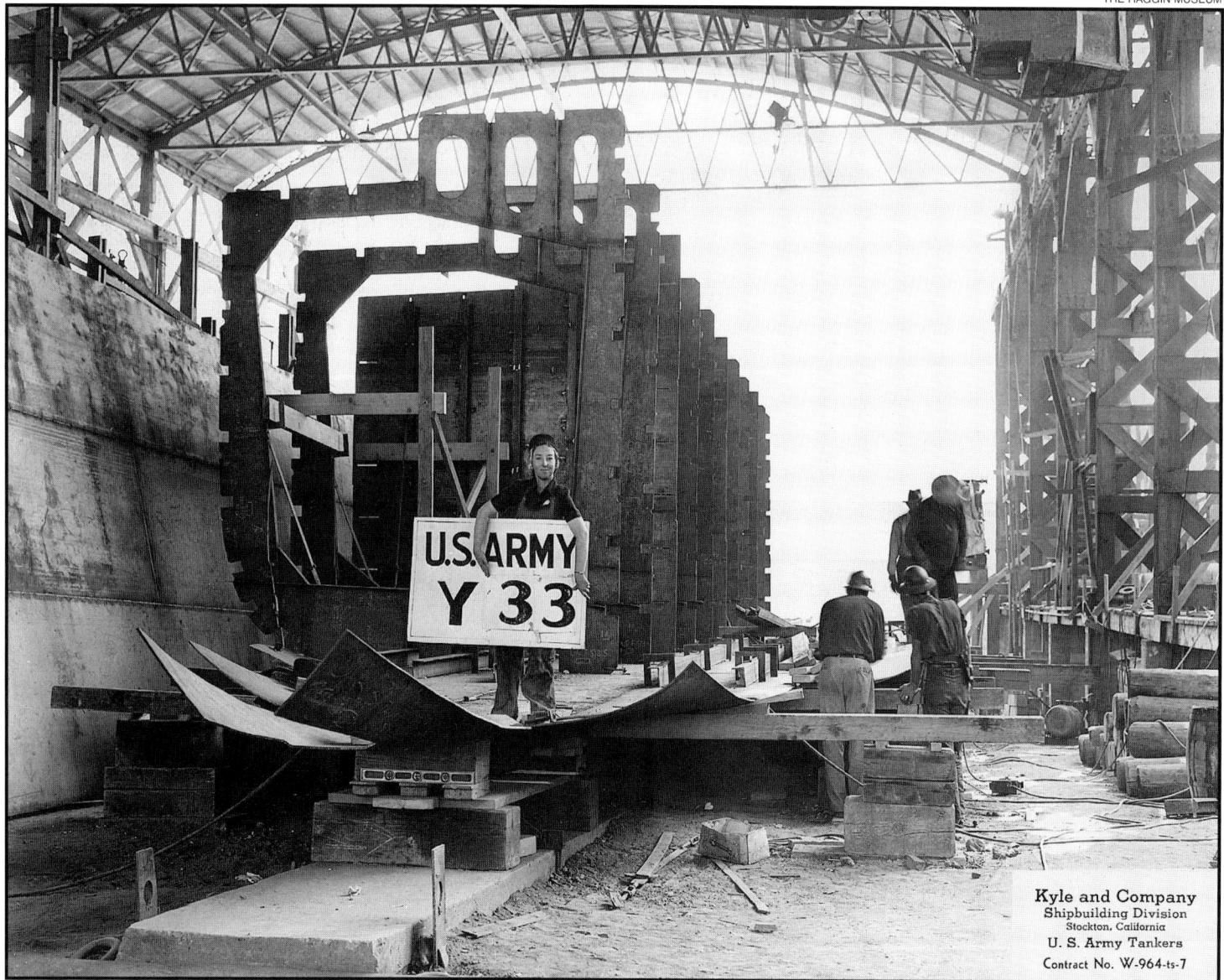

THE HAGGIN MUSEUM

Worker indicates hull number for the photographic record. October 1, 1943.

engine room ladders, wood and metal bunks, canvas sea anchors, mosquito nets, lumber slings, water tanks, and thousands of boxes used to ship bombs.

Martin Ship Service Company in San Francisco was a marine salvager and contractor in business since around 1900. The company's barges were equipped with huge vacuum systems for sucking sludge and refuse oil from ships, and special equipment for sandblasting metal surfaces. One of the company's main wartime jobs, besides general marine maintenance, was sandblasting hull bottoms in dry docks.

American Brass & Copper Company in Oakland had been around for sixteen years as a distributor of metal fittings, fasteners and specialty products when America entered the war. With huge warehouses and well-established contacts with metals manufacturers, American Brass & Copper was in a good position to hit the ground running in 1941 when demand soared due to the growing Bay Area shipbuilding industry. Their job was to channel valuable parts made from brass, copper, stainless steel, bronze, aluminum, lead and zinc in a steady flow to local shipyards. Their diversified stocks included nuts, bolts and washers, tubing, wire, rods, screening and plumbing parts, some of the millions of small, usually unseen parts that went into wartime vessels.

B. Simon Hardware Company, 8th and Broadway, Oakland, supplied mechanics tools to shipyards. Founded in 1900, the company became a leading tool distributor on the Pacific Coast. At the outbreak of war, local shipyards turned to them for a wide array of specialty tools in unprecedented quantities. As the shipbuilding industry expanded, B. Simon Hardware became known as a reliable source of high-quality tools and equipment.

Le Boeuf-Dougherty & Company of Richmond specialized in keeping ships on an even keel. Begun in 1941 to supply ballast for ships built at the Kaiser yards, the company produced a high-density crushed rock ballast weighing 230 pounds per cubic foot. Iron ore from Nevada gave the aggregate extra density so that less valuable space aboard ship was consumed. By adding the aggregate mix from belts and traveling buckets in small, well-placed amounts, workmen could stabilize a vessel for sea within

THE HAGGIN MUSEUM

Kyle and Company
Ship Building Division
Stockton, California

The LAUNCHING of the
U. S. Army Tanker Y 28
Contract No. W-964-tc-7
June 26, 1943

Tanker hull in gleaming fresh paint nears completion at Kyle and Company as a sister ship rises alongside.

48 hours. This job was done at the outfitting docks while other work was under way. The company expanded its operations to other areas, pile driving, dock work and towing. Following the Port Chicago disaster in 1944 when a loaded ammunition ship exploded, Le Boeuf-Dougherty got involved in the salvage operation. The company built the greatest barge crane on San Francisco Bay at that time. With its 250-ton lifting capacity, the crane helped clear the ammunition dock site at Port Chicago of submerged wreckage, a dangerous and exacting job.

Small shipyards as well as large ones in the Bay Area relied on suppliers and subcontractors from a widespread area. Stockton Steel Fabricators, a pool of small foundries, machine shops, tool makers and metal fabricators from the Stockton area and as far away as Bakersfield and Redding, made Stockton their assembly point. Output of these small shops was trucked to warehouses of the Stockton Iron Works at the foot of Harrison Street at the Channel. Here, larger sub-assemblies were fabricated and barged down river to the Kaiser yards in Richmond or other yards in Alameda.

Suppliers from other places included Birnie Electric Company and Korktone Company of Los Angeles. Their employees worked on the outfitting docks at Richmond installing electrical systems and radar for attack transports. Korktone made insulating material, granulated cork on bare metal used to combat condensation in powder magazines and ammunition handling rooms aboard ship.

Shipyards large and small across America benefitted from an experimental program set up by the War Production Board beginning early in 1942. A Contract Distribution Branch of the WPB coordinated work of thousands of small shops throughout the country. The plan was to involve every back-yard garage, home workshop and tiny manufacturing plant in war production. Test programs demonstrated that the idea, although fraught with difficulties, worked. In time, many more small production facilities converted with government assistance to war production, relieving home workshops from similar work. A medium-sized shop with a sub-contract to produce parts would in turn sub-contract with even smaller shops, each contributing a machining, cutting or assembly operation. Hundreds of thousands of parts used in Bay Area shipyards came from thousands of these micro sub-contractors.

THE HAGGIN MUSEUM

Moments after a fore-and-aft tanker launch at Kyle and Company, the Stockton Channel seems narrower than ever. Drag cables bring the hull up short to keep it from crashing into the warehouse opposite the yard.

Kyle and Company shipyard seen from the Channel with one of the 162-foot tankers, *Y34*, at the outfitting dock. On the ways are *Y45* on the left and *Y46* on the right These versatile craft served throughout the war and long after, supplying fuel and other liquid cargo to small ports from the Aleutians to the South Pacific. May 1, 1944.

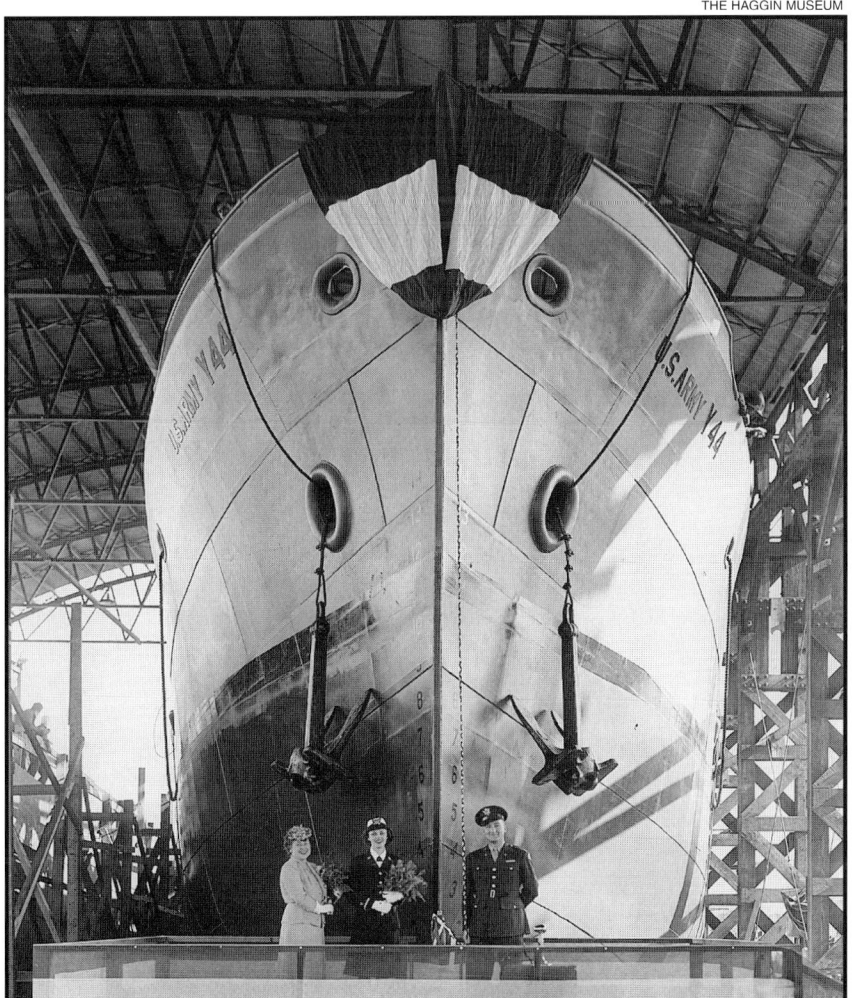

The launching ceremonies at small yards were briefer than those at the big yards and the crowds smaller too, but the events represented as much pride of accomplishment. Kyle and Company, April 22, 1944.

WOODEN CRAFT

Wooden craft played an important role in World War II. Among combat vessels, wooden minesweepers were perhaps the most effective use of wood because their non-magnetic hulls offered protection from magnetic mines. Patrol and picket boats were made both from steel and wood. The most famous World War II wooden vessel was the PT or Patrol-Torpedo boat. Fast and heavily armed, PT boats caught the public fancy after daring exploits in the South Pacific. Scores of noncombatant wooden vessels gave valuable service but without as much fanfare. These included Army and Navy tugs, tenders, repair and rescue vessels, small auxiliary craft and thousands of barges and pontoons. The Navy and Army shipbuilding programs took full advantage of experienced wooden boat builders, assigning contracts to small yards on both coasts and on inland ports.

Below: These 63-foot Navy Airplane Rescue Boats, called simply "crash boats" by those who used them, were made in great numbers by several yards throughout the United States and rescued downed airmen wherever American forces operated. Fast and highly maneuverable, they were popular with sportsmen after the war and appeared in coastal waters for decades after this photo was taken in 1943. A 104-foot version of the crash boat was built by Stephens for the Army.

Right: The busy Stephens yard looks calm in this 1943 photo showing some of the output for the year. The two larger vessels at center are 103-foot Army Aircraft Rescue Boats and the smaller vessels are 63-foot Navy Aircraft Rescue Boats. Stephens also built 72-foot tugs with a combination of bent and sawn frame construction, and 136-foot wooden minesweepers.

THE HAGGIN MUSEUM

Stephens Brothers' boats, Stockton Channel, 1943.

BUILD SHIPS!
Wartime Shipbuilding Photographs
San Francisco Bay
1940-1945

by Wayne Bonnett

America was at war. American ships were being lost to enemy action faster than new ships could be built. The directive was clear: Build the weapons of war—aircraft, tanks, guns—and build them fast. And build ships. In the San Francisco Bay Area, where ship-building was an old but fading tradition, people rose to the unprecedented challenge.

When the urgent call BUILD SHIPS! went out at the beginning of World War II, the San Francisco Bay Area responded by creating the greatest shipbuilding complex in the world. Older established boatyards on the Bay and its tributaries, and big shipyards that had turned out ships during World War I, geared up for action. New "ship factories," hastily built for rapid production, joined in as America built an armada larger than any the world had ever seen or will ever see again. From the giant Kaiser yards in Richmond to the small wooden-boat builders on the Stockton Channel, over 200,000 shipyard workers produced on average a ship a day for the duration of World War II, more than 1,400 vessels in 1,365 days.

Fortunately, this amazing construction feat was well documented by professional photographers under contract to the shipyards, the U.S. Maritime Commission and the U.S. Navy. The photographs in this book, selected from this collective historic archive, chronicle the "works-in-progress" activities of wartime San Francisco Bay Area shipyards during a fascinating and unique episode in Bay Area history.

Over thirty local shipyards produced and repaired an extraordinary variety of warships, tankers, freighters, landing craft, small boats and barges. Included here are photos of the Kaiser yards in Richmond, Bethlehem Ship-building, Western Pipe and Steel, and Belair in San Francisco; Moore Dry Dock Company in Oakland; Bethlehem, United Engineering, and General Engineering and Dry Dock Company in Alameda; Mare Island Naval Shipyard, Hunters Point Naval Dry Docks, and the Stockton shipyards of Hickinbotham Brothers, Stephens Brothers, Kyle & Company, Pollock-Stockton, Colberg Boat Works, D.W. Nicholson, and Clyde W. Wood, Inc. The photographs in BUILD SHIPS! are presented through the courtesy of the San Francisco Maritime National Historical Park, The Haggin Museum in Stockton, the Richmond Museum of History, the Sausalito Historical Society and private collections.

Wayne Bonnett is a writer and maritime artist and a collector of regional historic maritime photographs for over thirty years. His other works include *A Century of Maritime Photography* (Chronicle Books), *San Francisco By Land & Sea*, *The 1894 San Francisco Directory*, and *City of Dreams: The 1915 Panama-Pacific International Exposition* (Windgate Press).

WINDGATE PRESS

P.O. BOX 1715, SAUSALITO, CA 94966
PHONE 415 332 0912   FAX 415 332 4874

ISBN: 0-915269-20-1   CASEBOUND $45   © COPYRIGHT 1999 WINDGATE PRESS

THE HAGGIN MUSEUM

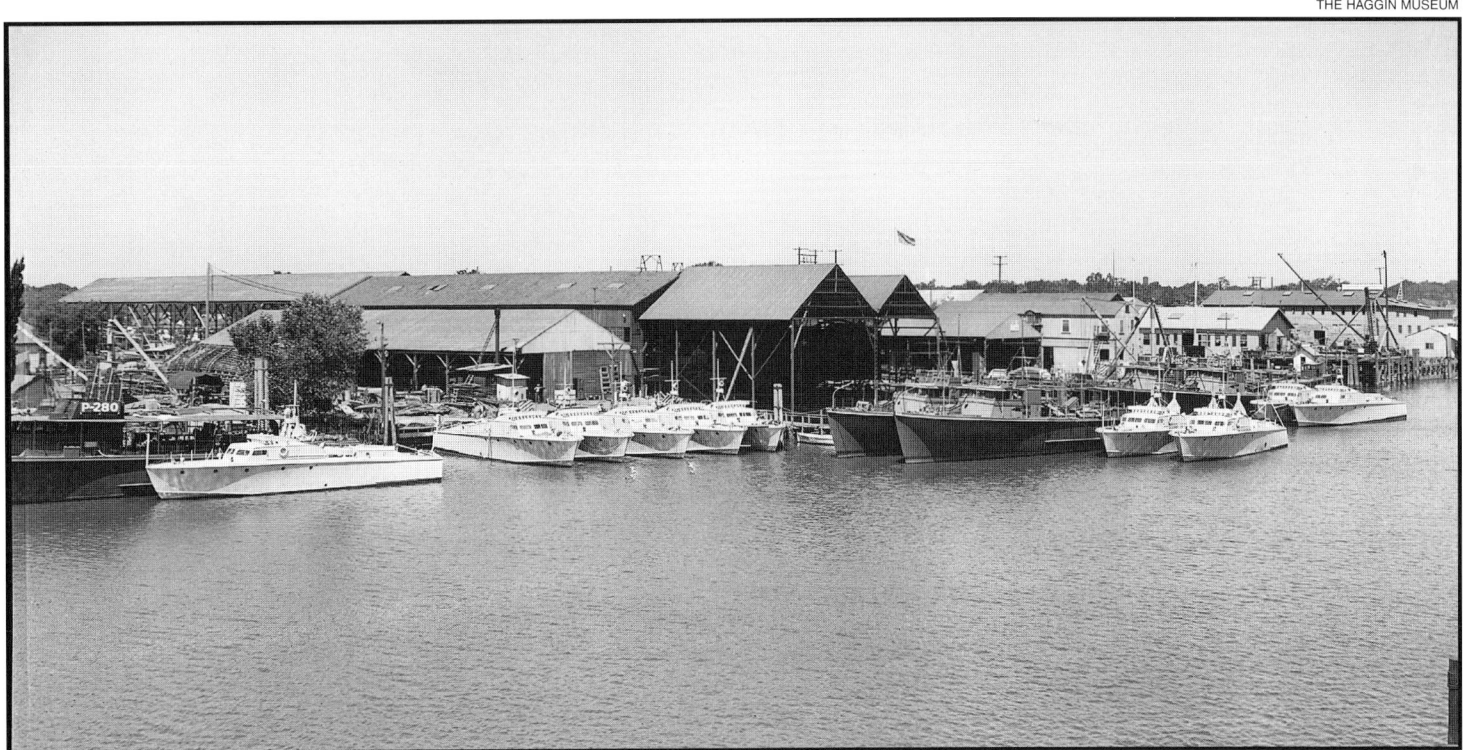

Stephens Brothers' yard, Stockton Channel, 1943.

THE HAGGIN MUSEUM

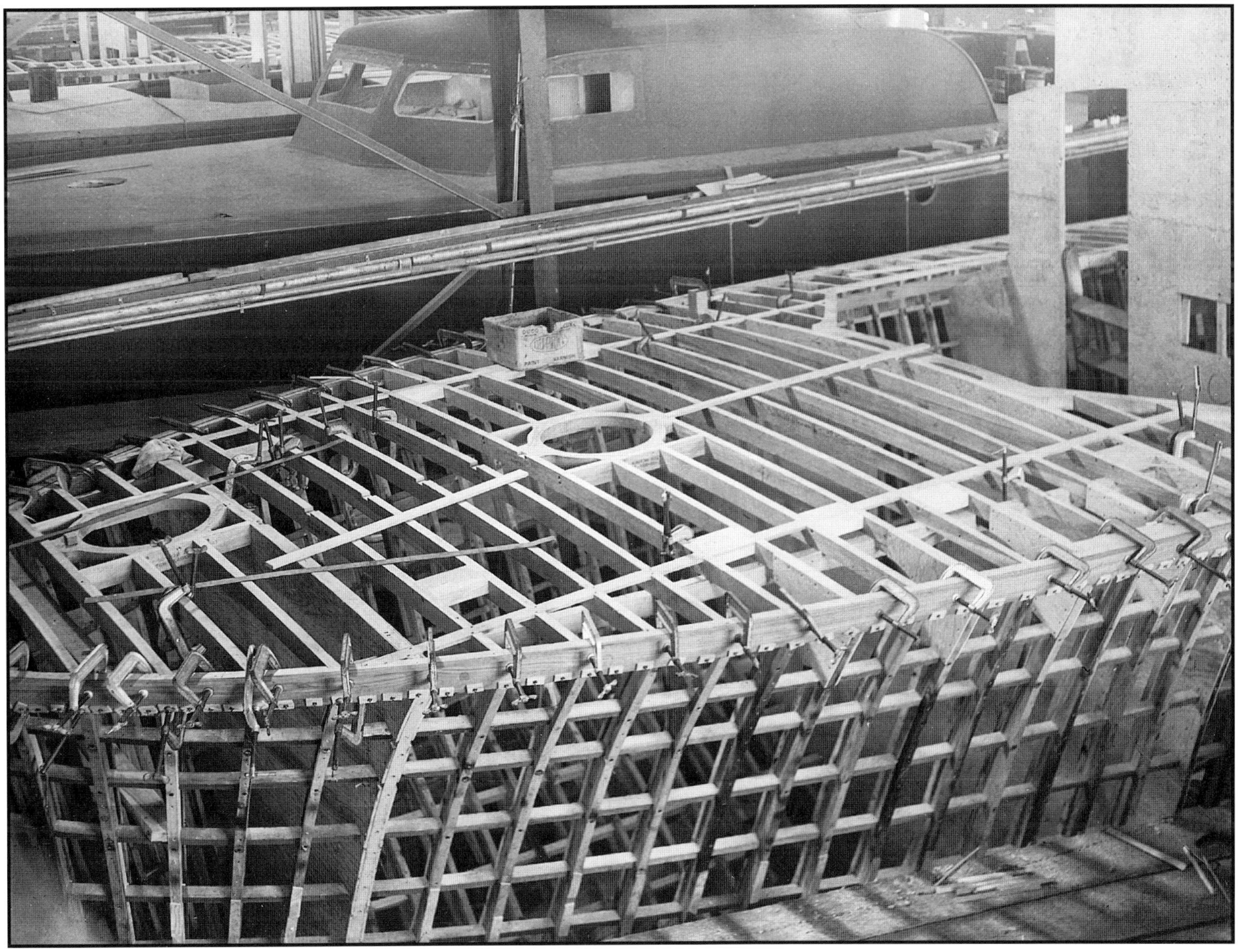

A 63-foot Navy rescue boat under construction at Stephens Brothers, 1943.

THE HAGGIN MUSEUM

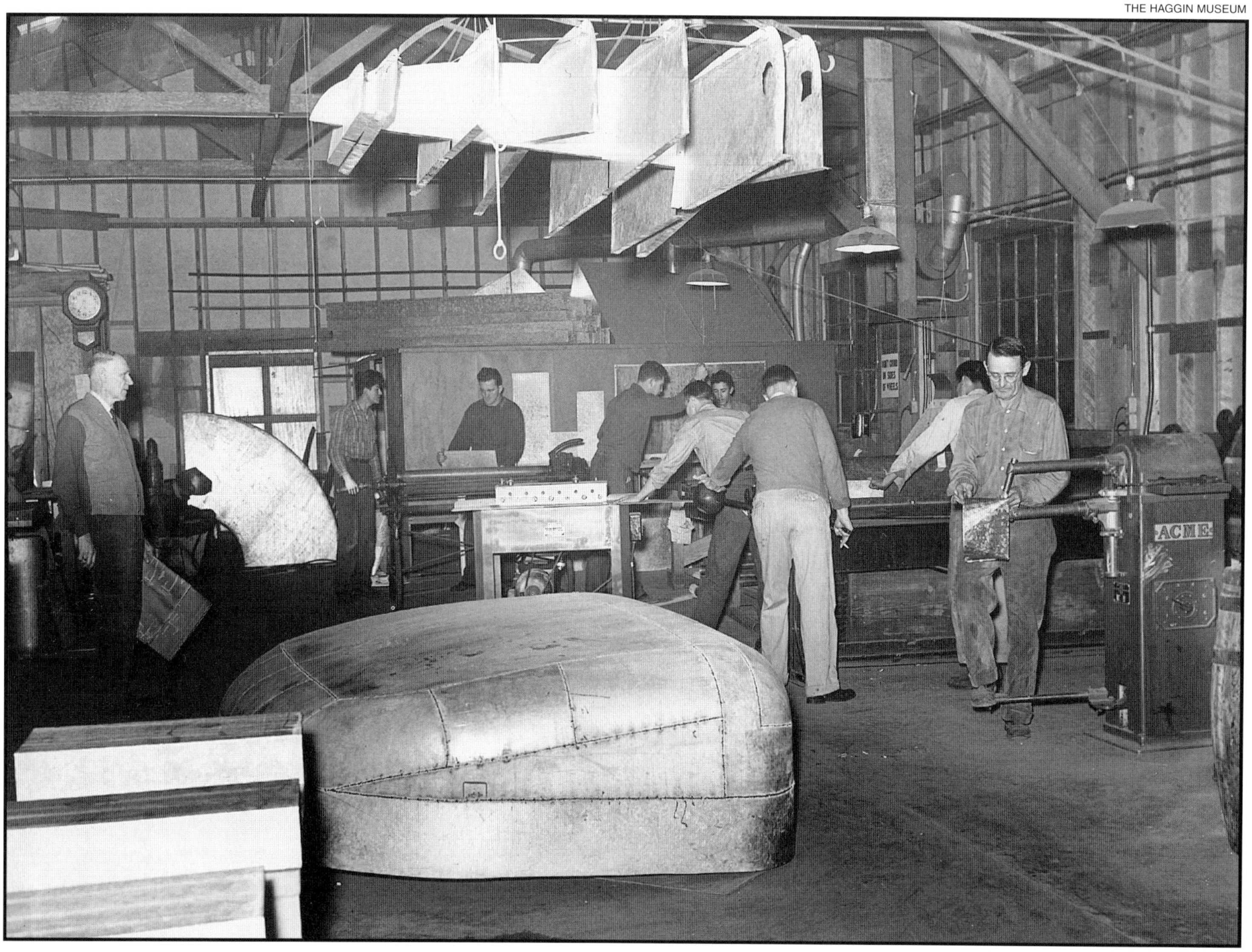

Above: The sheet metal shop at Colberg where the forward canopy is formed.

THE HAGGIN MUSEUM

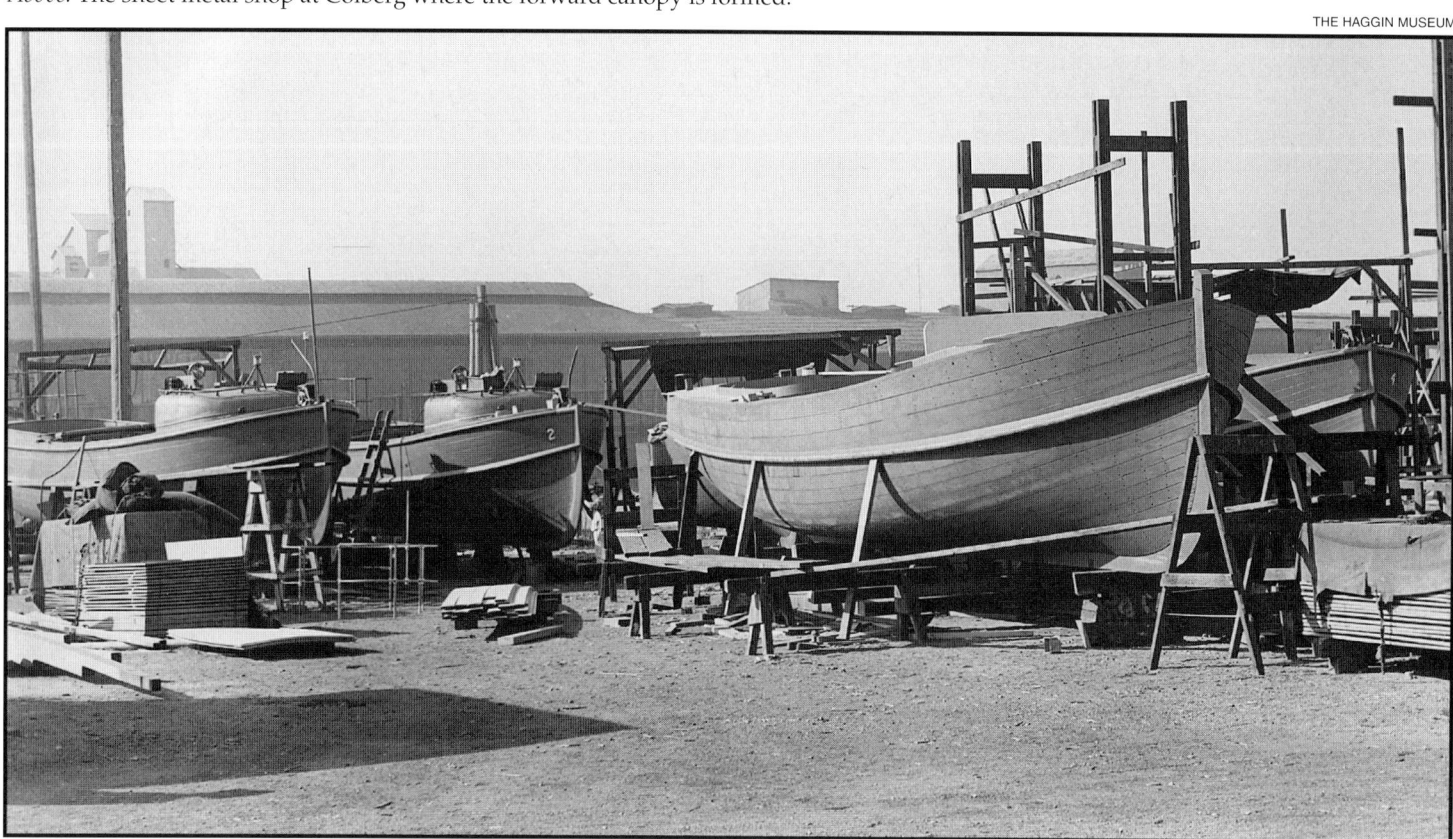

Above: Boats receiving their canopies in the Colberg yard. A finished view of one of these boats is on Page 165.

Colberg Boat Works in Stockton built, among other wooden craft, 42-foot seaplane fueling boats, shown here under construction. These specialized vessels combined traditional wooden boat-building skills with modern steel fabrication and sheet metal work. The company also built salvage vessels that had wood hulls and steel superstructures.

Other Stockton wooden vessel builders in addition to Stephens Brothers and Colberg were Clyde W. Wood, Inc., Pollock-Stockton and D.W. Nicholson Corporation who built 130-foot wooden barges for the Army (see Page 134). Clyde W. Wood built wooden tugs shown on the following pages and a 400-ton, 150-foot wooden floating drydock for docking ships under construction. Pollock-Stockton (see Page 132) was the largest shipyard in the Stockton area with over 5,000 employees. George Pollock, an engineer and contractor since 1918, had helped build Shasta dam and the Tower Bridge in Sacramento. He had built docks and dry docks at Pearl Harbor, Alameda, Mare Island, and San Pedro. In early 1942, his company converted a carrot field along the Stockton Channel into a specialized yard with two deep basins for the construction of sectional dry docks. Pollock also built wooden and steel barges and wood-hulled net tenders.

THE HAGGIN MUSEUM

Above: A sheet metal worker in Colberg's Grant Street shop reveals the more intimate working conditions of smaller yards.

THE HAGGIN MUSEUM

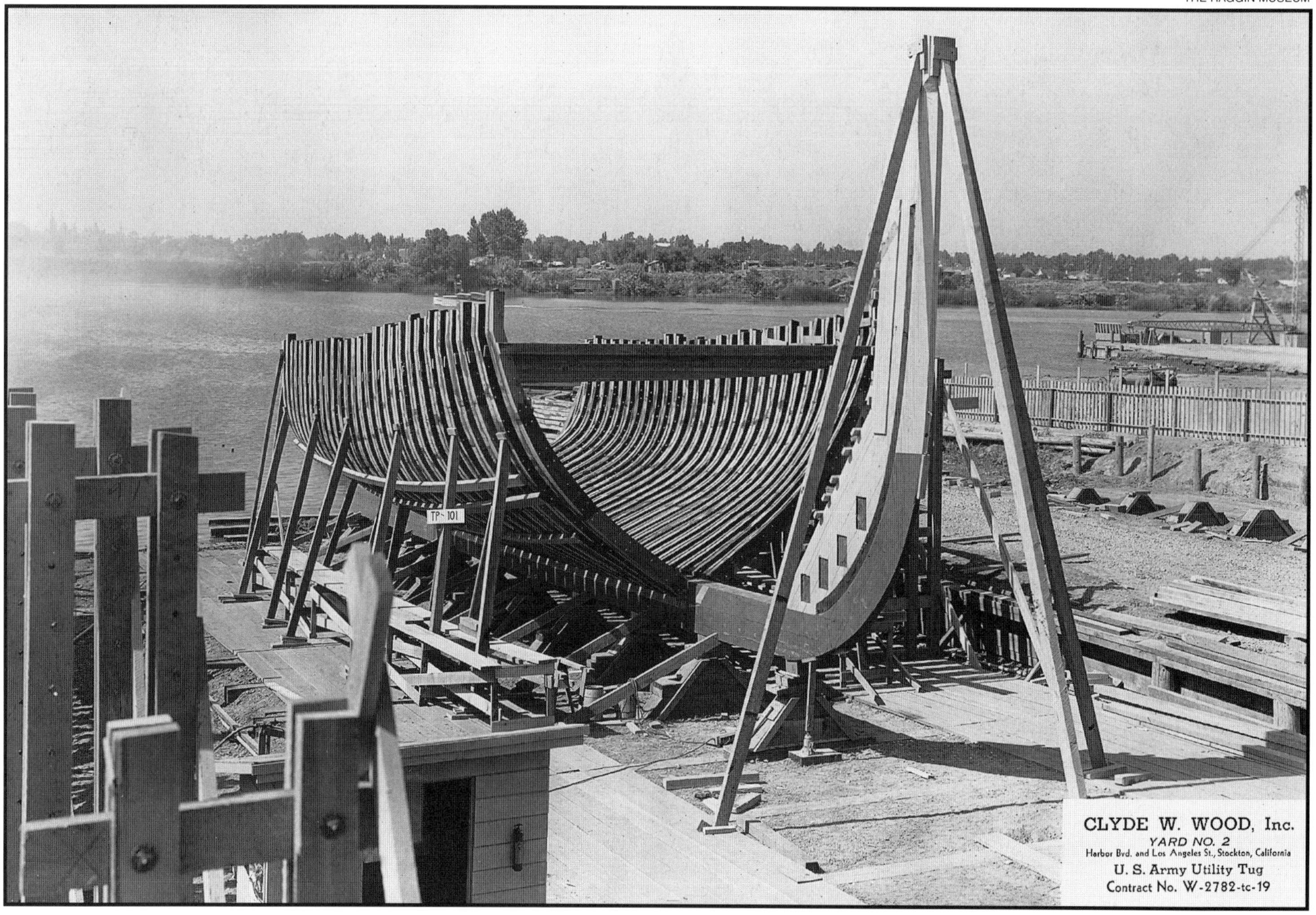

THE HAGGIN MUSEUM

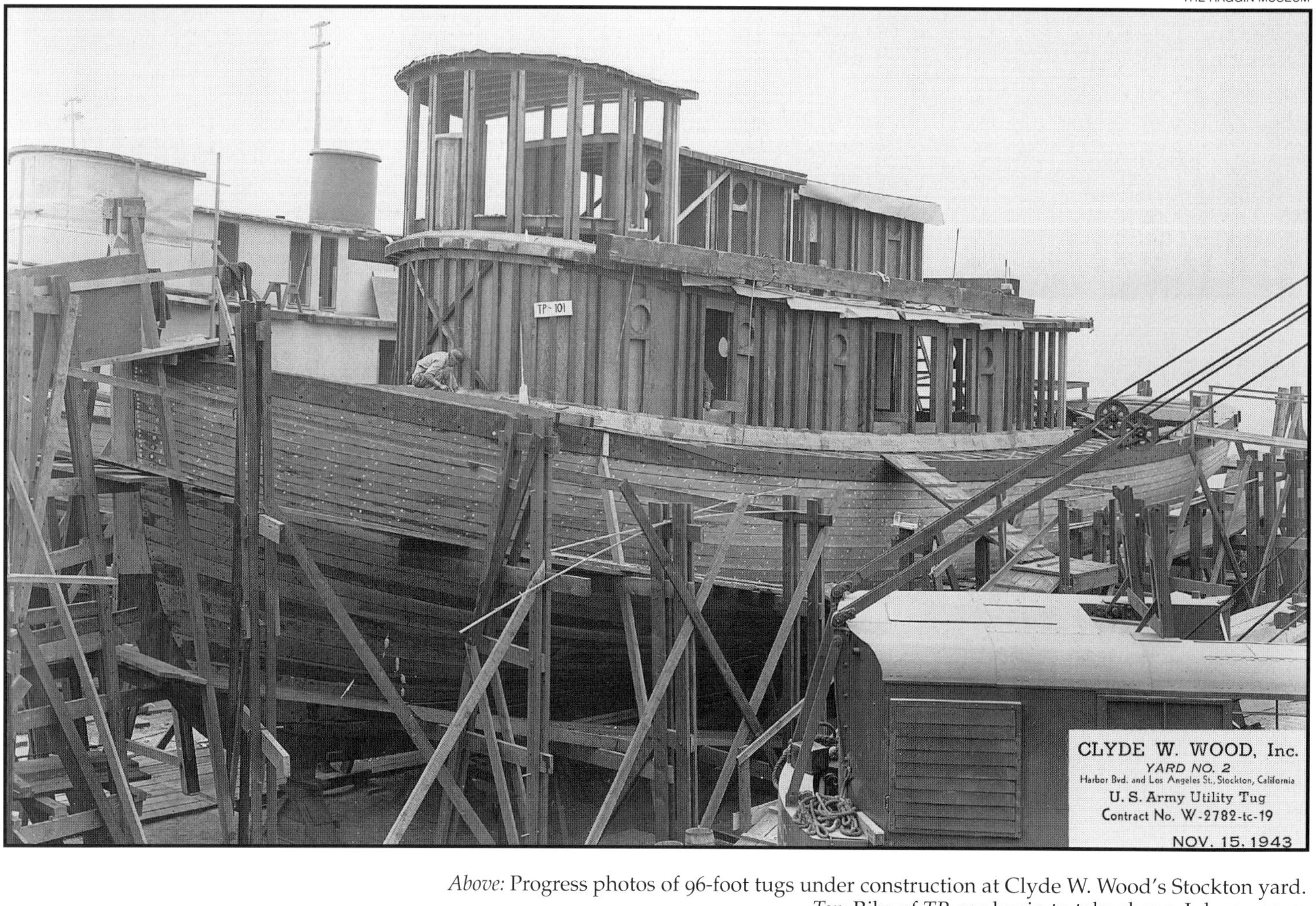

Above: Progress photos of 96-foot tugs under construction at Clyde W. Wood's Stockton yard.
Top: Ribs of *TP-101* begin to take shape, July 15, 1943.

Top: By September 15, 1943, framing is almost complete.
Bottom: These all-wood tugs had 450 horsepower Fairbanks-Morse diesel engines.

THE HAGGIN MUSEUM

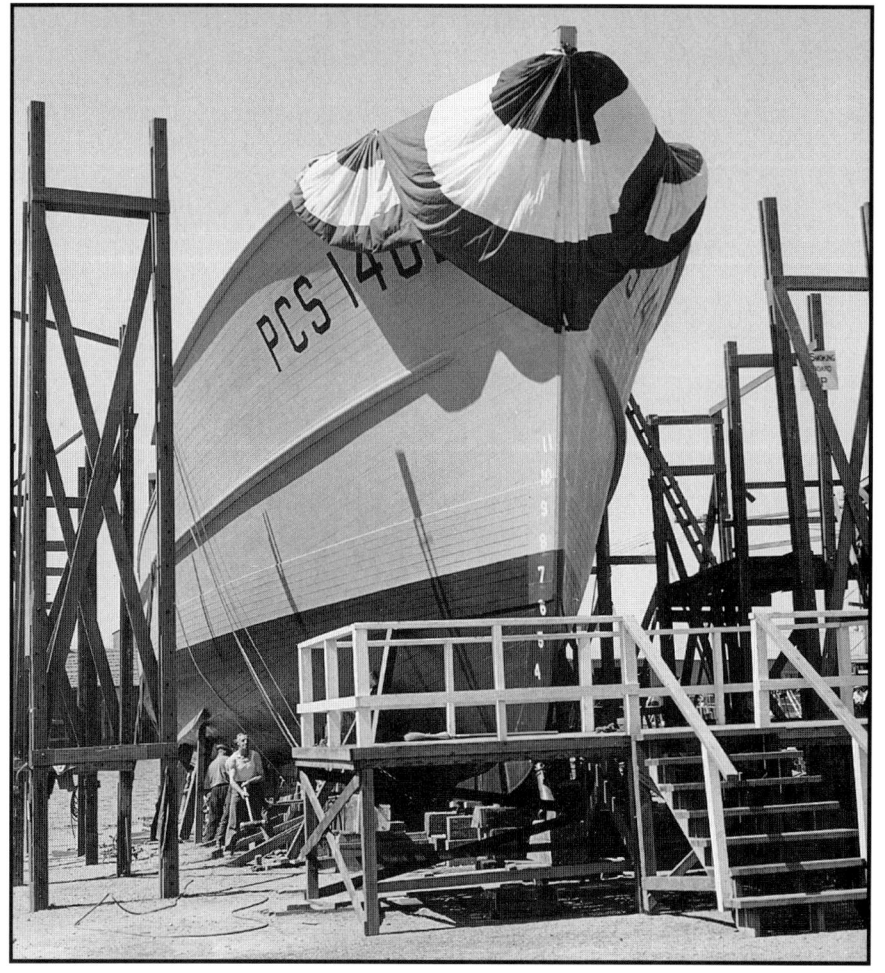

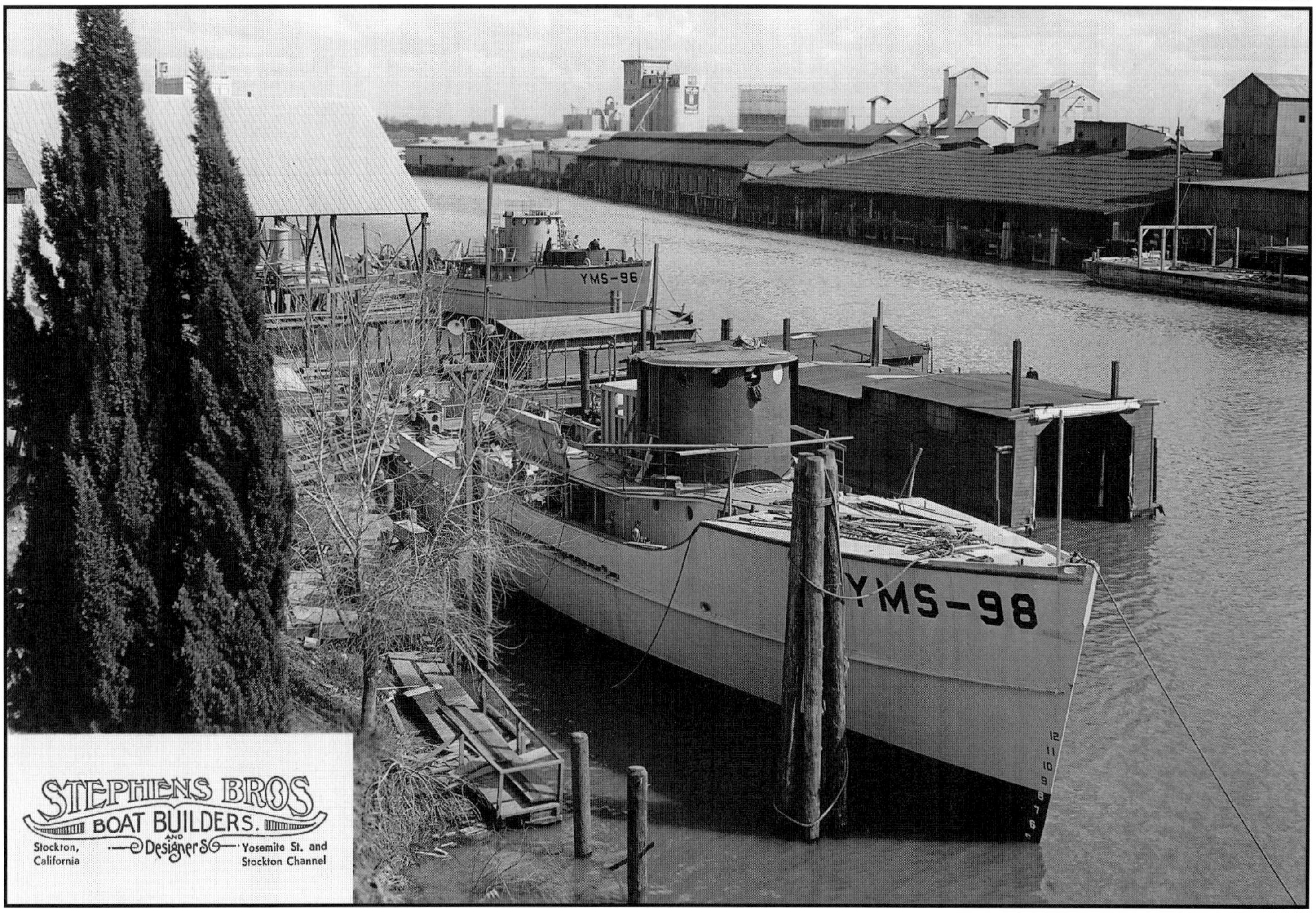

THE HAGGIN MUSEUM

Above: The largest boats built by Stephens Brothers during World War II were these 136-foot wood minesweepers powered by General Motors diesels. March 12, 1942.

Right: A wooden-hulled 136-foot sweeper-type sub chaser at Colberg Boat Works ready for launching. Workers are driving wedges to lift the hull onto sliding ways for the launch. Before the war, Colberg built, among other wooden vessels, big tuna clippers. The design was modified to become a refrigerated supply vessel for use in the Pacific (see Page 160).

Above: Close up of Stephens Brothers 63-foot Aircraft rescue boat in 1943. One local wag speculated that these boats might prove useful after the war for duck hunting on the Delta.

SHIPYARD MORALE

High worker morale at Bay Area shipyards was vital to production. Immediately after Pearl Harbor, enthusiasm for the defense effort ran higher than ever before. In time, however, the tedium of repetition set in. Much of shipyard work was hard and dangerous, made more so by worker inexperience and the grueling pace of production. Wartime shipyards were a forced melting pot of ethnic, religious and cultural prejudices and attitudes common to America at the time. Although almost all workers believed in a common goal, some acted in ways that hurt production. Employees and management joined in finding ways to maintain *esprit de corps*. Their efforts took many forms and, in general, despite worker complaints and hardships, petty thievery, strained racial, sexual and labor relations, morale remained high throughout the war. Most yards participated in special programs designed to boost worker morale, especially in the areas of recruiting and training workers, safety and labor and employee relations. Because so many new workers were far from their homes and in unfamiliar working conditions, off-hours entertainment and recreational activities were given higher priorities than ever before in American workplaces. Shipyards encouraged formation of organizations such as baseball, bowling and boxing teams, the War Fathers Club, Stage Door Canteens and the Bond-a-Week Club. In addition, workers were encouraged to join charity drives for the Red Cross, War Chest, March of Dimes and Christmas donations for children's and veteran's hospitals.

Shipyard gatherings, as long as they didn't interfere with production schedules, were encouraged. These included birthday and engagement parties, impromptu and organized lunch-time shows with singers, dancers, musicians, and visiting celebrities. The big yards had a surprising number of talented musicians and other performers who willingly gave of their time.

Shipyards staged special events to help break the monotony and keep the focus on winning the war. Posters and company magazines kept workers informed as much as security would permit. Worker incentives included rewards of war bonds for outstanding time- and cost-saving ideas put into production.

RICHMOND MUSEUM OF HISTORY

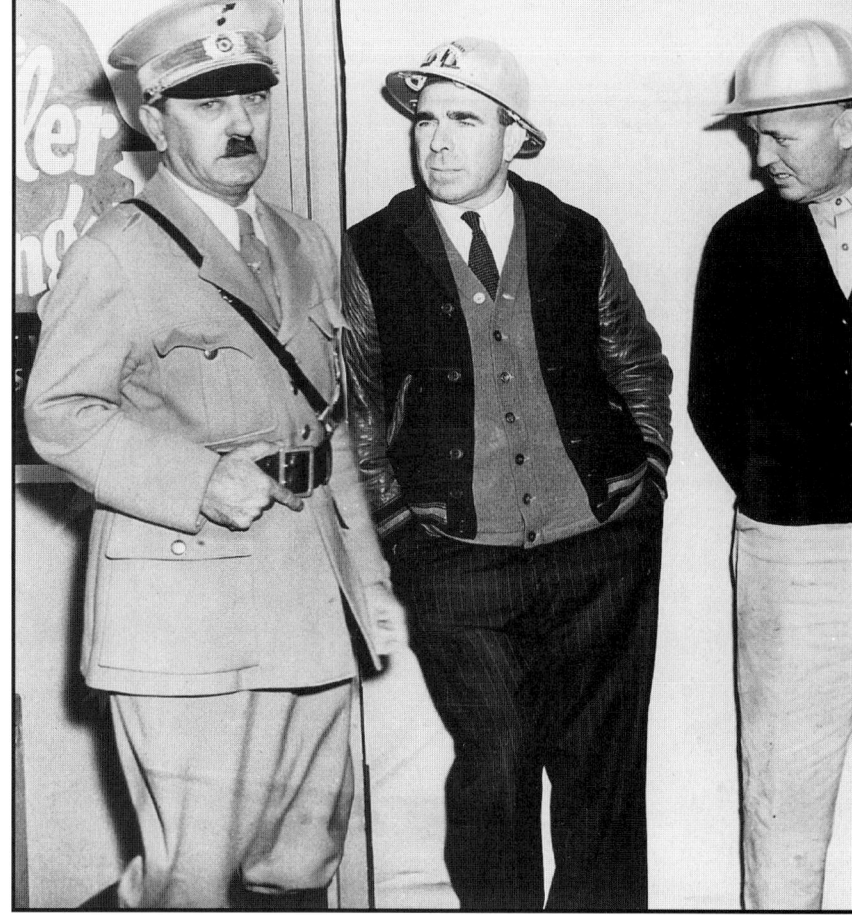

Right: A suspicious character visits the Richmond Kaiser yards under the baleful gaze of two employees. Promotions and stunts ranged from patriotic and openly sentimental to humorous.

Below: Traditional launch ceremonies took on new significance as they gave shipyards an opportunity to honor special people and recognize outstanding effort. Sponsors, who got to swing the bottle, were almost always women in accordance with maritime tradition. The list included workers, war widows, administrator's wives, celebrities and women in uniform.

RICHMOND MUSEUM OF HISTORY

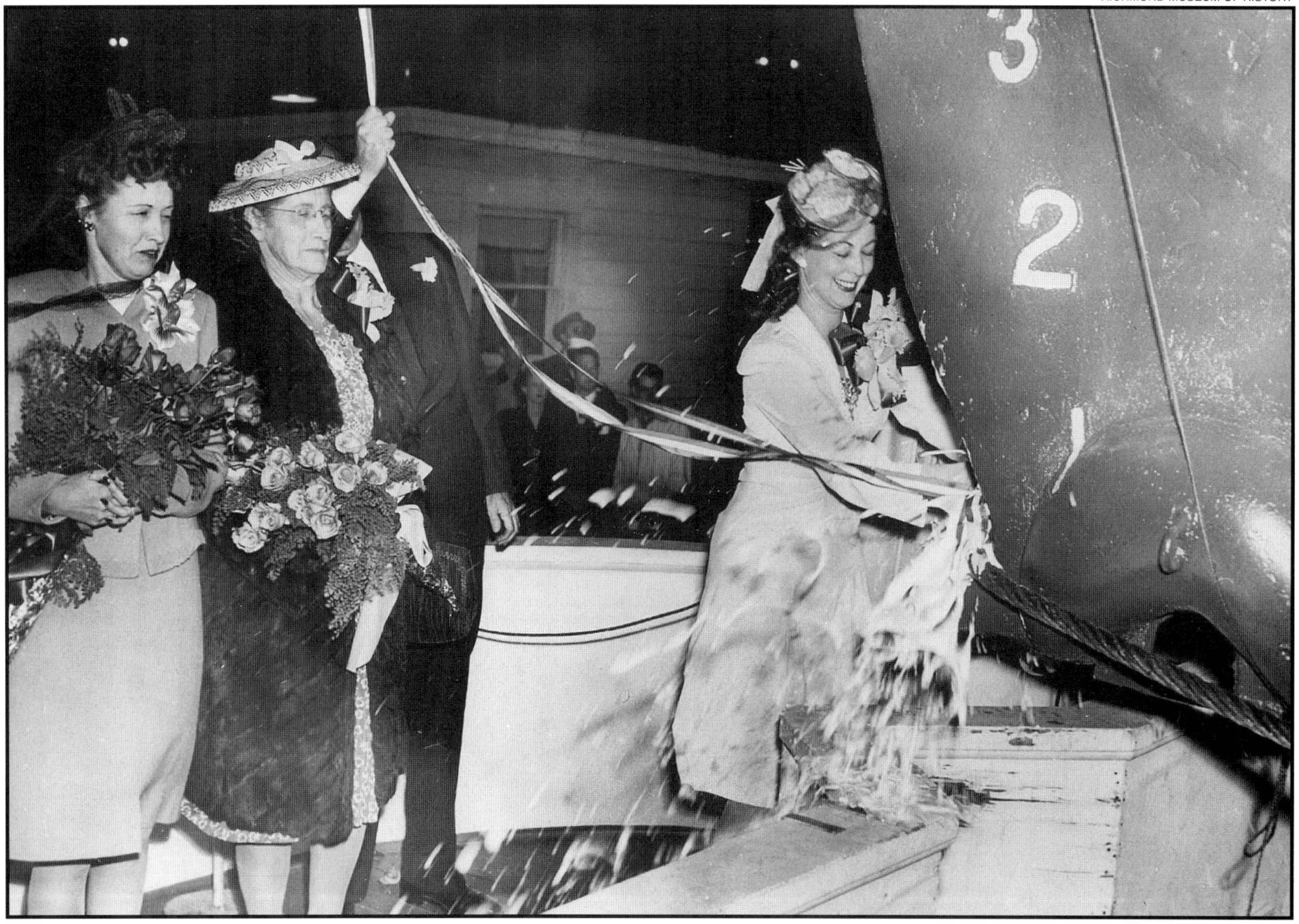

RICHMOND MUSEUM OF HISTORY

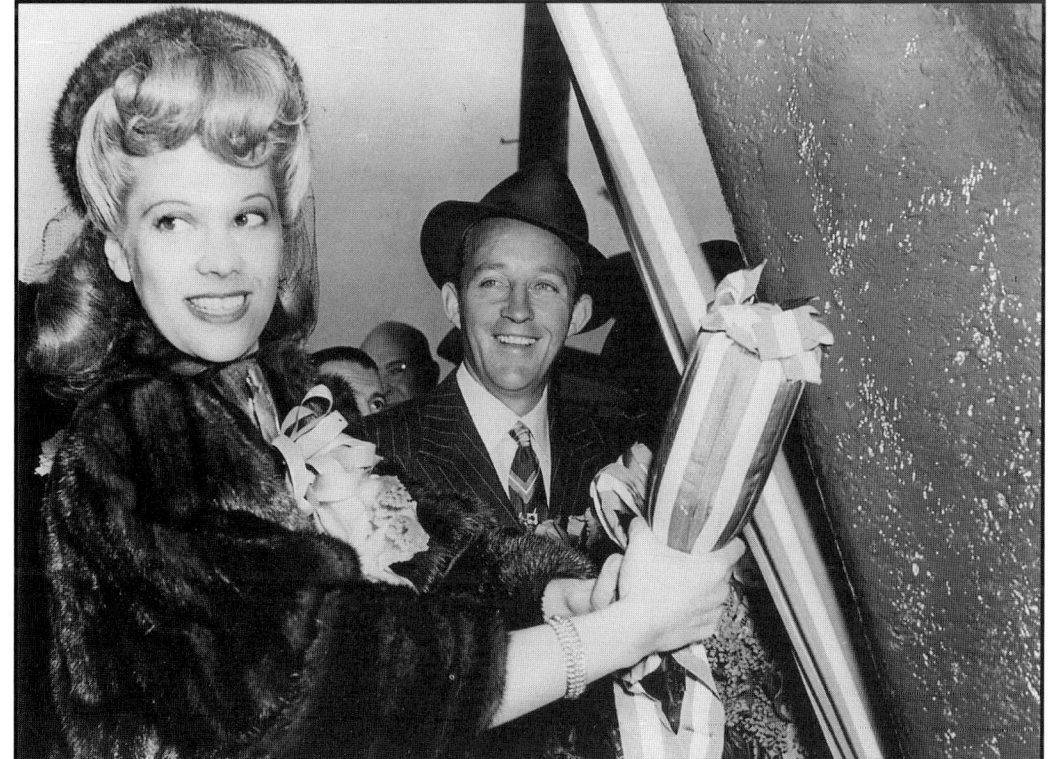

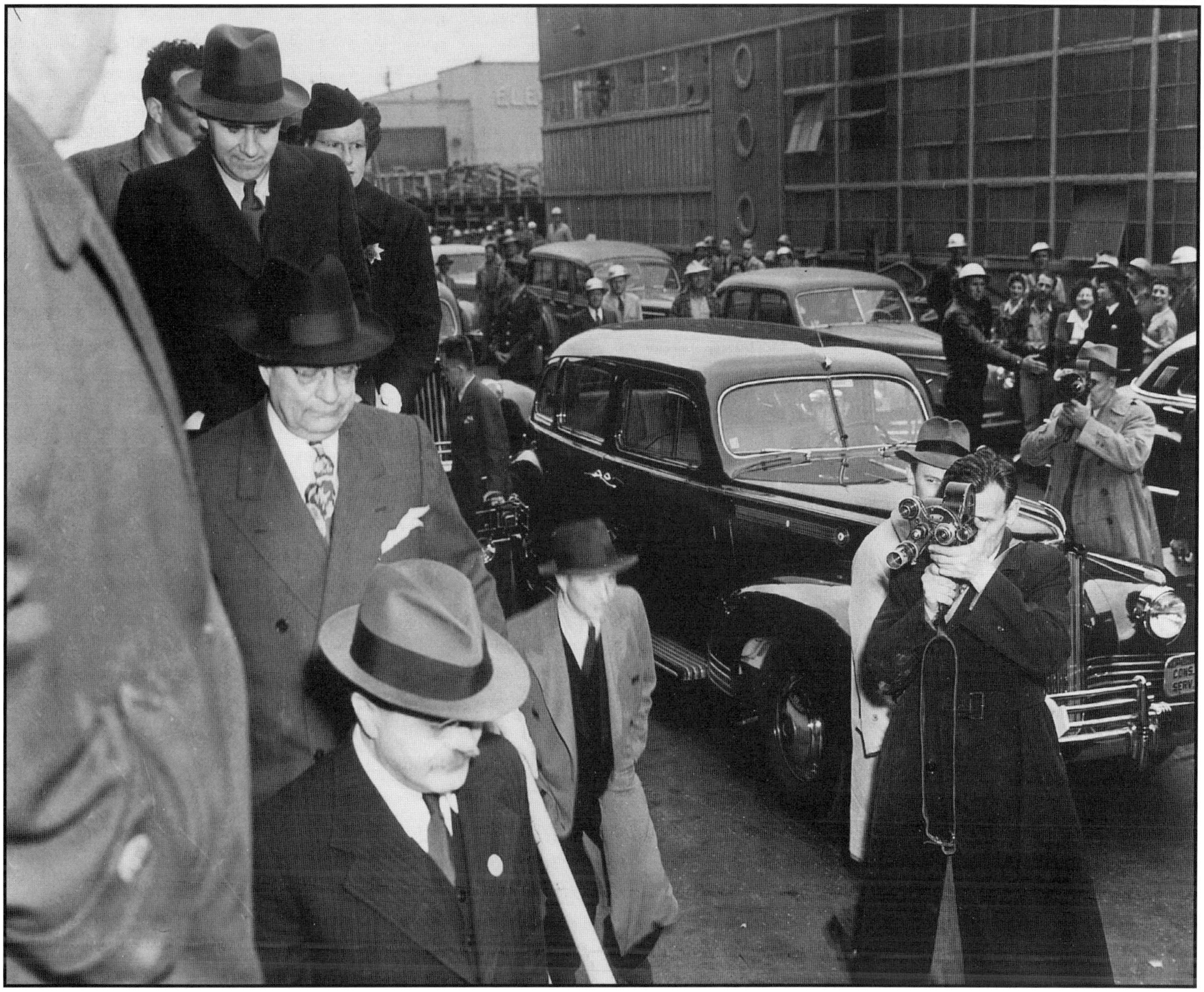

RICHMOND MUSEUM OF HISTORY

Above: Fast-moving Henry J. Kaiser hurries past security guards at Kaiser #3 with visiting dignitaries from the Soviet Union. Kaiser is sandwiched between Foreign Minister Molotov, front, and Ambassador Andrei Gromyko, rear. This probably was taken when Soviet representatives were in San Francisco for the founding of the United Nations in 1945.

Left: Movie stars and other celebrities boosted morale with their presence at launches. Here, Dinah Shore and Bing Crosby join the launch of Liberty ship *John R. Park* at Kaiser #2, February 20, 1943.

SAN FRANCISCO MARITIME NHP P79-071a Scr55:y pl.6563

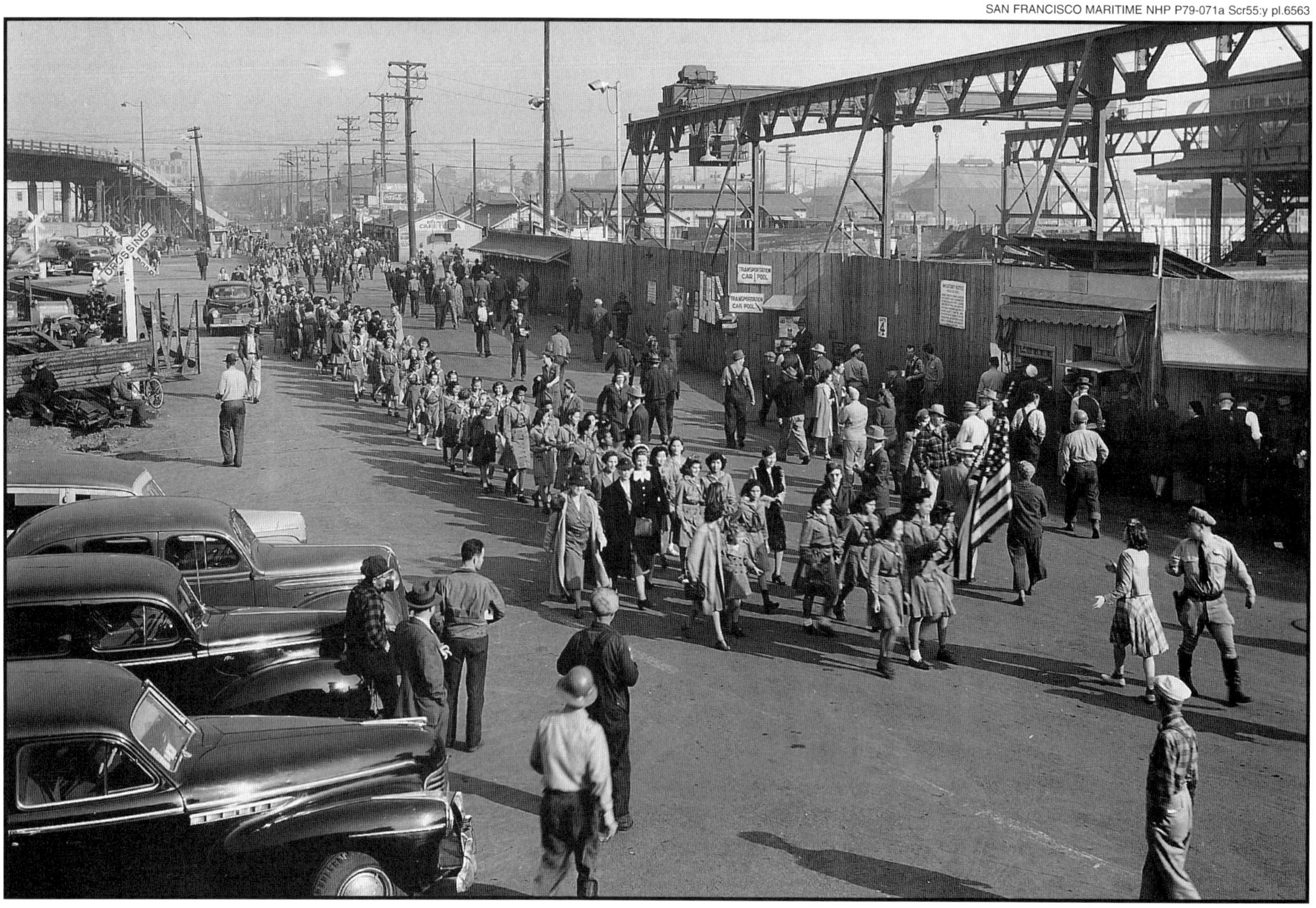

WINDGATE

Above: Sailors arrive at Colberg Boat Works in Stockton to pick up Christmas packages gathered by the local steamfitters' union for overseas servicemen, and to spur the Third War Loan campaign, September 22, 1943.

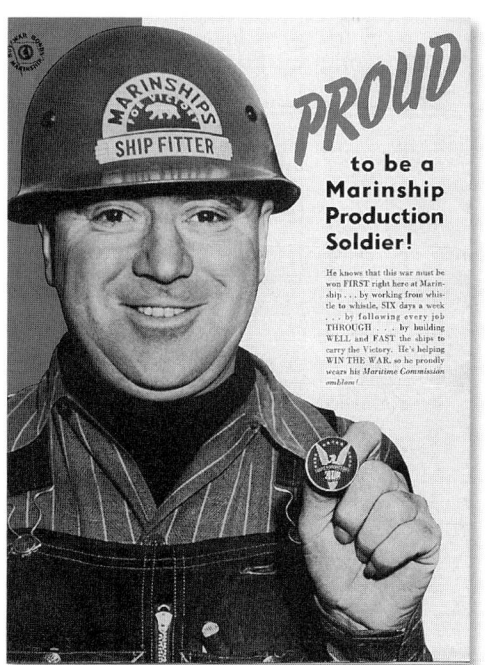

Above: Back cover of the January 19, 1943 issue of *The Marin-er*, Marinship's official publication.

Above left: Oakland Girl Scouts arrive at Moore Dry Dock to witness the launching of C2 freighter *Rainbow*, November 27, 1943.

Below left: A pickup band at General Engineering and Dry Dock in Alameda provides a musical interlude in 1944.

Above: Chabot Terrace in Vallejo, across the channel from Mare Island, served workers and families of military personnel. It was less-than-affectionately known by residents as "Shabby Acres." c.1944.

Above: Naval dependents in Vallejo housing project, 1943. The influx of women workers and dependent families to the Bay Area called for special programs for small children, from day care centers to emergency school rooms.

Right: The big shipyards operated twenty-four hours a day, every day. The day shift was 8 A.M. to 4 P.M., swing shift 4. P.M. to midnight, and the graveyard shift midnight to 8 A.M. Many women shipyard workers with husbands overseas, shared accommodations or boarded with families in the area. Marinship, 1944.

Marin City, adjacent to Marinship was a complete community with 1500 family houses and apartments and 1200 dormitory rooms, plus school, recreation center and shopping. c.1944.

HOUSING AND TRANSPORTATION

Closely linked to worker morale was the necessity for wartime housing and transportation. Even before Pearl Harbor, expansion of shipbuilding and other defense industries in the Bay Area had generated a housing shortage. Workers naturally wanted to live near the yards and the early new employees occupied all available rental housing. After Pearl Harbor, with massive expansion of shipyards plus the new yards at Richmond and Sausalito, the Bay Area housing shortage became acute. Tens of thousands of workers and their families needed immediate housing and had to settle temporarily for house-trailer camps, tents in parks, make-shift quarters in auditoriums and other public buildings. As workers had to live farther and farther from their workplaces, local transportation systems were strained. Obviously the federal government had to address the housing and transportation problems and act quickly to avoid serious slowdowns in shipyards and other war production plants. Two new agencies, the Office of Defense Transportation (ODT) and the National Housing Agency (NHA) were formed. The first helped coordinate existing transportation and assist in getting transport equipment whenever possible. The second coordinated various existing housing groups and formulated new housing programs.

High priority for new housing was given to Army and Navy needs, with Maritime Commission shipyards lower on the list. Because of low priorities for NHA housing, the possibility arose that the new shipyards in Sausalito and Richmond might be ready for operation before housing could be found for the workers. In time, however, Marin City was constructed on vacant land just north of Sausalito for Marinship, and family units were set up in Richmond and Oakland. In addition dormitories for single workers in Richmond were built and managed by the Kaiser shipyards.

The Bay Area saw the biggest concentration of shipbuilding anywhere in the country and with it, the greatest demand for housing and services. Schools and processing centers, hospitals and clinics were needed as well as housing. At the end of 1942, over 10,000 applications for family housing were on file in Richmond. The population of Richmond mushroomed from 23,000 in 1940 to 100,000 in 1943, largely due to the Kaiser shipyards. Thousands of other Kaiser workers lived in communities all around the Bay and commuted to Richmond. The small town of Sausalito doubled its population to 7,000, quickly absorbing all available houses and apartments. By the end of 1943 an additional 6,000 residents lived in nearby Marin City. Small rental units, often single rooms, were squeezed into existing small hillside homes in Sausalito.

Close by every wartime production center were temporary housing developments. Stockton had several "villages" to accommodate many of the 10,000 defense workers new to the area.

RICHMOND MUSEUM OF HISTORY

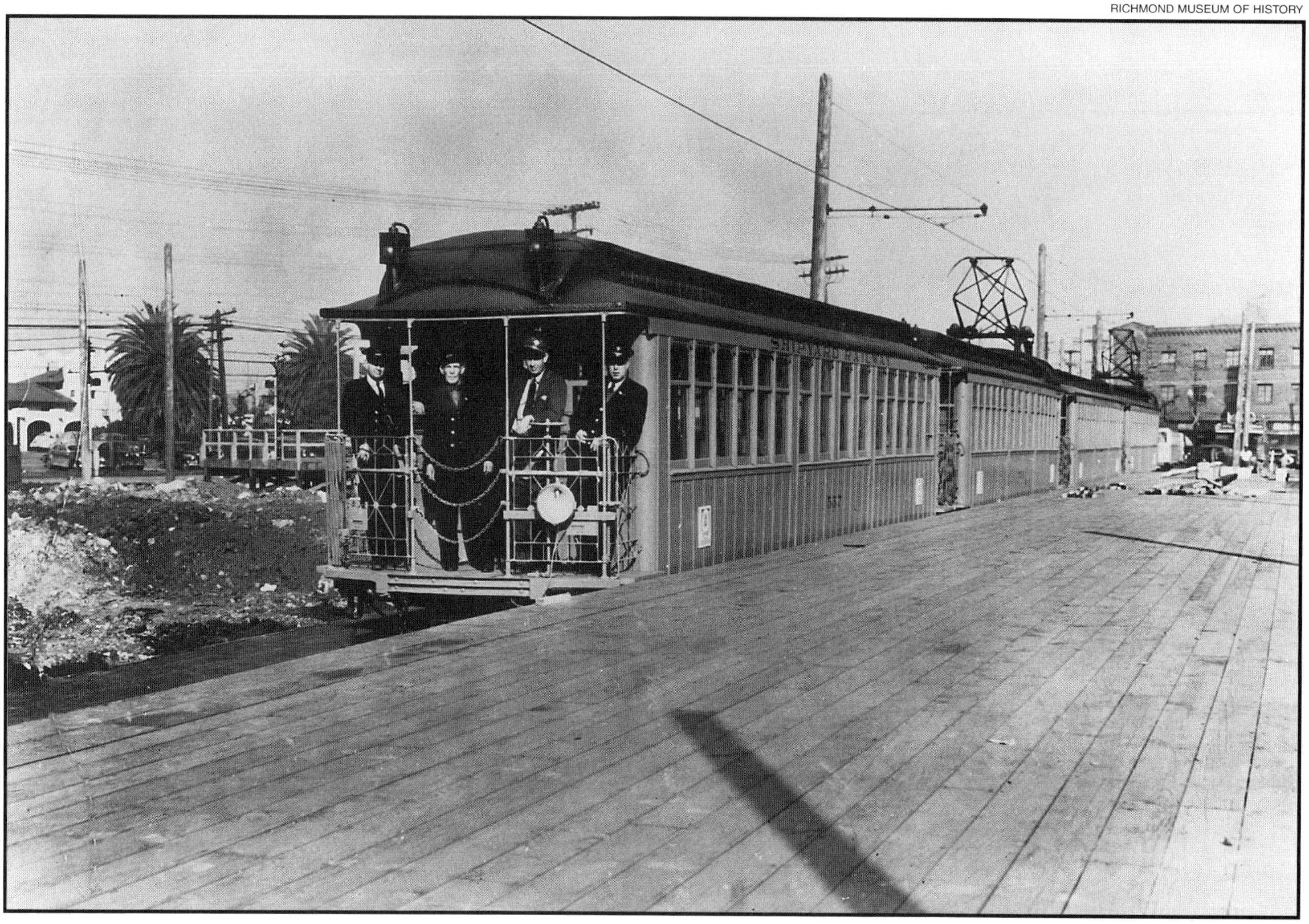

Above: The "Shipyard Special," using obsolete cars from the elevated railway in New York, ran over old Key Line trackage from Oakland to the Kaiser yards in Richmond. c. 1945.

SAUSALITO HISTORICAL SOCIETY

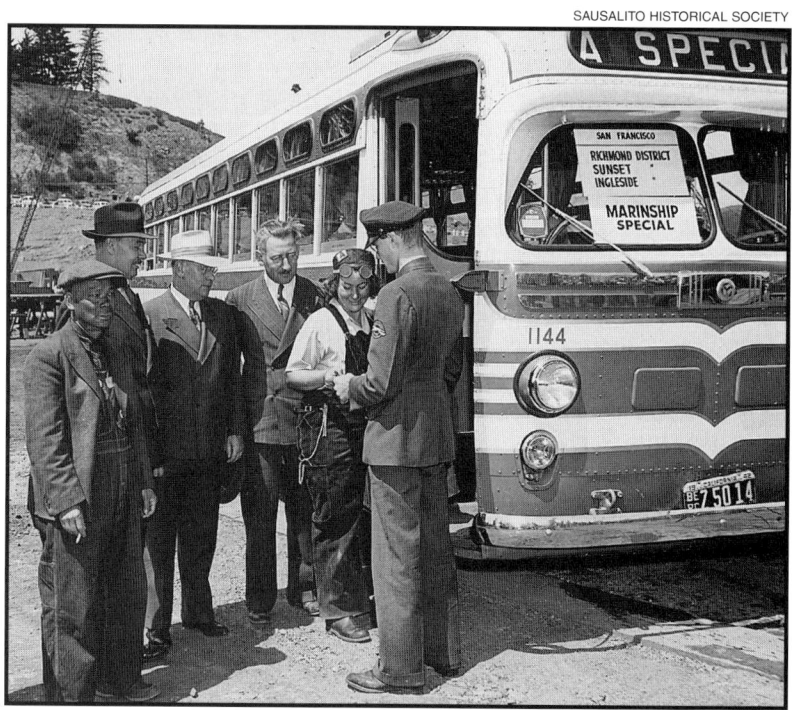

Greyhound and other carriers shuttled workers to the major shipyards with special wartime routes. c. 1943.

As with most supply and demand problems during World War II, housing and transportation shortages grew more complicated with every effort to solve them. Each shipyard had its own transportation needs and no single solution fit every situation. Each yard developed a transportation plan coordinated by the Office of Price Administration, which controlled gasoline rationing nationwide. Pacific Greyhound set up special bus routes to provide commuter service but a national rubber shortage threatened to curtail bus operations. Ferry boats were requisitioned to serve Richmond and Marinship. Special commuter trains served Richmond and Moore Dry Dock Company. Fortunately the rubber shortage was not as serious as projected and many workers who had to commute did so in car pools.

WINDGATE

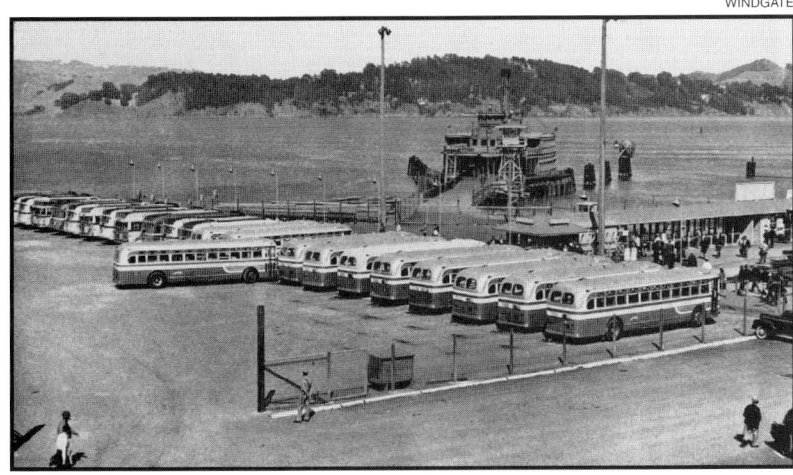

Left: The old SP ferry *Yerba Buena* was called to service at Marinship in 1942. The boat ran between a special slip within the shipyard and the foot of Hyde Street, San Francisco. By early 1945, the ferry was phased out due to lack of riders.

SAUSALITO HISTORICAL SOCIETY

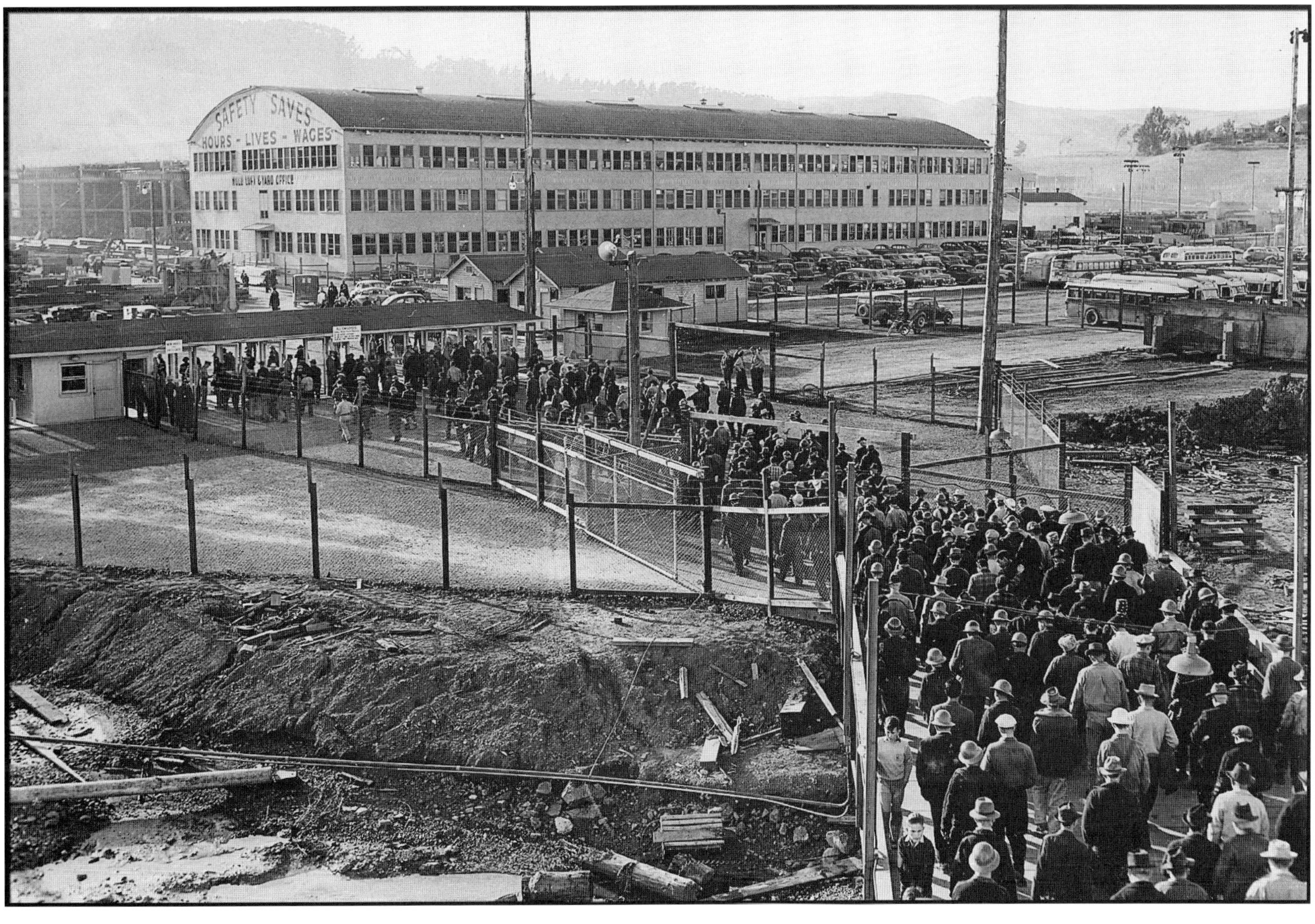

Workers streaming from the ferry at Marinship pass through security gates. The large wooden building is the mold loft.

SPECIAL VESSELS

World War II introduced a new type of vessel, the invasion or landing ship. Since the war was mainly fought on enemy-held foreign soil, there were few friendly ports in which to disembark troops and supplies from traditional transports and freighters. Military planners recognized that forced landings on hostile beachheads would be the standard means of taking war to the enemy. That meant developing new vessels and building them in unprecedented numbers.

From that early determination came a fleet of 25,000 landing craft of various types ranging from sixteen-foot rubber boats to 4,000-ton ocean-crossing tank carriers. This achievement of design and construction within a two year period from 1941 to 1943 is one of the greatest achievements of naval construction in history. Without these vessels, America would have been unable to conduct war in Europe and the South Pacific. They made possible successful Marine landings on Guadalcanal, Tarawa and Iwo Jima in the Pacific and the invasions of North Africa, Italy and Sicily and the D-Day landings at Normandy.

Although these vessels were used in "amphibious operations," most were not true amphibians, that is, capable of functioning in water and on land. Most were water-borne vessels capable of being safely beached to disgorge cargo or troops, then refloated. Landing craft were of two types, sea going vessels and those carried on board other vessels. The latter type, some of which had sea-going capabilities, were built in greater numbers. Vessels came in several configurations and sizes and were designated according to their specific uses. They were unnamed but given numbers and a prefix, LC for Landing Craft, or LS for Landing Ship. The most common were LCP, Landing Craft Personnel; LCV, landing Craft Vehicle; LCVP, for carrying a jeep or light tank along with personnel; LCM, Landing Craft Mechanized for landing light or medium tanks in initial assaults; and LCT, Landing Craft Tank, the largest vessels carried as deck loads on larger ships. Added to those were boats armed with rockets and machine guns such as LCS, Landing Craft Support.

Ocean-going landing vessels were larger and designed to deliver themselves to the invasion site rather than be carried on board ship. These were the LCI, Landing Craft Infantry, over 150 feet long capable of carrying about 200 infantrymen, LST, Landing Ship Tank, over 300 feet long with swing-open bow doors, capable of being powered right onto a beach; and the LSD, Landing Ship Dock, about 450 feet long designed for docking operations in hostile waters.

Tracked amphibious vehicles designated LV, Landing Vehicle, rounded out the invasion fleet. Standard tanks were fitted with snorkel apparatus to permit diesel engines to operate below waterlines; the LVT, Landing Vehicle Tank called the "Alligator" had fins on its treads allowing it to "swim" ashore. The "Duck" was an amphibious truck with six wheels to carry it over reefs and rocks. One of the most famous amphibious vehicles, developed in top secret, was the "Amtrak," an armored, tracked landing vehicle used in many Pacific island invasions.

SAN FRANCISCO MARITIME NHP P85-030.582

Above: Launch of USS *Belle Grove*, one of eight LSD's built by Moore Dry Dock Company. A Landing Ship Dock (LSD) was 457 feet long at 4,500 tons. Their special feature was a huge enclosed bay with hinged stern ramp. On reaching its destination, the LSD became a floating dock by flooding the bay and lowering into it by crane fully-loaded landing craft. The boats then exited by the lowered stern ramp and made for the shore. Boats were retrieved by the same means. February 17, 1943.

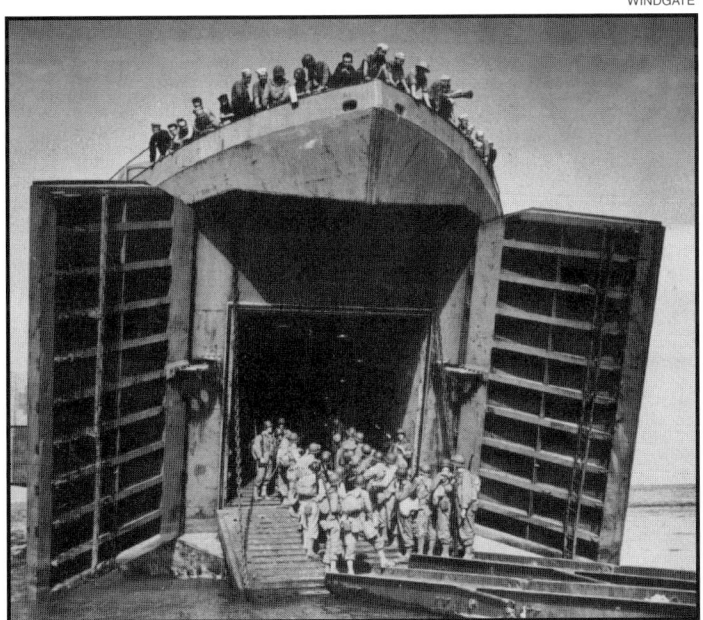

Above: LST with bow doors open.

Above: LSD with stern ramp closed.

Left: LST's carried invasion troops and vehicles onto the beaches in some of the heaviest fighting of the war. Kaiser #4 at Richmond built fourteen of these specialized vessels. This one, built by American Bridge, shows the large open deck area that could be used for storage. The key feature of the LST was its huge swing-open bow used to disgorge cargo. The vessel had flooding tanks to lower the bow to the beach or create a list to side-launch large landing craft from the deck. Two cradled landing craft are seen on the LST.

Landing craft made in the largest numbers were those with drop ramps at the bows. Built in a number of sizes from 36 feet to 300 feet and designed to carry soldiers, jeeps, trucks and even tanks, they evolved rapidly during the war based on combat experience. While small invasion boats used by armies to cross rivers date back to before Napoleonic times, development of specialized landing craft is modern by comparison. Designed to transport heavy artillery and horses across rivers, special barges were used by several warring nations in the late nineteenth century. During World War I the British attempted to land large numbers of troops at Gallipoli with small boats and assorted craft. Difficulties in getting the boats on shore and disembarking troops left the soldiers vulnerable to withering defensive fire. The terrible losses incurred demonstrated the need for specialized craft.

By the end of World War I experimental gasoline-powered boats with bow ramps had been tested successfully in combat conditions. Between the wars further development took place both in Europe and America. The Japanese in their assaults on China and Southeast Asia in the 1930s again demonstrated the value of landing craft. The U.S. Navy decided to design and build self-propelled invasion craft that could be carried aboard large transports. This was the birth of the modern landing craft that became such an essential element of World War II amphibious landings.

Moore Equipment Company, a pre-war road-building machinery manufacturer in Stockton, built over two hundred tank lighters and other invasion barges for the Navy. Hundreds of other landing craft were manufactured in Denver, Colorado, and shipped by rail to Mare Island for launching. In the Bay Area, McDonough Steel Company, Judson Pacific-Murphy and others built landing craft.

D-Day landings, Normandy, June 6, 1944.

Tank lighters at Stockton for the Army. The small armored wheel house is evidence that these boats are intended to hit the beach under heavy enemy fire.

WINDGATE

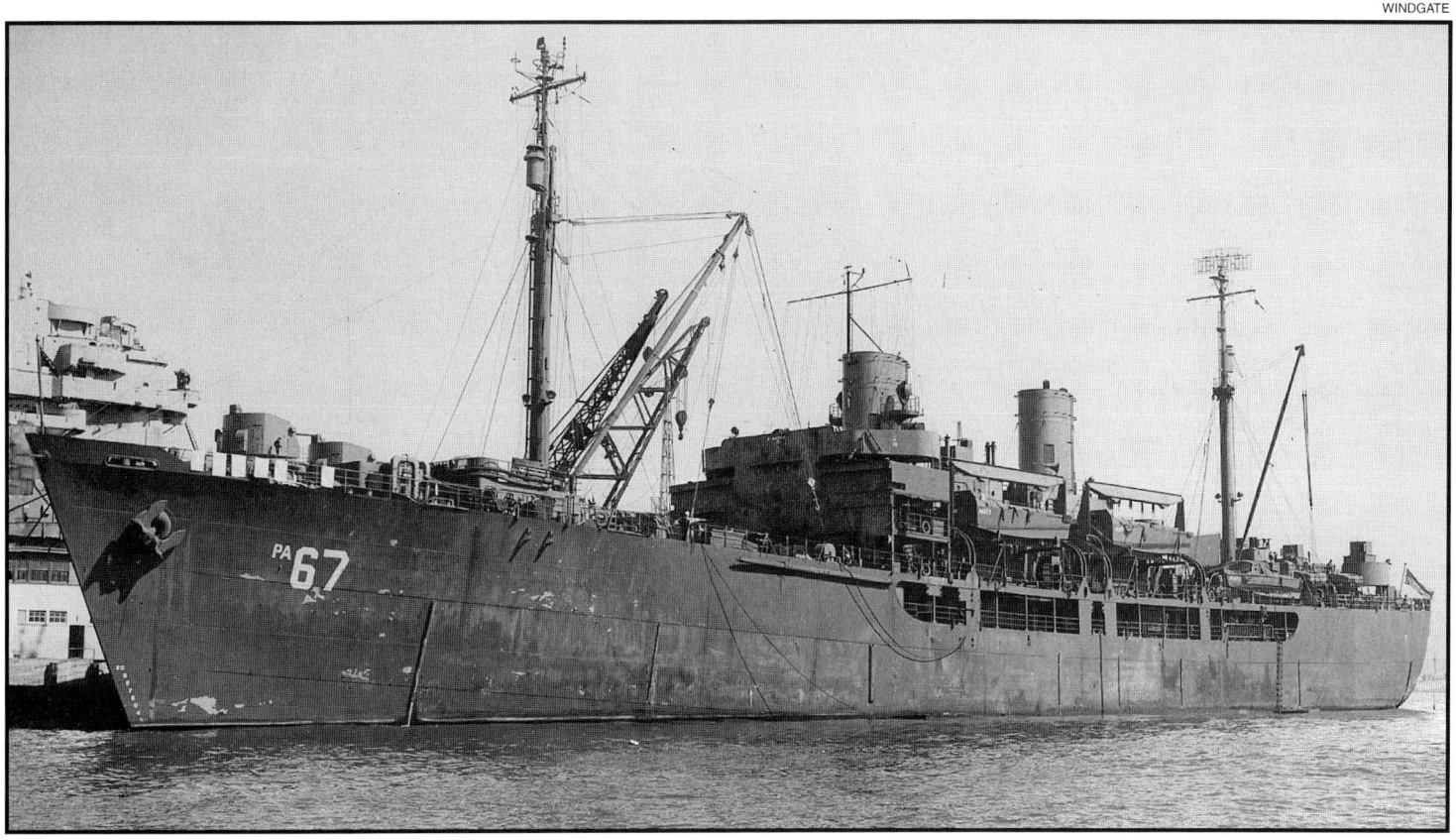

Small landing craft were delivered to the battle zone aboard specially equipped attack transports. The attack transport *Bruleson*, shown here, carries landing craft on davits.

THE HAGGIN MUSEUM

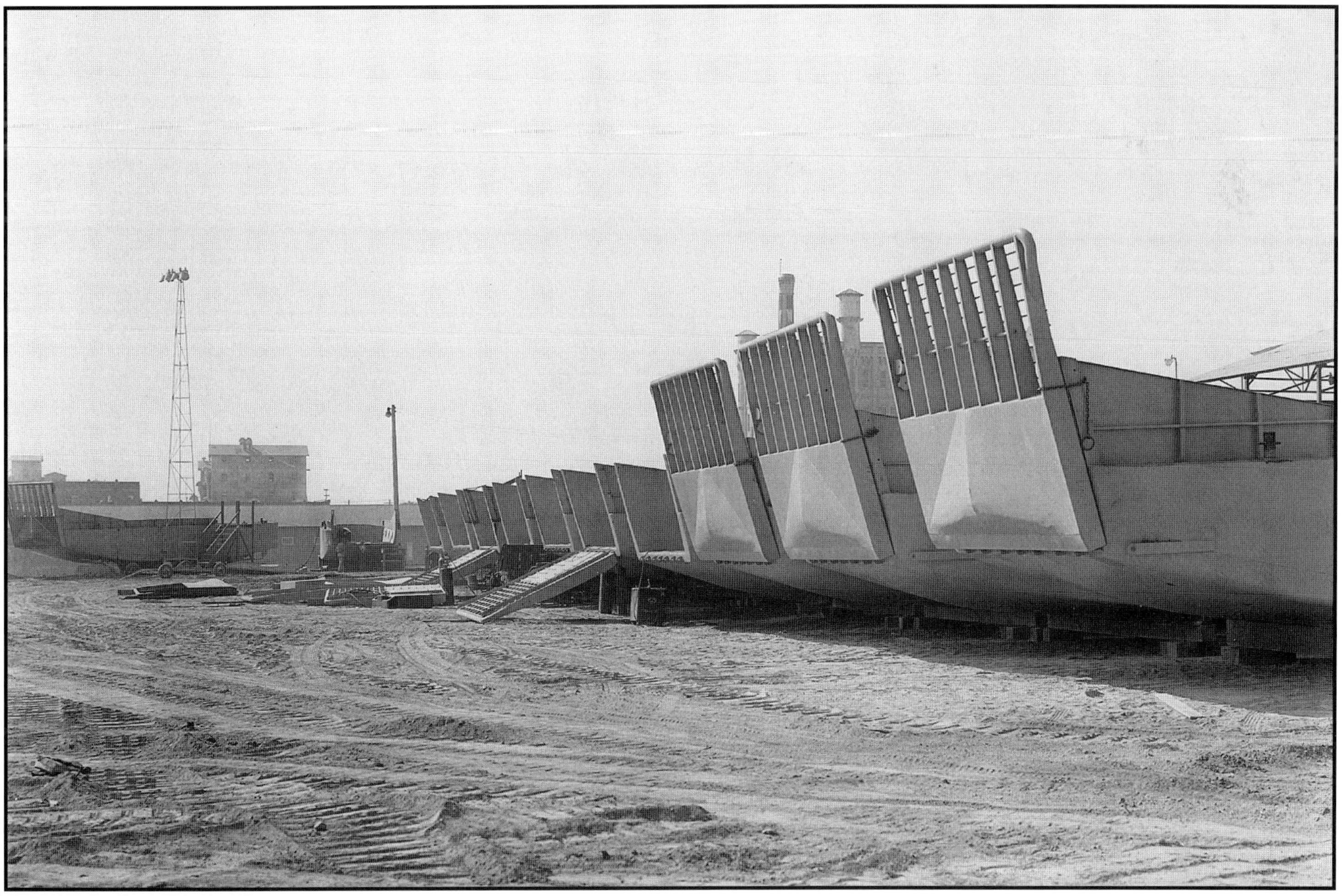

Landing craft were manufactured by scores of shipyards all over the country. These fifty-foot Army tank lighters at Hickinbotham Brothers in Stockton are receiving hinged bow ramps. September 25, 1942.

Arrival of Section 1C of Hull #58 at Yard #4, December 22, 1943.

Kaiser #4 in Richmond was an example of how conduct of the war rapidly changed shipbuilding strategies. In 1941 Kaiser constructed his first Richmond shipyard to built thirty cargo ships for England. Just two days after the first keel was laid in April, 1941, the Maritime Commission directed Kaiser to build a second shipyard in Richmond for Liberty ships and have it operational by September. Pearl Harbor, December 7, 1941, changed priorities again; on January 9, 1942, the Maritime Commission and Kaiser began a third shipyard at Richmond to build big C4 troop transports. By this time yards one and two were building the British freighters and Liberty ships, although none had yet been launched. By May 14, 1942, the first keel was laid at Kaiser #3.

By the spring of 1942, war planners had decided on a course of island invasion in the Pacific and recognized the necessity of massive European invasions. Landing craft and invasion ships, needed with all urgency, moved up the priority ladder. Just as the first ship slid down the ways at Kaiser #1 in June, 1942., Kaiser got a call to build yet another shipyard, this one for invasion ships.

All but exhausted construction crews began work immediately on yard 3-A, as it was called. The type of ships to be built there, initially cloaked in secrecy, were LST's.

Several eastern yards besides Kaiser in Richmond and the Kaiser yard in Vancouver, Washington were contracted to build LST's. In all, 982 were completed during the war including 15 by Kaiser, Richmond, and 30 by Kaiser, Vancouver. Over 100 were converted to repair ships, casualty evacuation ships, boat tenders and service craft.

Kaiser #3-A was renamed Kaiser #4 as construction began. This yard was unique among Bay Area shipyards in that it came closest to an auto-type assembly line for big ships. Subassemblies were built at Kaiser and at a number of other shops and yards around the Bay, including Independent Iron Works an Oakland, Clyde W. Wood and Stockton Steel Fabricators in Stockton, and Pacific Coast Engineering Company in Alameda. Components were delivered to the three building ways at Richmond and lifted into position by overhead crane. As one ship was completed and launched, another moved forward into launching position. When the LST contract was completed, Kaiser #4 switched to frigate escort vessels (S2-S2-AQ1) based on the British and Canadian Corvette. After building twelve of these, the yard turned to another type, the C1-M-AV1 coastal cargo ship shown under construction on these pages. By war's end, Kaiser #4 had launched 51 ships including 24 coastal cargo carriers.

Hull #64, looking aft, sub-assembly area, Yard #4, June 29, 1944.

Hull #59, looking forward, on Way #2, Yard #4, April 29, 1944.

A completed C1-M-AV1 coastal cargo ship. These compact vessels were called "pint-size Liberties" by workers. They proved useful for at least two decades after World War II.

Above: Twin-engine Balloon Barge Leader, April 1, 1944.

Above right: The steel barges were all-welded construction and as alike as peas in a pod. Balloon barges also were made by Kyle & Company's Fresno yard.

These little-known craft are balloon barges designed to anchor aerial gas-filled barrage balloons deployed to protect invasion beaches and other facilities from low-flying aircraft. In theory, enemy aircraft dropping down below the balloons to strafe or bomb the beach would risk striking the balloon support cables. Each non-powered barge contained a cable reel and winding gear to raise and lower a balloon. The barges were strung together as needed and towed into position by a motorized version called a "barge leader." Balloon barges were delivered to overseas locations on the decks of cargo ships.

Balloon barge ready for shipment to Mare Island, January 3, 1944.

THE HAGGIN MUSEUM

THE HAGGIN MUSEUM

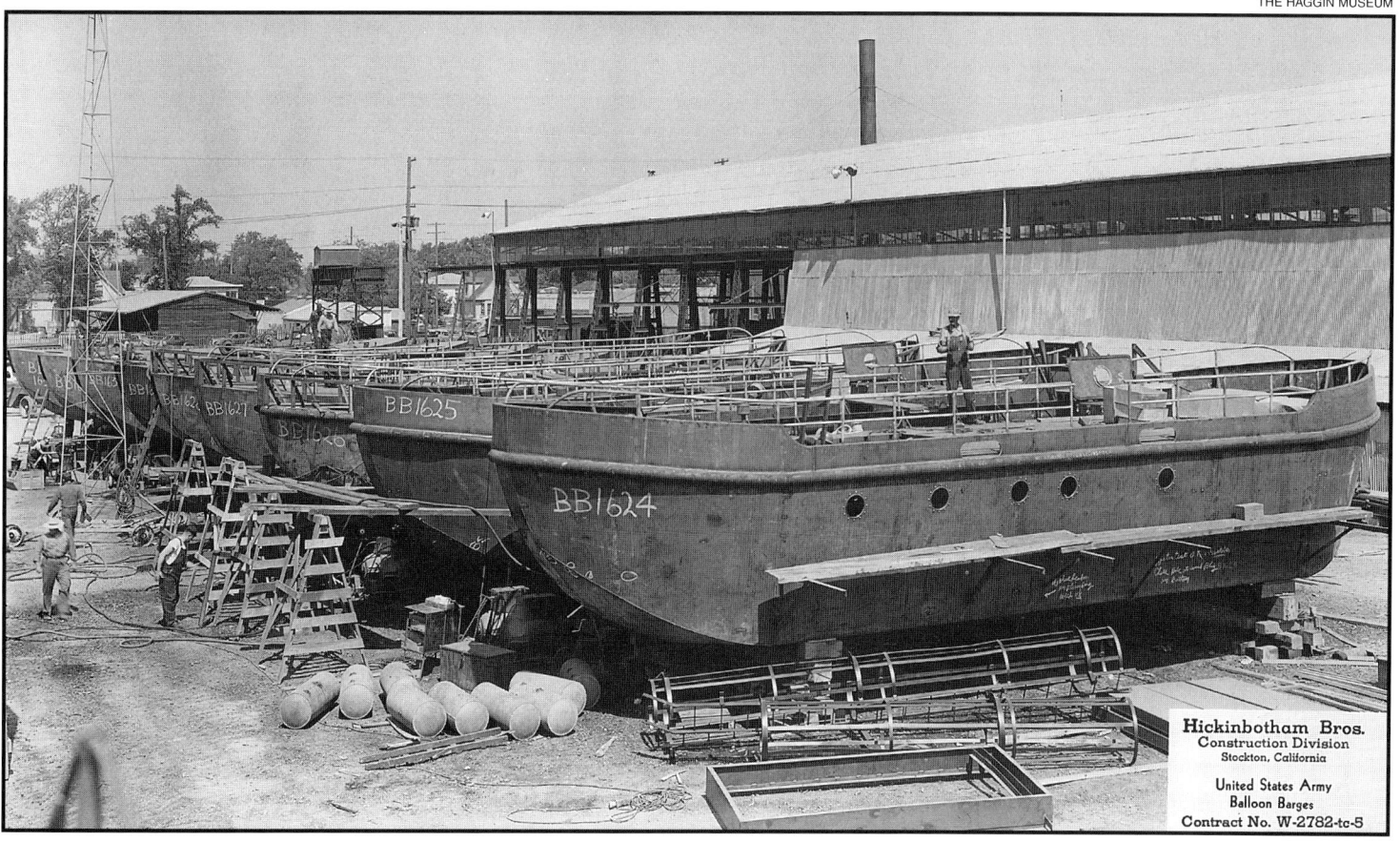

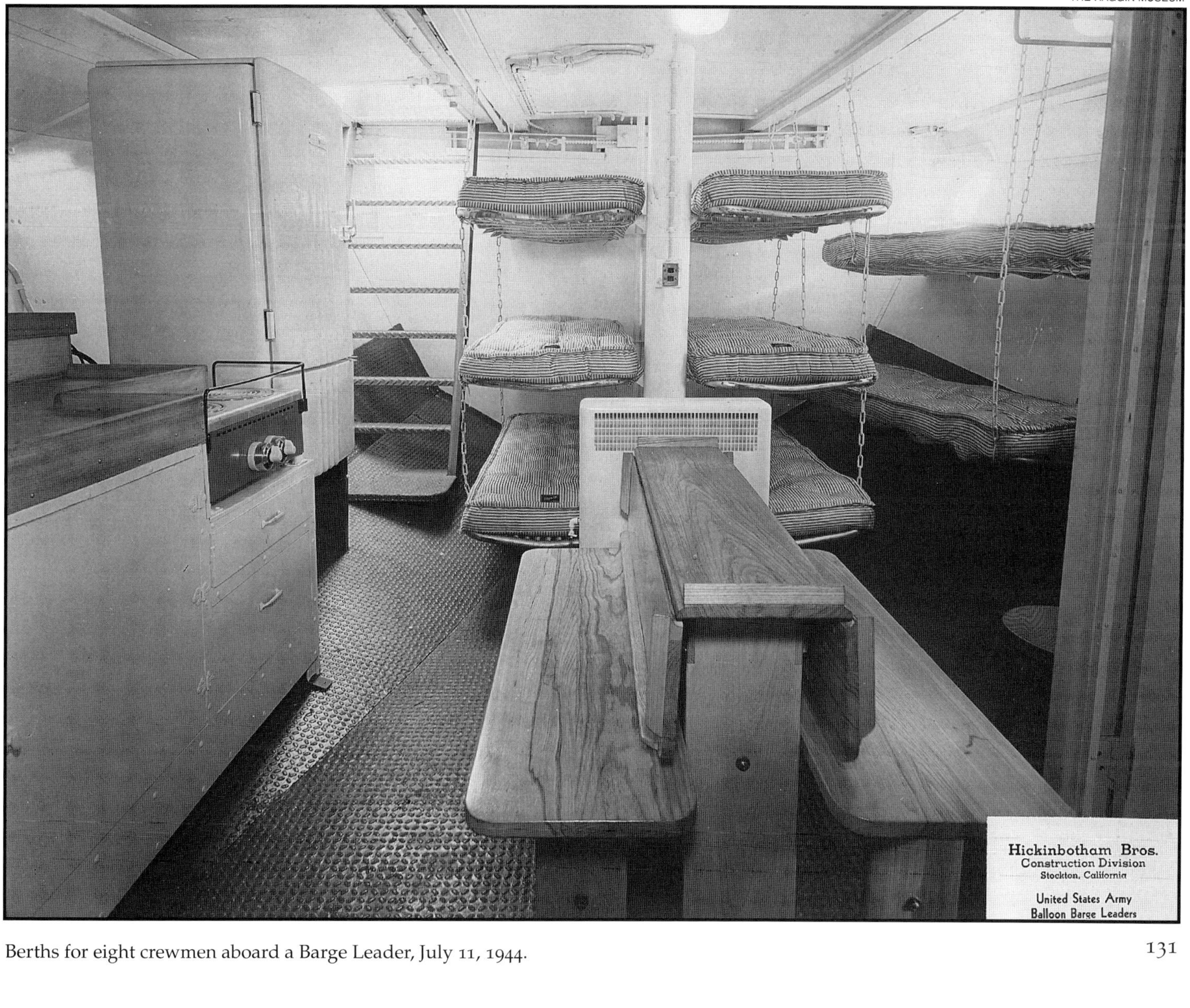

Berths for eight crewmen aboard a Barge Leader, July 11, 1944.

THE HAGGIN MUSEUM

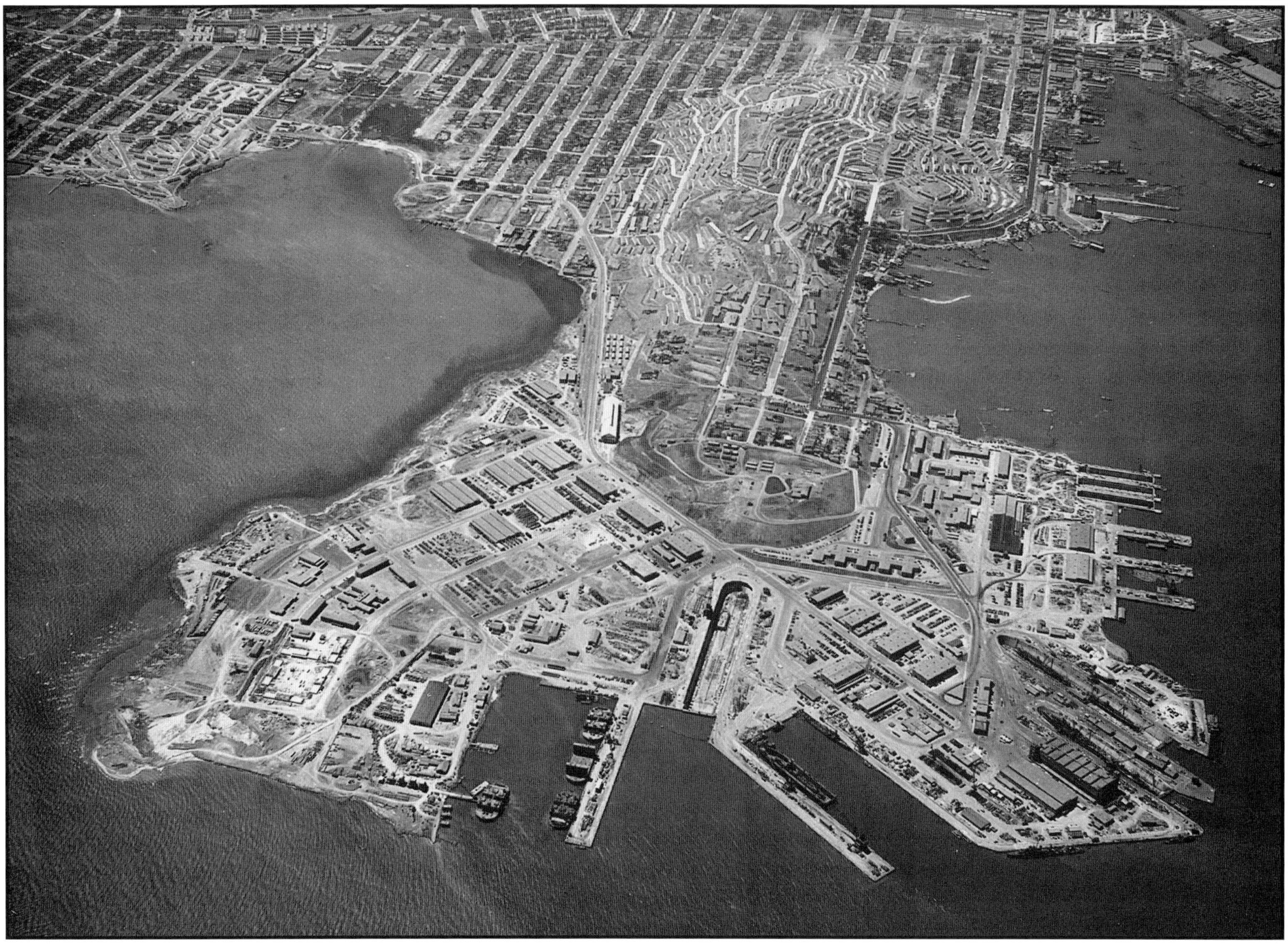

Pollock-built dry dock sections were towed to Hunters Point, above, before being towed to the South Pacific. Four of the bulky sections are visible in the holding basin, center foreground, c.1944.

DRY DOCKS

Another innovation in World War II was the floating sectional dry dock. Since ships in the Pacific war zone were far from mainland repair facilities, repair capability had to be taken to the ships. The sections were towed across the Pacific and linked together to form dry docks capable of handling the largest battleship or aircraft carrier. At sea, the huge upright "wings" of each section were folded flat on the deck, then raised at the assembly point. Each section contained living quarters and diesel engines used to raise and lower the wings, operate cranes and pumps needed for flooding and refloating. These ungainly monsters and other movable docks made a valuable contribution to victory.

THE HAGGIN MUSEUM

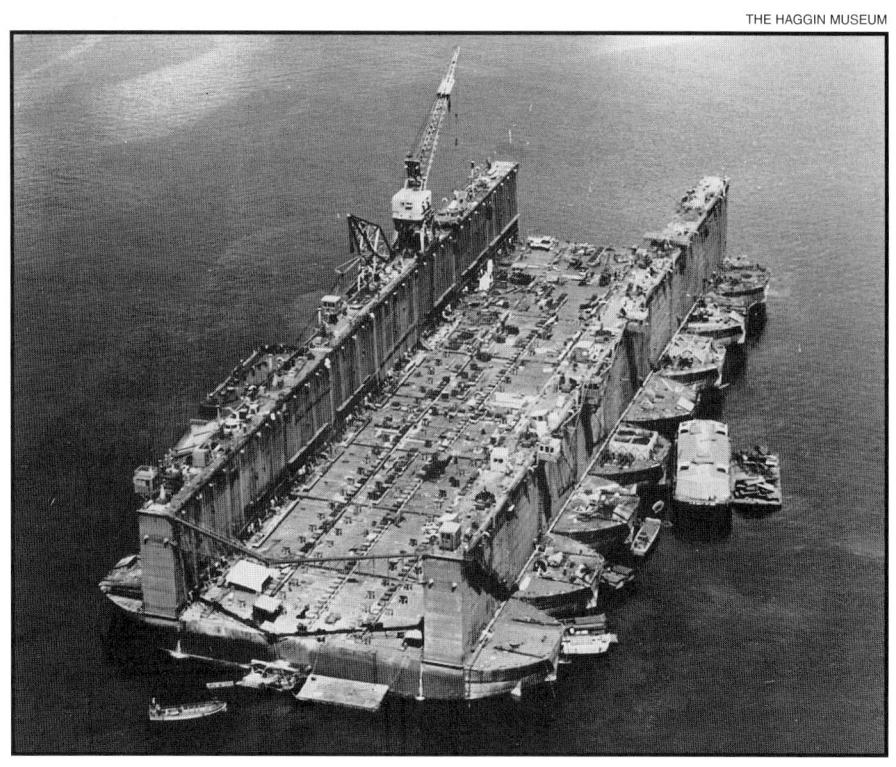

Above: Eight ABSD sections built by Pollock-Stockton linked to form a single dock capable of holding a 600-foot ship.

Floating dry dock built by Pollock-Stockton, c. 1944.

Pollock-Stockton Shipbuilding Company delivered sixteen huge sectional dry dock ABSD (Advance Base Sectional Dock) units. Each was 256-feet long by 80-feet wide. Pacific Bridge Company, a specialist at building shipyards and dry docks, built four ABSD sections in Alameda.

Below: Stern view of a barracks ship at the Pollock outfitting dock. These were used in combat areas as post-invasion temporary quarters for workers and emergency crews. Similar vessels served in several Bay Area shipyards as temporary housing for workers. Colberg Boat Works at one time housed 1,200 men in wooden barracks built on an old, unseaworthy barge.

THE HAGGIN MUSEUM

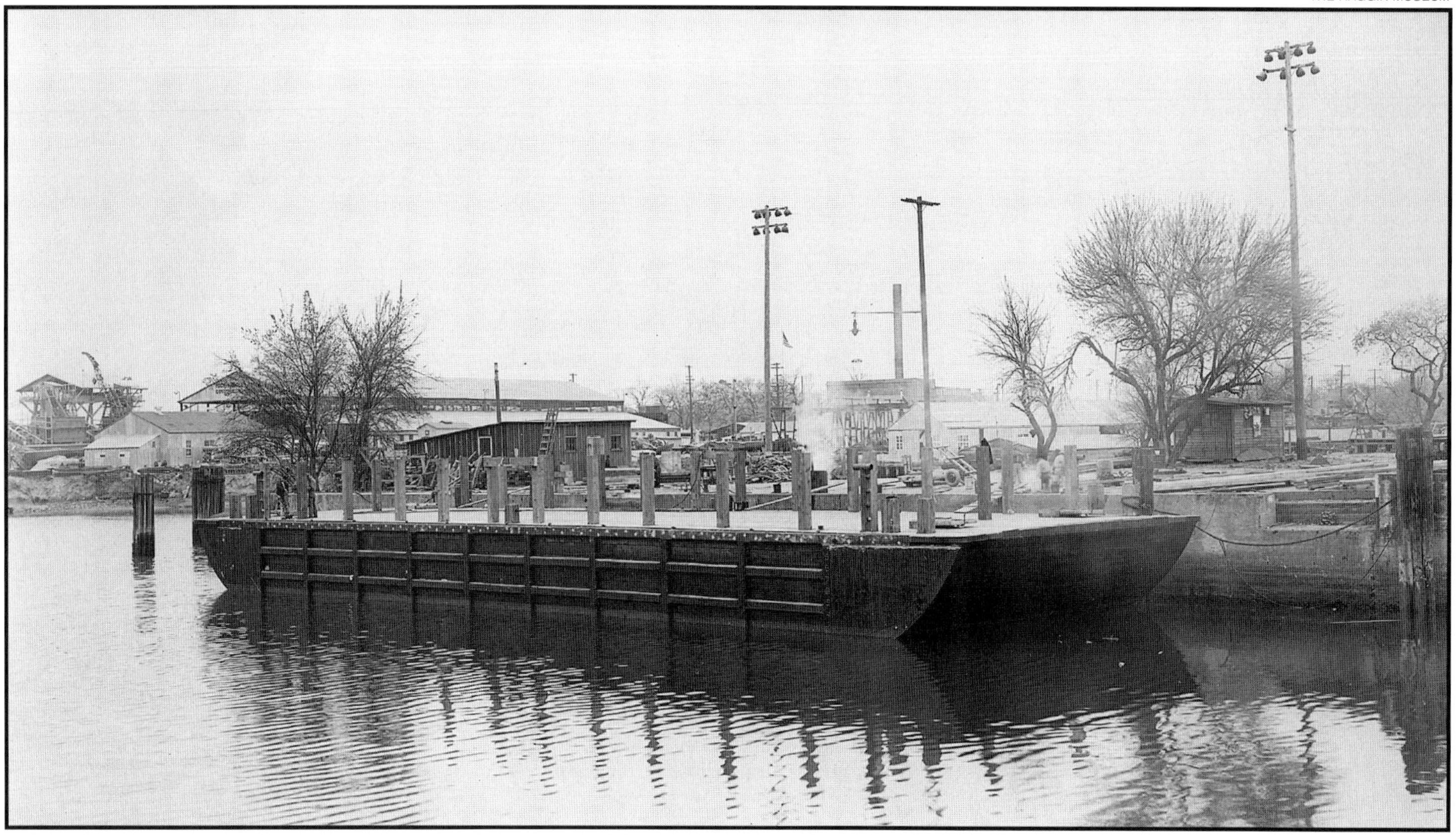

Above: One of the wooden barges built by D.W. Nicholson in Stockton for the Army, April 1, 1944.

THE HAGGIN MUSEUM

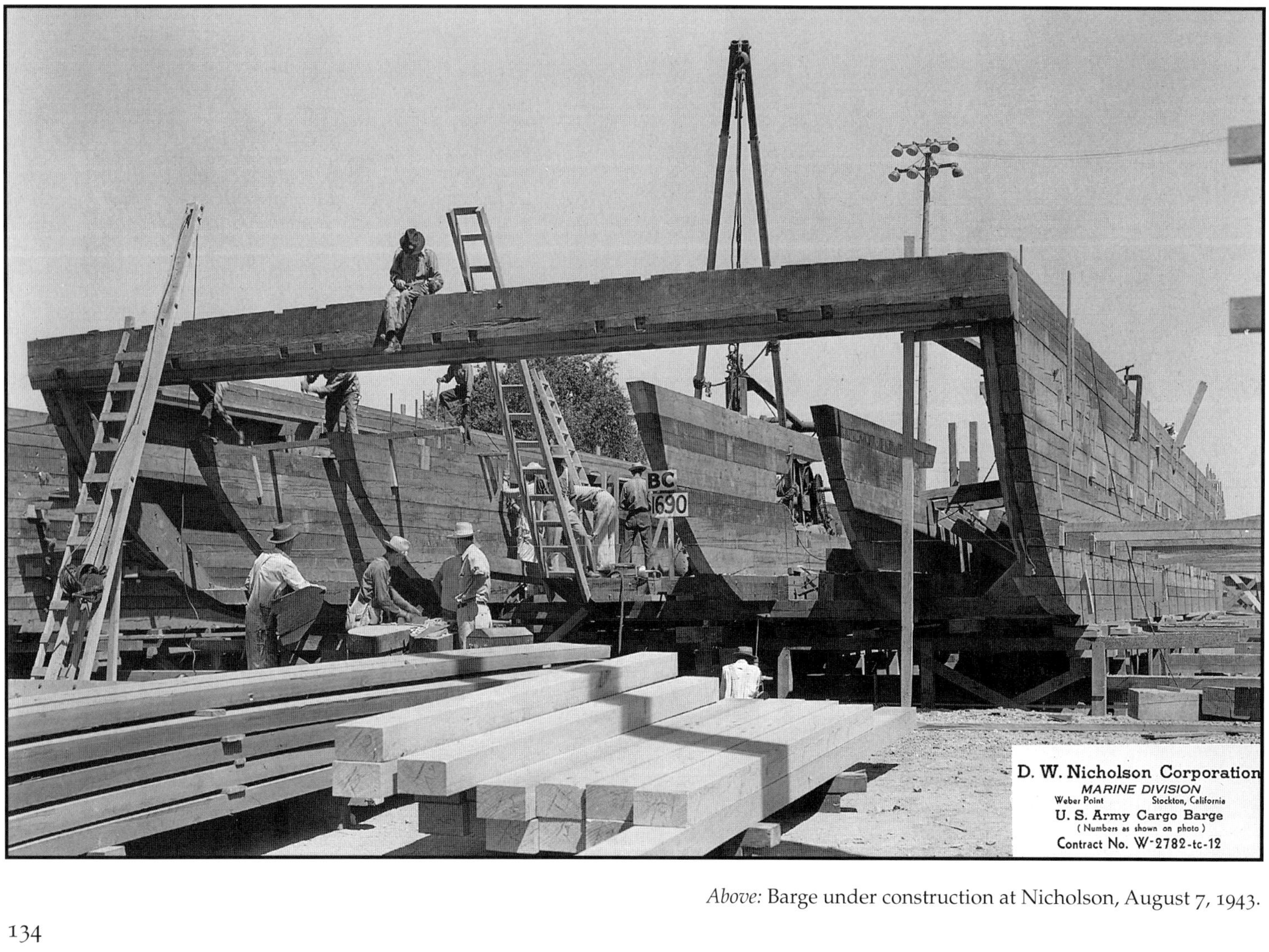

Above: Barge under construction at Nicholson, August 7, 1943.

THE HAGGIN MUSEUM

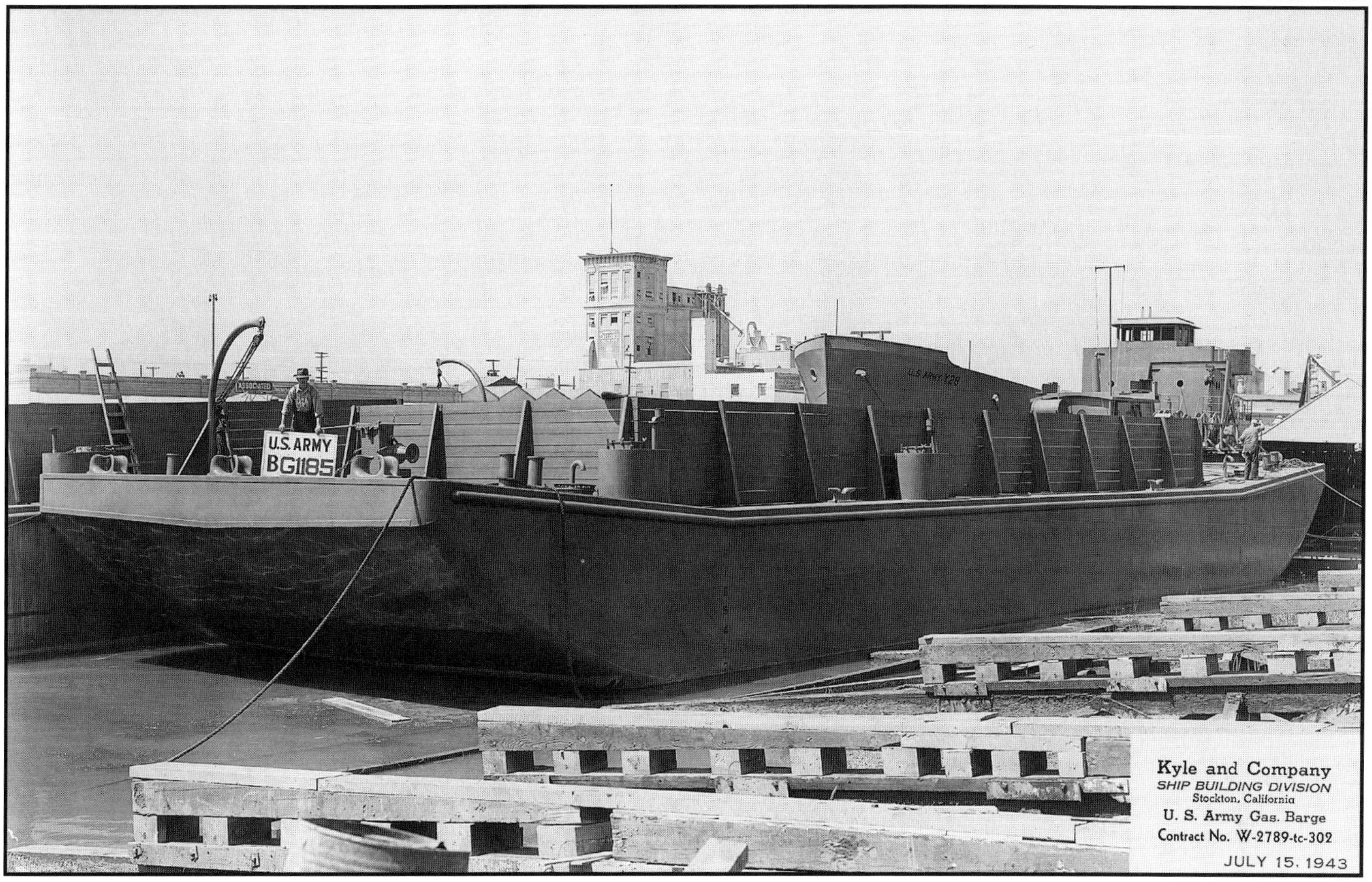

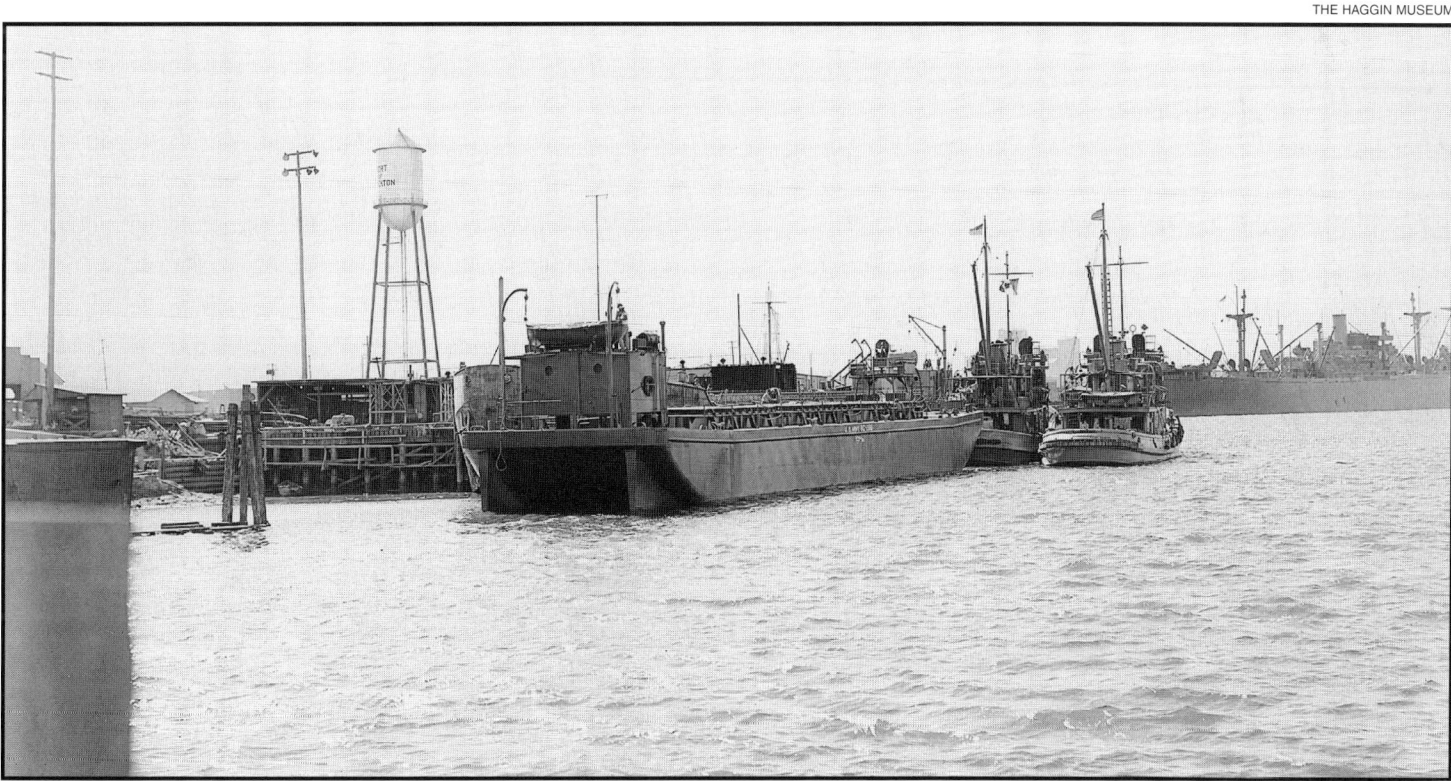

Kyle and Company made these all-welded steel barges.

Bay Area shipyards, experienced in both wooden and steel barge construction, responded quickly as new types of water-borne carriers were needed. Fighting a two-ocean war necessitated thousands of barges to transport and store water and fuel as well as dry cargo. Barges also were low-cost platforms for repair and maintenance facilities for all branches of the service. Naval and Maritime Commission shipyards needed barges for day-to-day operations.

THE HAGGIN MUSEUM

This 130-foot cargo barge was one of several built by Clyde W. Wood.
Stockton Channel, September 30, 1944.

THE HAGGIN MUSEUM

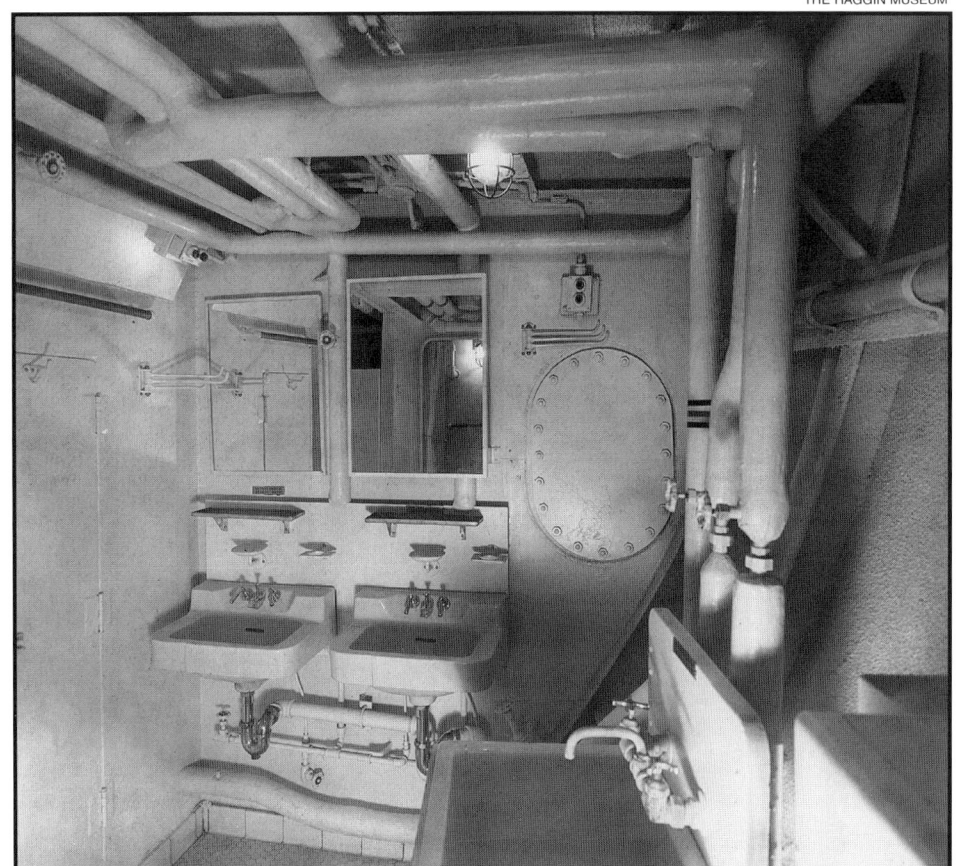

Small freighters and tankers for use in makeshift harbors and inter-island supply were in great demand by both the Army and Navy. These four photos show Hickinbotham Brothers cargo vessels under construction.

Left: This shot of the crew's head in one of the 176-foot freighters shows how every inch of the compact hull is used. October 20, 1944.

Top right: No wasted space in the Hickinbotham yard. As each vessel is side-launched, the next is moved closer to the water, January, 20, 1945.

THE HAGGIN MUSEUM

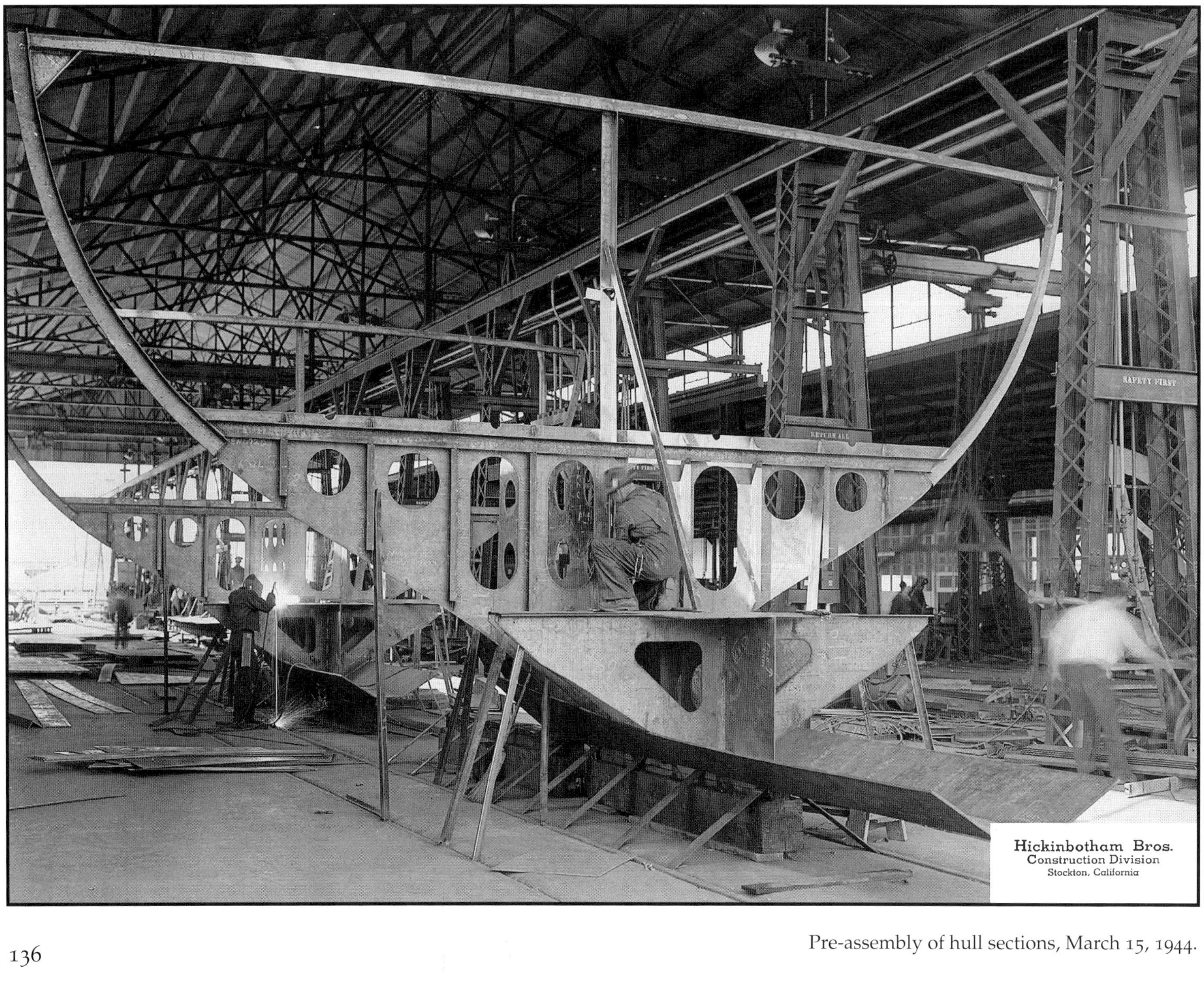

Pre-assembly of hull sections, March 15, 1944.

THE HAGGIN MUSEUM

THE HAGGIN MUSEUM

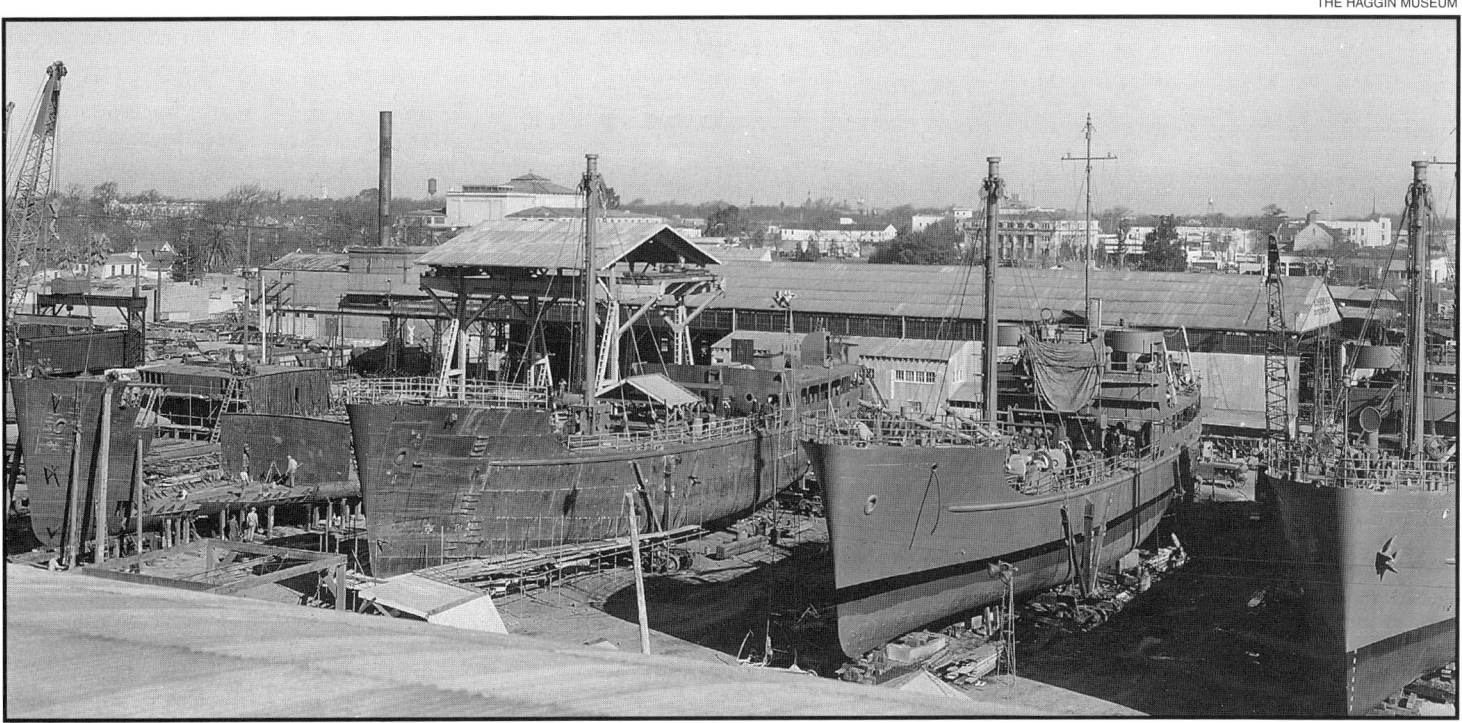

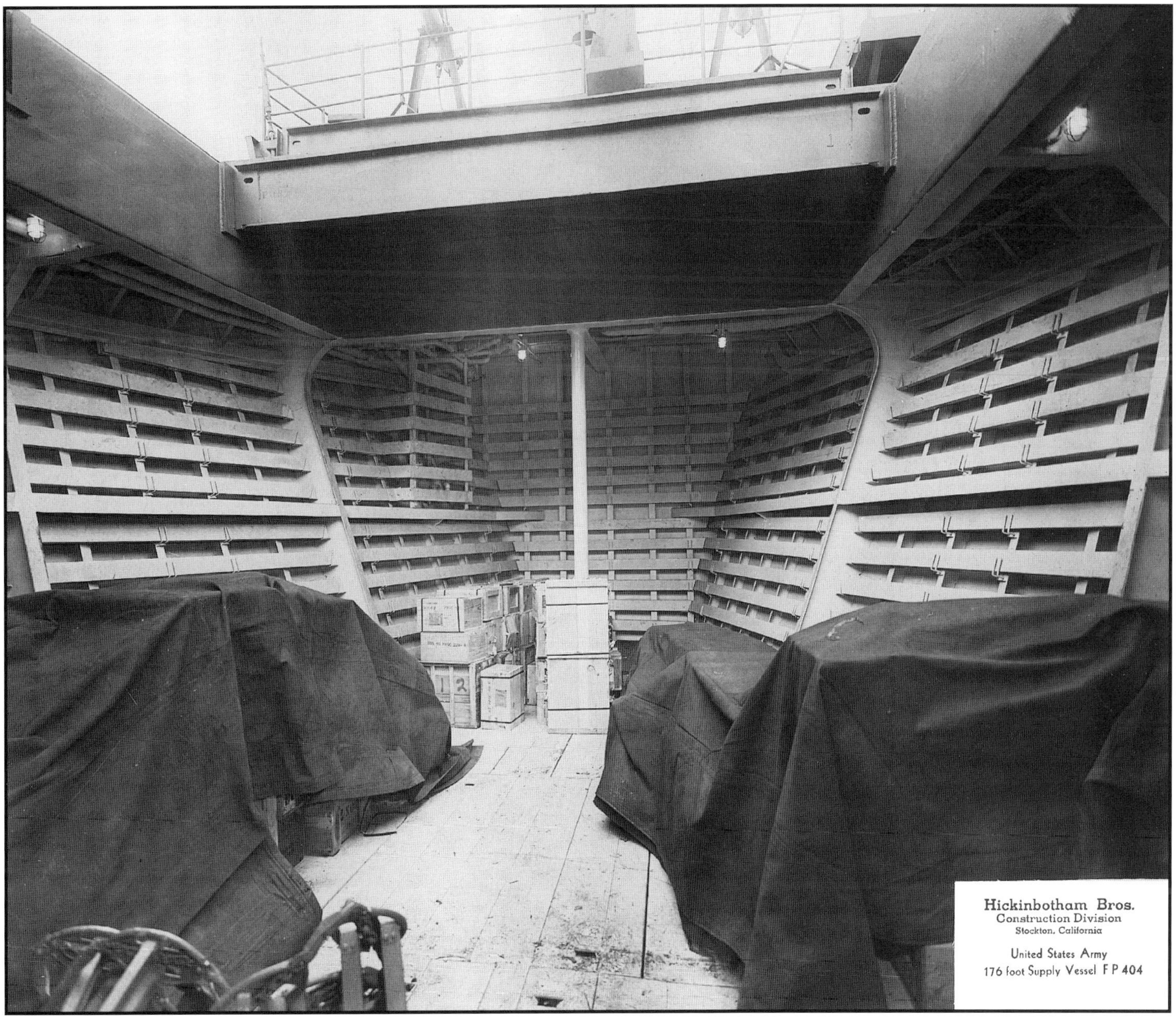

Cargo hold, looking forward, October 20, 1944.

The Moore-built C2 freighter *War Hawk*, in service with the Navy, receives a new 22-ton prefabricated stem to replace the battle-damaged original. Moore Dry Dock Company, April 18, 1945.

Above: Evacuation transport USS *Pinkney* being inspected at General Engineering and Dry Dock repair yard, Oakland, by two sailors posed to show human scale to the otherwise unidentifiable twisted steel structure, June 23, 1945. The *Pinkney*, launched by Moore Dry Dock in 1941, was evacuating wounded soldiers from Okinawa in 1945 when she was struck by a Japanese suicide plane. Bomb and torpedo damage in the Pacific war zone and fire caused massive damage and loss of life to some vessels that managed to stay afloat long enough to return to the Pacific Coast. Others were repaired or made seaworthy in battle-zone floating dry docks, then returned to Pearl Harbor or the Bay Area.

REPAIR AND CONVERSION

In addition to shipbuilding, most Bay Area yards were heavily involved in ship repair during World War II. When America entered the war, existing Bay Area yards had experienced men and up-to-date facilities to handle almost any kind of repair and rebuilding. As the war progressed, all repair facilities were strained to the limit not only by American battle-damaged ships, but allied ships that sought refuge in San Francisco Bay. Bethlehem, for example, repaired or converted over 2,500 vessels from eleven countries including captured Italian and German ships. Moore Dry Dock, Hunters Point, and Mare Island Naval Shipyard repaired thousands of other vessels. In addition to battle-damage repairs, routine maintenance and overhauls were a staple of Bay Area shipyard operations throughout the war.

USS *Hazelwood*, Mare Island Naval Yard, June, 1945.

Battle-damaged ships began arriving in Bay Area yards shortly after Pearl Harbor and the endless stream never let up until the war ended. In addition to the big shipyards, small operations joined in making repairs. Hurley Marine Works of Oakland, for example, repaired over 400 damaged hulls using their single electric marine railway haulout. Their joiner shop, when not occupied making damage-replacement parts, turned out large orders of wooden mess tables and seats for Liberty ships. In the spring of 1944, the Navy announced that five yards had been reconverted to handle repair work exclusively; Bethlehem, Moore Dry Dock, Hurley Marine Works, Kaiser #3 and United Engineering in Alameda.

Left: At Mare Island, the Kamikaze-stricken destroyer USS *Hazelwood*, built by Bethlehem, San Francisco, shows horrific destruction to bridge and forward batteries. On April 29, 1945, off Okinawa, *Hazelwood* was struck by a suicide plane from the stern. The plane grazed over the top and careened into the bridge, where the aircraft's bombs exploded killing the captain, the executive officer and 36 crewmen. After temporary repairs in the South Pacific, *Hazelwood* made it home to San Francisco in the condition shown here. A censor's pen has cross-hatched the damaged radar antennas on the 5-inch gun director and crumpled mast. June, 1945.

Above: USS *Bush,* sistership of *Hazelwood,* on trials at Bethlehem, May 15, 1943, shows what a Fletcher Class destroyer should look like. *Bush* served in the Pacific from the Aleutians to New Guinea and the Philippine invasion to Okinawa. On April 6, 1945, she was struck by three suicide planes off Okinawa. After a gallant fight to save her, *Bush*'s crew abandoned her to heavy seas and the ship sank.

Above: Bethlehem, San Francisco, seen here from overhead in 1945, (north is at top) was a multi-purpose shipyard capable of handling almost any job. Two shipways where many destroyers were built are set on an angle at upper left, next to three additional medium-sized ways. Four larger shipways are at the bottom of the photo. Shown also are four dry docks and a variety of outfitting berths. Bethlehem, San Francisco, was the only privately-owned ship-repair yard in the country to operate a submarine repair base. Between 1943 and the end of the war, thirty-one submarines were overhauled in the 16th Street yard.

Below: Anytime a fighting ship returned from a battle zone, it was refitted with the latest weapons and equipment reflecting the rapid changes brought about by wartime experience. Official photos were made of each vessel modification. Here, USS *Suncock*, a steel-hulled net tender similar to the wooden-hulled versions made by Pollock-Stockton and General Engineering and Dry Dock, lies alongside a pier at Bethlehem, San Francisco, June 19, 1945. The numbers refer to changes made while the vessel was in the yard. 1. Added twin 20 MM machine guns, port and starboard. 2. Added 50-gallon gasoline tank. 3. Added twin 20 MM machine guns on center line. 4. Freeboard enlarged, port and starboard. 5. New ensign staff locker.

Above: The attack cargo ship *Suffolk* undergoes refit at Bethlehem, San Francisco. Alongside to the right is a Fletcher class destroyer and next to that a C2 transport. Forward of the *Suffolk* is an unidentified light cruiser of the type made at Bethlehem. The ship at far left is a troop transport with landing craft aboard. Possibly all the ships in this 1945 photo are being prepared for an invasion task force.

Bay Area yards became expert at converting vessels from one type to another as the demands of war changed. Some conversions occurred before launch, some immediately after, and many after months or years of sea duty.

Costa Rica Victory at outfitting berth, Kaiser #3, June 26, 1944. The Victory ship was a general purpose cargo vessel that was converted into several specialized types, including water and fuel tankers and troop transports.

SAN FRANCISCO MARITIME NHP P85-030.102

SAN FRANCISCO MARITIME NHP P79-071a Scr55:h pl.2163

Tankers built at Marinship returned for refits and repair of worn or damaged piping. Old pipe was salvaged as scrap. In all, the 78 Marinship tankers incorporated over 1,000 miles of piping.

At the beginning of the war, Bay Area shipyards converted passenger ships into transports. Bethlehem, San Francisco, tackled the Matson liners *Lurline*, *Mariposa*, *Monterey* and *Matsonia*, hurriedly converting them into much needed troopships. As the war ended and in the years immediately after, some Bay Area yards were heavily engaged in reversing the process, converting troop transports to passenger liners.

Top left: The Italian luxury liner *Conte Biancamano*, built in 1925, was seized by the United States when Italy declared war in 1941. She was converted into the Navy transport *Hermitage*, shown here, and returned to Italy after the war.

Left: A few old tankers, such as this one, SS *Vacuum*, built by Moore & Scott in 1920 for the World War I emergency program, were converted into station tankers during World War II. Too slow for front-line sea duty, the ships served behind the lines as floating refueling depots.

After victory in Europe in May, 1945, Bay Area shipyards focused more than ever on the Pacific war with Japan. Plans called for invasion of the Japanese home islands with an armada larger than the one amassed for the D-Day invasion of Normandy. Workloads in some local yards shifted to invasion barges and related craft. After the atomic bombs were dropped on Hiroshima and Nagasaki, Japan surrendered; the planned invasion and all work on special invasion craft halted.

Right: These floating "Dagwood' steel caissons, 230 feet long by 70 feet wide and 60 feet deep, were to contain concrete ballast and flooding tanks. They would be towed to Japan and sunk to form breakwaters and unloading platforms for the invasion fleet. The first load of steel for the first Dagwood arrived at Marinship the day of the Japanese surrender. None were built.

Below: Marinship invasion barges. Thirty were to be riveted, twenty to be bolted together and shipped to forward island bases, there to be riveted on site. A shortage of available riveters forced a change in construction to combination welded and riveted hulls. Only seven of these barges were completed before the war ended.

WINDGATE

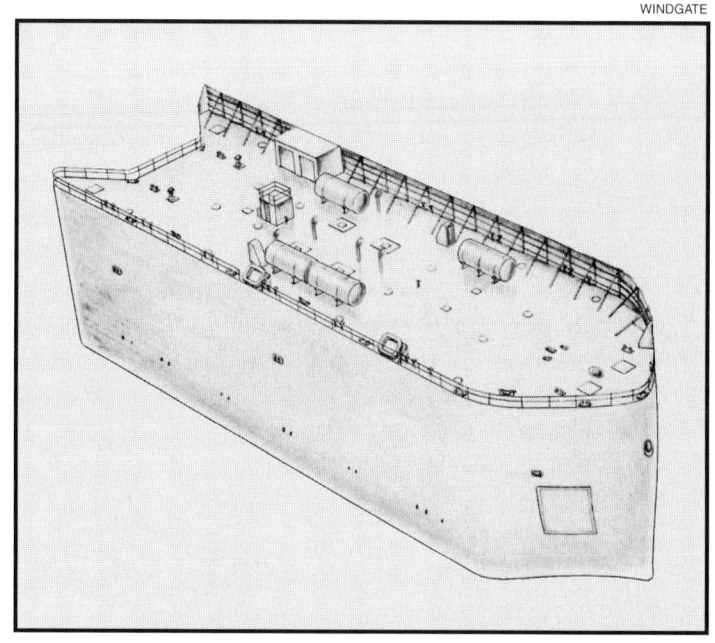

Above: Marinship received a top-secret contract in 1945 for a special vessel code-named "Dagwood."

SAUSALITO HISTORICAL SOCIETY

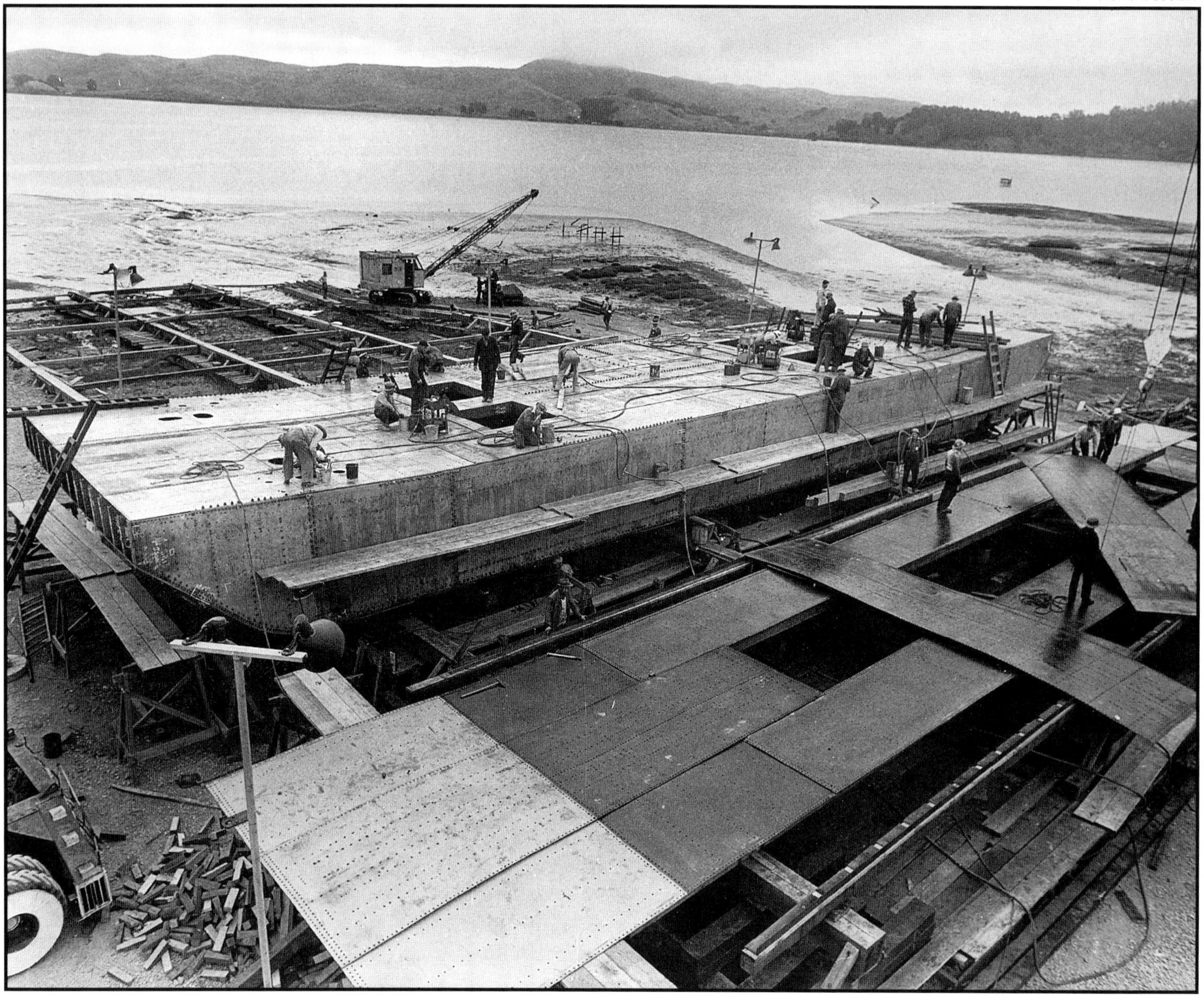

Above: In the summer of 1945 Marinship added a special mini-shipyard to the Sausalito yard to build 104-foot Army invasion barges.

SAN FRANCISCO MARITIME NHP P79-071a Scr55:bb pl.7417

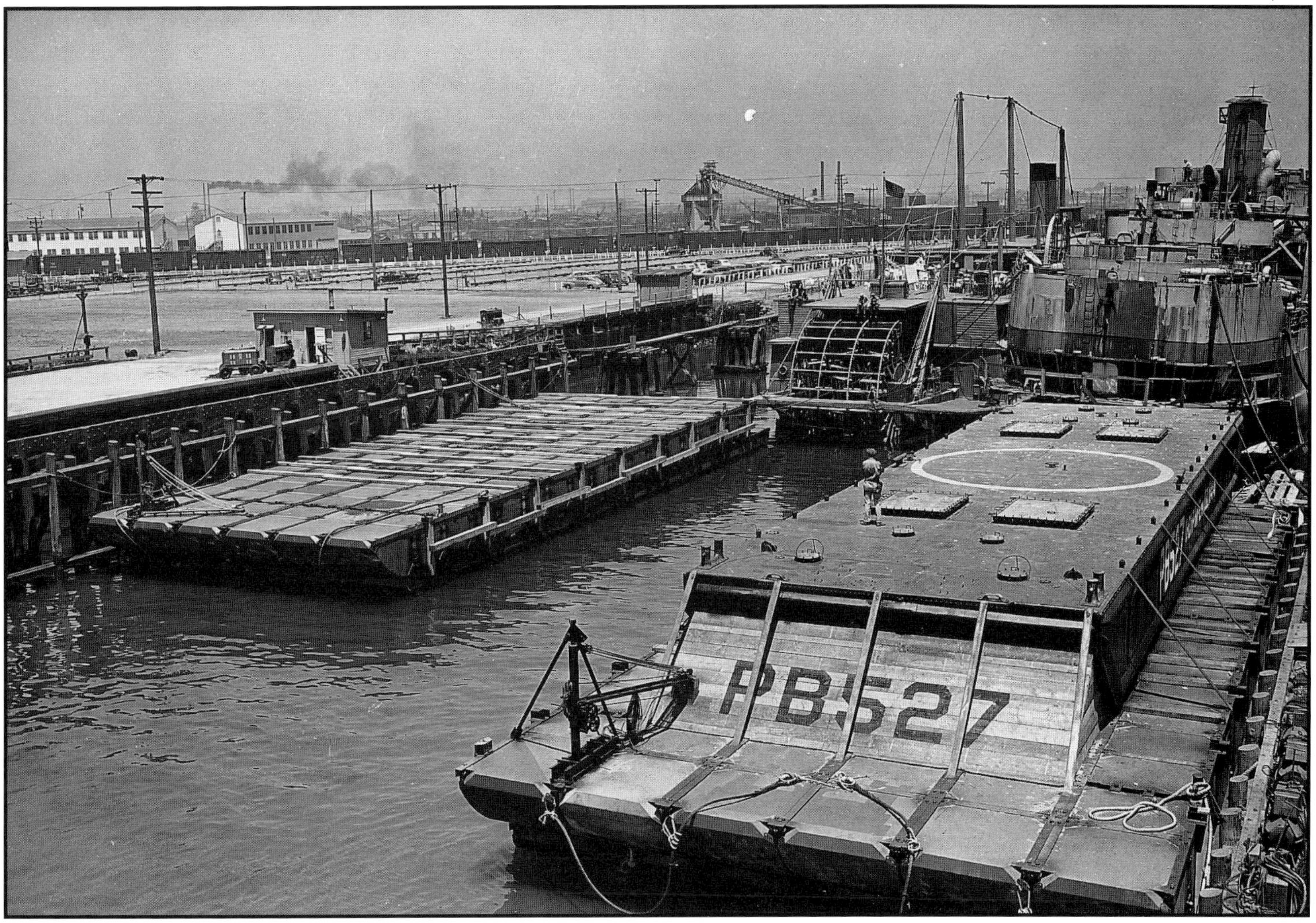

Above: Pontoon barges built for the U.S. Army Corps of Engineers at Moore Dry Dock's West Yard in July, 1945. These sea-going units could be lashed together to serve a variety of needs. The pontoon barge at right carries a smaller steel barge for delivery somewhere in the Pacific.

SAUSALITO HISTORICAL SOCIETY

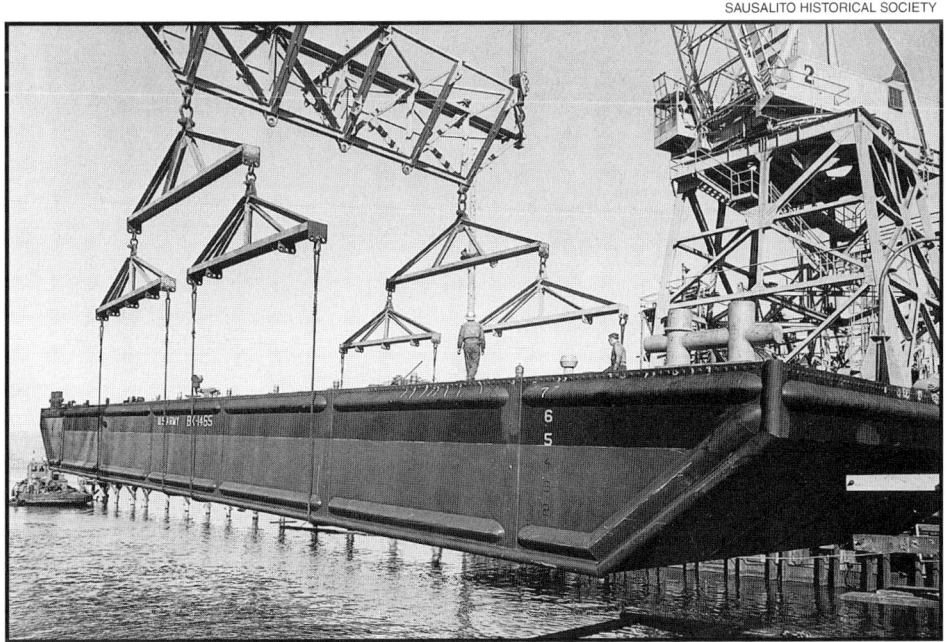

A strongback and gantry crane at Marinship lift an invasion barge from the building way to deep water.

SAUSALITO HISTORICAL SOCIETY

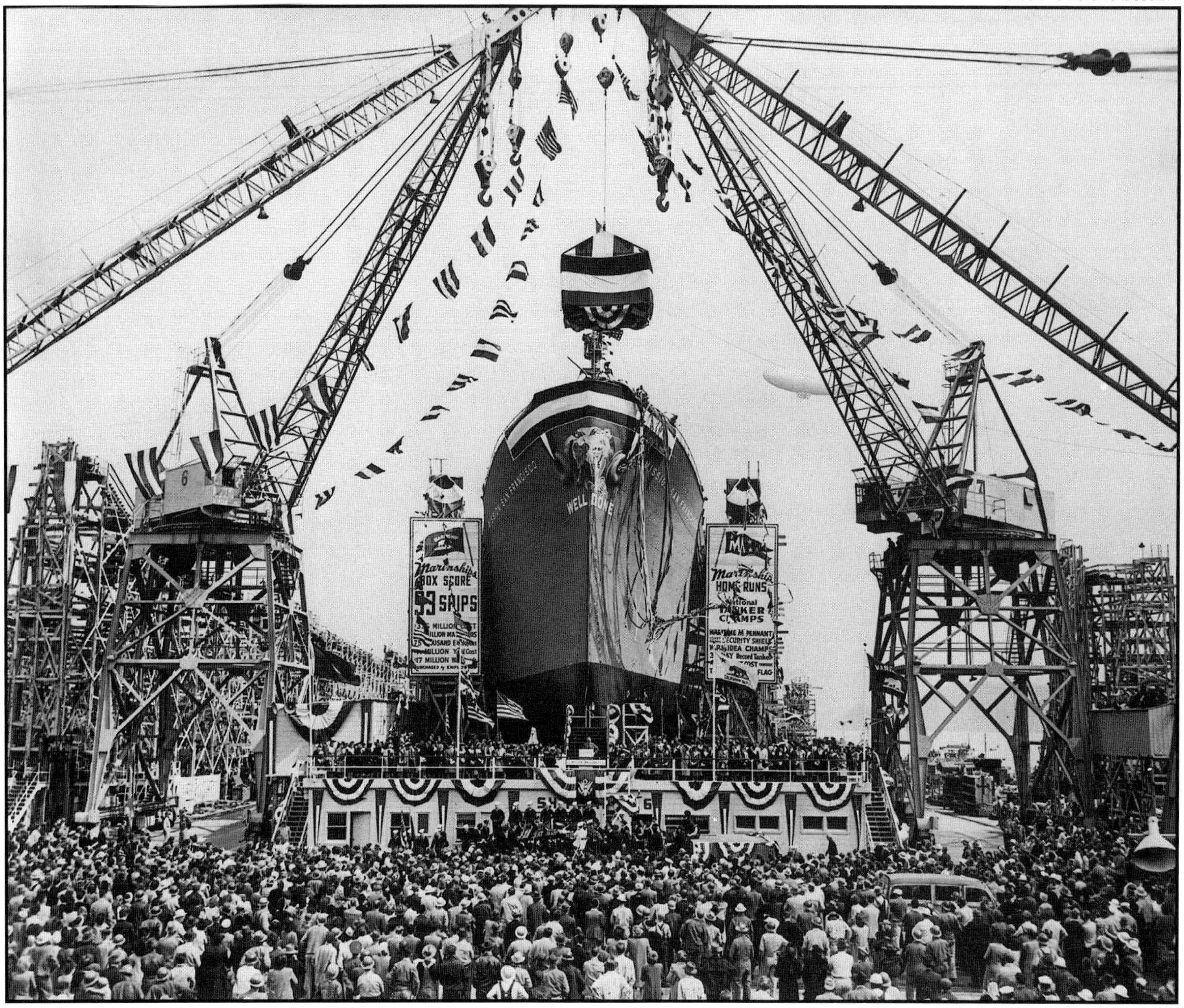

At Marinship, the last tanker under contract to be completed was launched with unusual fanfare. September 8, 1945.

As victory in the Pacific seemed certain, workers in Bay Area shipyards knew that a shipbuilding era was coming to an end. Many hoped that yards would remain open after the war, if for no other reason than to maintain the huge fleet of American ships, yet most knew that the majority of workers would not be needed. Layoffs began even before the war ended as contracts were scaled back or canceled.

Opposite page, top: At Kaiser #4 in March, 1945, this launching of the C1 freighter USS *Flagler* marked a new 46-day construction record. Three months later, the last vessel was launched from this yard.

Opposite page, bottom: As the end drew near, workers gathered mementos, exchanged photographs and addresses, and shared their pride in work accomplished. For thousands, wartime shipbuilding would be the experience of a lifetime creating memories that would last a lifetime. Kaiser #2, c 1945.

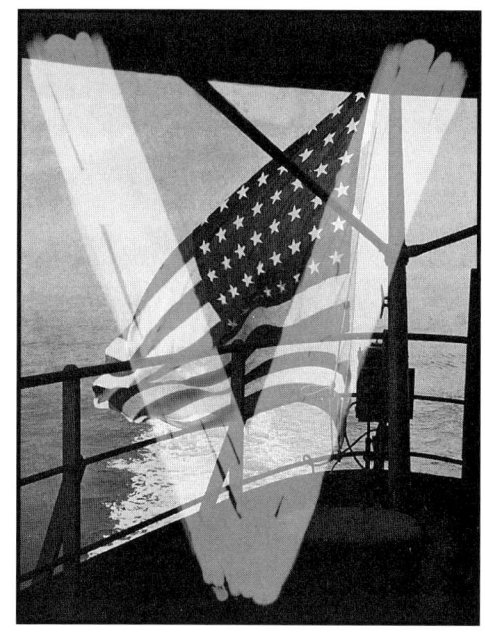

SAN FRANCISCO MARITIME NHP P82-019a.2772pl

RICHMOND MUSEUM OF HISTORY

These two P2 troop transports outfitting at Bethlehem, Alameda, were completed as luxury liners *President Cleveland* and *President Wilson* for American President Lines. 1946.

After the Japanese surrender, the Maritime Commission and Navy decided case-by-case, which ships under construction to finish and which to scrap. Likewise, decisions had to be made by government and private industry which shipyards would remain open and which would close. Conversion work kept some yards busy for several years but the era of major shipbuilding in the San Francisco Bay Area was over.

American President Lines *President Cleveland* ready for launch in civilian colors in 1946.

VESSEL TYPES BUILT IN SAN FRANCISCO BAY AREA SHIPYARDS, 1941-1945

Following are examples of major vessel types built in Bay Area shipyards during World War II. Additional types are pictured in the body of this book. Many small landing craft variations are not included nor are modified cargo vessels that were similar in appearance to standard types. In all, over thirty shipyards launched some 1,400 vessels in the Bay Area between 1939 and 1946, not counting the hundreds of landing craft manufactured elsewhere and launched by Bay Area yards. By far the most numerous type of vessel produced in the Bay Area were Liberty ships built by Kaiser and Marinship. Most major warships, including aircraft carriers, battleships and heavy cruisers were built in eastern shipyards. Fifty escort aircraft carriers were built by Kaiser in Vancouver, Washington.

Atlanta Class Light Cruiser USS *Flint*, Bethlehem, San Francisco, September 8, 1944. One of four built in San Francisco: *Oakland*, *Reno*, *Flint* (ex-*Spokane*), and *Tucson*. 6,000 tons, 541.5 feet by 54.5 feet. All served with distinction in the war.

S2-S2-AQ1 Frigate, one of twelve built by Kaiser #4 in 1943. Seventy-five frigates were Coast Guard manned for escort duty. 1,430 tons, 304 feet by 37.5 feet.

Benson Class Destroyer USS *Gillespie*, October 2, 1942. 1,620 tons, one of nine built by Bethlehem, San Francisco.

Fletcher Class Destroyer USS *Hoel*, August 3, 1943. 2,050 tons, one of sixteen built by Bethlehem, San Francisco.

Buckley Class Destroyer Escort USS *Damon M. Cummings*, July 8, 1944. 1,400 tons, one of twelve built by Bethlehem, San Francisco.

C1-B Maritime Commission Freighter SS *Alcoa Patriot*, Bethlehem, San Francisco, August 11, 1941.

C3 Maritime Commission Freighter SS *Mormacsea*, ex *Sea Panther*, Moore Dry Dock, March 10, 1941, wearing peacetime colors and neutrality flags.

Gato Class Submarine USS *Blenny* (built by Electric Boat), fifteen of this type were launched at Mare Island, 1943-45.

C2 Maritime Commission Freighter SS *Trade Wind,*, Moore Dry Dock, April 28, 1943.

AS-19, USS *Proteus*, Navy Submarine Tender, Moore Dry Dock, 1944.

T2 Tanker *Mission Dolores*, April, 1944, one of seventy five built by Marinship.

Navy Hospital Ship USS *Tryon*, Moore Dry Dock, September 19, 1942.

USS *ASR7*, Submarine Rescue Vessel, Moore Dry Dock, December 14, 1942.

USS *482*, LST (Landing Ship Tank), Kaiser #4, December, 1942.

C4 Transport (AP) *General M.M. Patrick*, Kaiser #3, June 21, 1944.

Navy Attack Cargo Vessel (AKA), USS *Whiteside*, based on C2 hull, Moore Dry Dock, September 6, 1944.

LSM 351 (Landing Ship Medium), (built by Pullman, Chicago) 520 tons, 203 feet long by 34.5 beam, type built by Mare Island. 1945.

THE HAGGIN MUSEUM

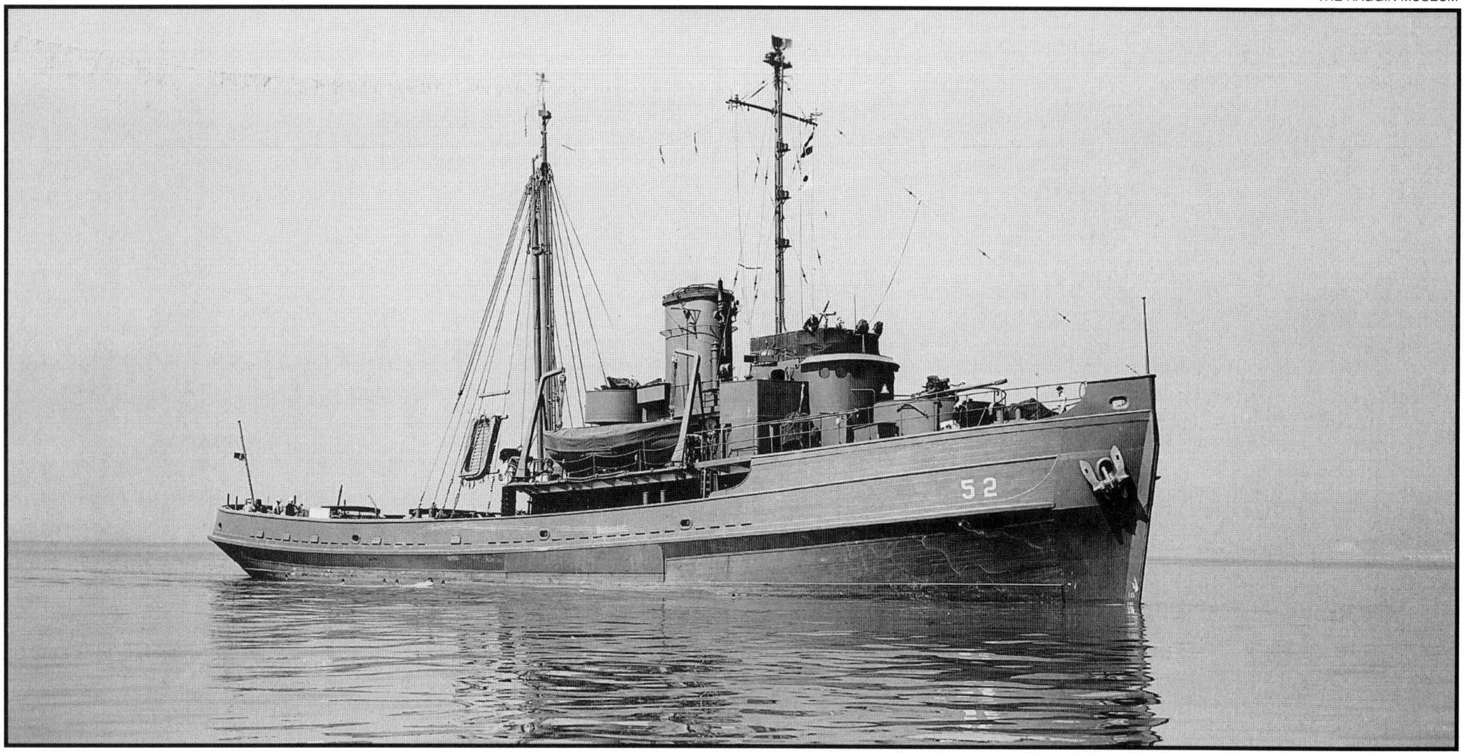

Rescue Tug USS *ATR52*, one of four by Colberg Boat Works, August 14, 1944. Six were built by Fulton Shipyard, Antioch.

THE HAGGIN MUSEUM

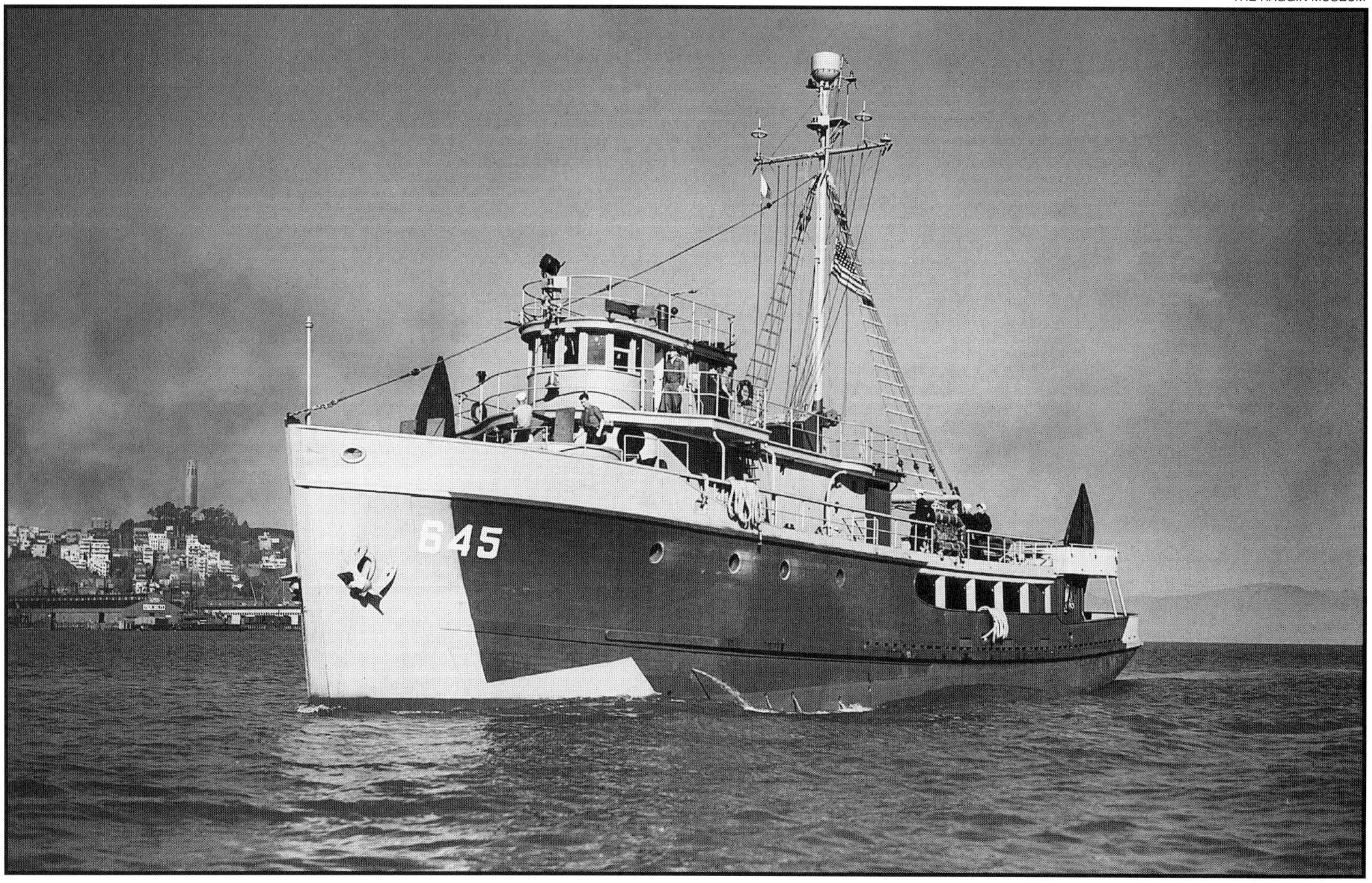

Refrigerated Supply Vessel, *YP645*, Colberg Boat Works, April 25, 1945.

THE HAGGIN MUSEUM

U.S. Army Patrol Boat, Stephens Brothers, c. 1944.

THE HAGGIN MUSEUM

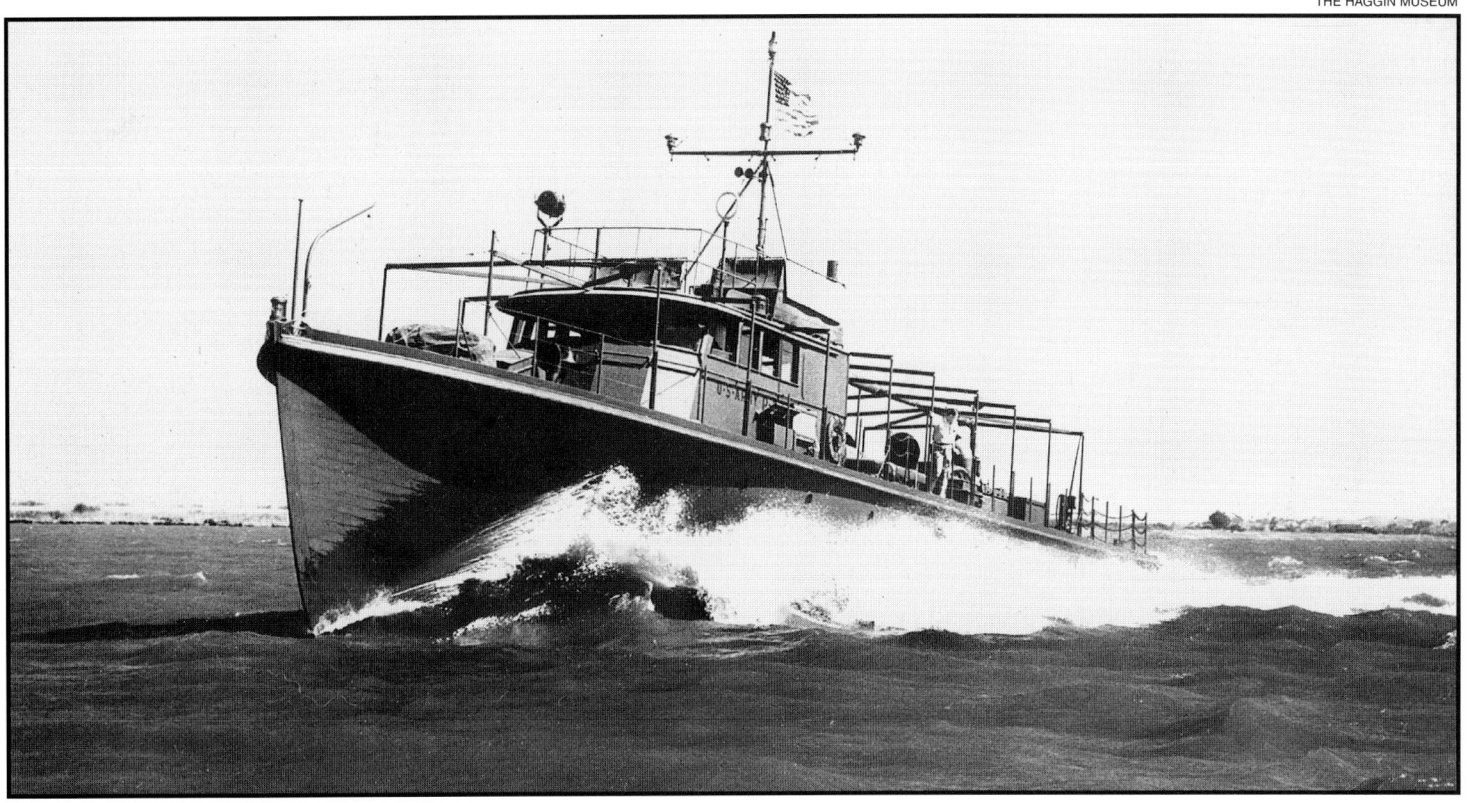

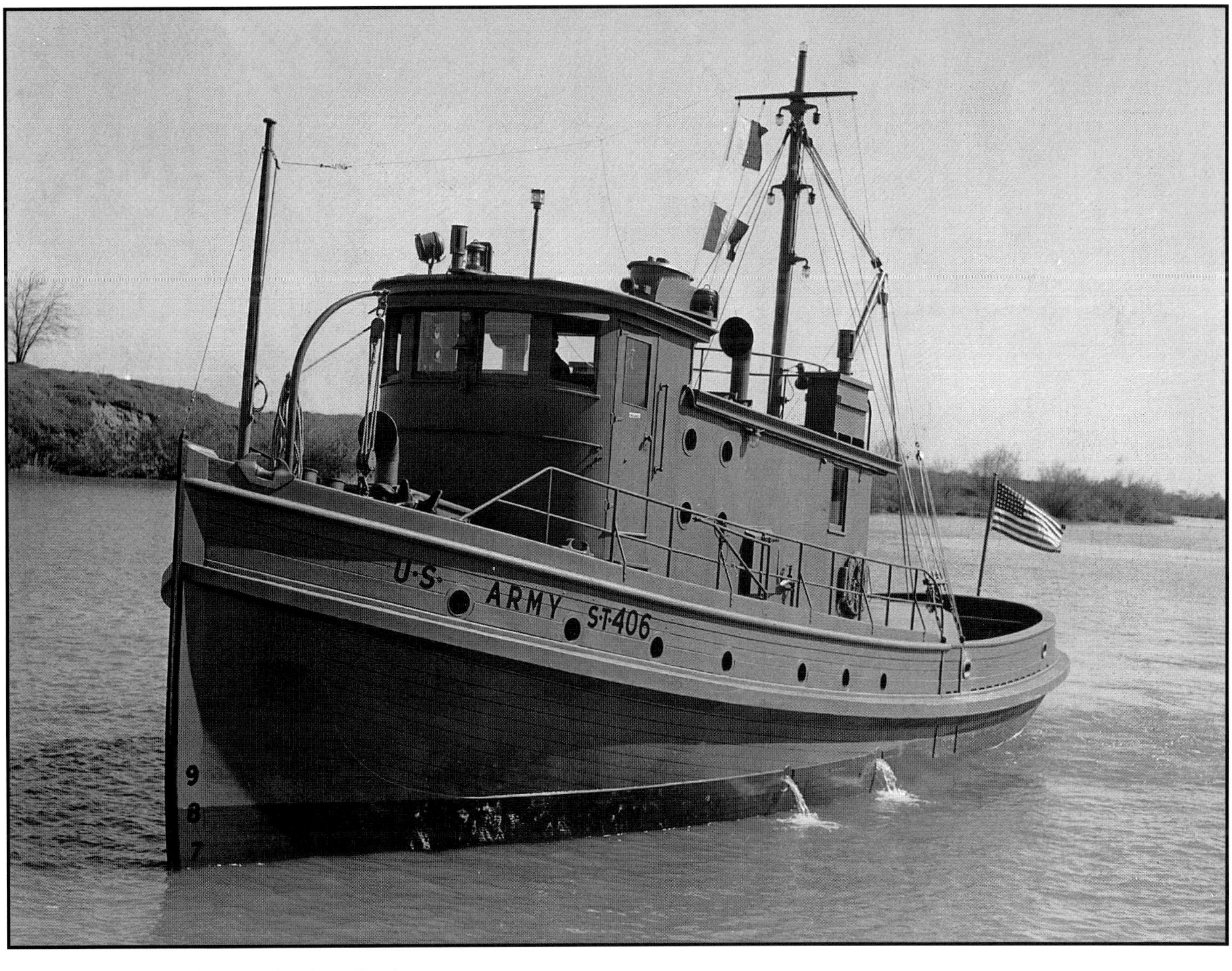

ST406, U.S. Army 72-foot tug, Stephens Brothers, c.1944.

SS *Ocean Vigil*, one of thirty "Ocean" type pre-Liberty ships built for British by Todd-California Shipbuilding Corp. (Kaiser #1, Richmond), November 9, 1941.

C1-M-AV1, Cargo Ship (called "pint size" Liberties), one of twenty-four built at Kaiser#4, 1944-45.

YF740, steel lighter, Pollock-Stockton, May 10, 1945.

EC2-S-C1 Liberty ship, 519 built by Kaiser #1 and Kaiser #2, 18 built by Marinship, 1943-1944. Speed 11 knots, 441 feet long, by 57 feet beam, 10,000 deadweight tons.

VC2-AP3 Victory ship, 142 built by Kaiser #1 and Kaiser #2, 1944-1945. Roughly same size as Liberty but turbine-powered with speed of 15 knots.

APL Barracks Barge, Colberg Boat Works, c.1944. Served in post-invasion operations as temporary quarters for workers and emergency crews. Repair vessels similar in appearance built by Pollock-Stockton.

WINDGATE

Above: Navy Fleet Tug (ATF) USS *Serrano*, one of 17 built by United Engineering Company, Ltd., Alameda, and outfitted at Pollock-Stockton, 1942-1944.

Left: Salvage Vessel (ARS) USS *Gear*, one of 22 built by Basalt Rock Company, Napa, 1942-45. Basalt also built YF lighters, YC barges and small YO fuel oil tankers similar to those built by Hickinbotham.

Above: U.S. Army 50-foot Salvage or Utility Boat, Stephens Brothers, c.1945.

Motor Minesweeper USS *YMS383*, Colberg Boat Works, February 19, 1943, one of 12 built by the company. William F. Stone, Oakland, also built four of these 215-ton vessels.

42-foot Aircraft Fueling Boat, used to refuel seaplanes, Colberg Boat Works, 1945.

U.S. Coast Guard 38-foot Cabin Picket Boat, Stephens Brothers, April, 14, 1942. This same type was built in several yards across the United States.

C2 freighter SS *Bald Eagle*, awaiting launch, gazes down on a welder at Moore Dry Dock Company, May 7, 1942.

INDEX

A
Alcoa Patriot 156
Alcoa Pioneer 1, 3
Alloway 13, 54
American Brass & Copper Company 105
American Bridge 125
American Distilling Company 34
American President Lines 27, 152-53
Arago 10
USS *ASR7* 158
Atchison Topeka & Santa Fe Railroad 8
USS *ATR52* 160

B
balloon barges 130-31
B. Simon Hardware Company 105
Bald Eagle 93, 166
Banner Island 40
Barrett & Hilp 37
Basalt Rock Company 8, 164
Bath Iron Works 32
Bechtel Corporation (W.A. Bechtel Company)
    see Marinship 32, 35,
Belair Shipyard 36-37
USS *Belle Grove* 125
Benicia Arsenal 40
Benicia Shipbuilding Company 17
Bethlehem, Alameda 8, 82-83, 152-53
Belair Shipyard 8,
Bethlehem Shipbuilding Company 1, 3, 8, 9,
    10, 24, 25, 26, 29, 60, 66, 82-83, 88, 94-95,
    96-97, 98, 99, 139, 140, 141, 142, 143, 144,
    147, 155
Bethlehem Shipbuilding Corporation, Ltd. 12,
    13
Birnie Electric Company 106
USS *Blenny* 156
Bruleson 127
USS *Bush* 141

C
USS *Caldwell* 97
USS *California* 22-23
California Shipbuilding Company (Calship) 35,
    56, 57,
California Transportation Company 20
Cape San Martin 94-95
Capto 56
USS *Caughlan* 82
USS *Charleston* 11
USS *Chicago* 23
USS *Cincinnati* 22
Chabot Terrace 120
Clyde Iron Works 63
Clyde W. Wood, Inc. 38, 111, 112-13, 128, 135
Coco Solo Naval Base 18, 19
Colberg Boat Works 40, 65, 75, 78, 110-11, 114,
    119 160, 163, 165, 133
concrete vessels 17, 36-37
Conship (Concrete Ship Constructors) 37
Consolidated Western Steel Corporation 27
Conte Biancamano 146-47

Costa Rica Victory 145
Crosby, Bing 117

D
Dagwood 148
D.W. Nicholson Corporation 38, 111, 134
USS *Damon M. Cummings* 155
Dashing Wave 93
Dauntless 11
Delta King 20
Delta Queen 20
Donahue, Peter and John 10
Dravo Corporation 104
dry docks 132-3

E
Emergency Fleet Corporation 17

F
Fairbanks-Morse Diesel engines 113
Fir 62
USS *Flagler* 150-51
USS *Flint* 95, 154
USS *Florikan* 89
Flying Scud 93
USS *Foreman* 88, 98, 99
Frederic R. Kellogg 14
Fresno 12
Fort Cronkhite 30, 31
Fort Mason 8, 9
Fulton Shipyard 160

G
USS *Gear* 164
General Engineering &
    Dry Dock Company 20, 21, 118-19, 139
General M.M. Patrick 159
USS *Gillespie* 155
Great Republic 93
Gromyko, Andrei 117
Guntert & Zimmerman 40,

H
Hamilton Field 71
USS *Hazelwood* 140-41
Hermitage 147
Hickinbotham Brothers Construction Division
    38, 40, 41, 52, 53, 73, 76-77, 126-27, 130-31,
    136-7
USS *Hoel* 155
Hog Island Shipyard 18, 55
Hotspur 93
Hunters Point
Hunters Point Naval Drydocks 9, 19, 132, 139
Huntington Hills 70-71
Hurley Marine Works 141
Hyster 61, 79

I
Independent Iron Works 128
Inland Shipbuilding Association 39
Isherwood System 14

J

John R. Park 117
John S. McKim 10
USS *John W. Thomason* 82-83
Judson Pacific-Murphy 126

K

Kaiser Cargo Company 33
Kaiser, Henry J. 32, 117
Kaiser Permanente 33
Kaiser, Richmond #1 33
Kaiser, Richmond #2 33, 57, 117
Kaiser, Richmond #3 33, 141, 145
Kaiser, Richmond #4 33, 70, 128-29, 154
Kaiser shipyards 8, 9, 32-33, 43, 44, 45, 82, 116-7, 122, 125, 151
Kaiser, Vancouver 128, 154
Korktone Company 106
Kyle and Company, Inc. 38, 66, 104-7, 130, 135

L

L.A. Young Spring and Wire Corporation 104
landing craft 124-27,
USS *Langley* 19
launching ships 84-91
Lathrop Holding and Reconsignment Point 40
Le Boeuf-Dougherty & Company 105-106
USS *Leary* 13
USS *Lexington* 19
Liberty Fleet Day 47
Liberty ships 35, 46-49, 50, 56, 57, 163
USS *Lofberg* 82-83
USS *LSM 351* 159
USS *LST 482* 158
Lurline 147

M

Macaw 89
Malolo 28
Mare Island Naval Shipyard 8, 9, 11, 12, 13, 18, 22-23, 66, 82, 130, 141
Marin City 50, 121-23
Marin-er (periodical) 34, 119
Marin Hills 172
Marinship (W.A. Bechtel Co., Marin Shipbuilding Division) 4, 8, 9, 34-35, 41, 49, 50-51, 58-61, 62, 64-65, 68-71, 72, 74, 78, 79, 80, 86-87, 89, 92, 93, 119, 120-21, 146, 147, 148-49, 150, 154, 157
Mariposa 147
Maritime Commission (see United States Maritime Commission)
Martin Ship Service Company 105
Matson Line 28, 29
Matsonia 28, 29, 147

Matthew Turner Shipyard 17
USS *McCall* 88
USS *McCord* 99
McDonough Steel Company 126
Merchant Marine Act of 1936 24
merchant ship losses 31
Mission Dolores 157
Mission Purisima 71
Mission San Rafael 80
Mission Santa Barbara 4
USS *Mississippi* 19
Molotov, Foreign Minister 117
Monterey 147
Moore and Scott Iron Works 12, 13, 14, 16, 54, 56, 147
Moore Dry Dock Company 3, 8, 9, 21, 24, 25, 27, 42, 43, 53, 55, 60, 62-63, 70, 75, 80, 81, 85, 87, 89, 93, 100-103, 118-19, 125, 138, 139, 141, 149, 166
Moore Equipment Company 38, 126
Moore, James R. 42
Moore Shipbuilding Company 14,
Mormacsea 156
Mormacsun 3
Mount Tamalpais 34

N

National Housing Agency 121
Nicholson, D.W. *See D.W. Nicholson*
Nokatay 54
Northwestern Pacific Railroad 8, 34

O

Ocean Vigil 162
USS *Ocklawaha* 68-69
USS *Olympia* 11
USS *Oregon* 11
Oskawa 15

P

Pacific Bridge Company 133
Pacific Coast Engineering Company 128
Pacific Erecting Company 60
Pacific Greyhound 122-23
Pacific Rolling Mills 12
Palo Alto 17
Panama Canal 18, 59
Pan American Petroleum & Transport Company 14
Pearl Harbor 6, 7, 28, 29, 111
Peralta 21
USS *Pennsylvania* 7
USS *Pinkney* 139
President Cleveland 152-53
President Wilson 152

USS *Proteus* 157
Pollock, George 111
Pollock-Stockton Shipbuilding Company 38,
    111, 132-33, 143, 162, 163
Pullman Company 159

Q

R
USS *Raleigh* 22
USS *Reno* 94, 99
Richmond, city of 27, 32-33
Risdon Iron Works 11, 12,
riveted ships 14-16
Robert E. Peary 57
Rough and Ready Island 38, 39

S
USS *Saginaw* 10
St. Louis Steel Company 104
USS *San Francisco* (first) 11, (second) 23
San Joaquin River 38, 39, 90
USS *Saratoga* 19
Scott, Irving M. 10
Sea Arrow 85, 103
Sea Beaver 91
Sea Oriole 90-91
Sea Panther 156
Sea Phoebe 91
Sea Star 81
Sea Starling 91
Seattle-Tacoma Shipbuilding Corporation 32
USS *Sebago* 20
Sebastian Cermeno 35
USS *Serrano* 164
Sharpe General Annex 40
Sharpe General Depot, Stockton Annex 38
USS *Shaw* 7
shipyard cranes 62-67,
Shore, Dinah 117
USS *Shubrick* 13
South San Francisco 27
Southern Pacific Railroad 8
USS *ST406* 161
Stephens Brothers 38, 39, 40, 108-9, 114-15,
    161, 164, 165,
Stockton (tanker) 102
Stockton, city of 8, 9, 38-41, 121,
Stockton Channel 20, 38-41, 108-9, 126, 135
Stockton Naval Supply Depot 38
Stockton Ordinance Depot 40
Stockton, Port of 38-40
Stockton Steel Fabricators 38, 106, 128
Stone, William F. 165
Suffolk 144

Sun Shipbuilding & Dry Dock Company 74
USS *Suncock* 143

T
Todd-California Shipbuilding Corporation 32
Todd Shipyards 32
TP101 112-13
Trade Wind 157
Transportation, Office of Defense 121
USS *Tryon* 158

U
United Engineering Company, Ltd. 8, 141, 164
United States Army Corps of Engineers 51, 77, 149
United States Maritime Commission 24, 25, 32,
    35, 48, 50, 96, 104, 128, 152
United States Navy 18, 25, 29, 30, 152
United States Shipping Board 12
Union Iron Works 10, 11,
Union Iron and Brass Foundry 10

V
Vacuum 146-47
Vallejo 22, 120-21
Victory ships 44, 145, 163

W
Walnut 62
War Production Board, Contract Division
    Branch 106
USS *War Hawk* 80, 138
USS *Wedderburn* 99
welding 74-77,
Western Pacific Railroad 8
Western Pipe & Steel 8, 26, 27, 52, 90-91,
USS *Whitehurst* 99
USS *Whiteside* 159
World War I 12-17, 54, 56,

X

Y
Yaquina 15
Yerba Buena 123
Yellowstone 16
Y34 107
Y44 107
Y45 107
Y46 107
YF740 162
YMS383 165
Young America 100
YP646 65, 90, 160

Z

Acknowledgments

Many people have contributed their time and energies into making this book possible. The staffs of the San Francisco Maritime National Historical Park, The Haggin Museum, the Richmond Museum of History and the Sausalito Historical Society have been most helpful in locating and making available materials related to wartime shipbuilding. Special thanks to Taylor Horton, Mary Jo Pugh, Susan Benedetti, Tod Ruhstaller, Kathleen Rupley, Elizabeth Robinson, and Evert Heynneman, and to Joseph A. Moore and James R. Moore, who provided unique insights into wartime shipyard management.

An Informal Bibliography

Of the many hundreds of books and publications about America during World War II, the following were particularly useful in preparing *Build Ships!* Some of them are available in book stores; the older ones are out of print but can be found in various libraries with maritime collections, such as the J. Porter Shaw Library of the San Francisco Maritime National Historical Park in San Francisco.

Ships For Victory: A History of Shipbuilding Under The U.S. Maritime Commission in World War II, by Frederic C. Lane (Johns Hopkins Press, Baltimore, 1951). This is the single most comprehensive and informative book on World War II shipbuilding in the United States. It describes in detail the formation and operation of the United States Maritime Commission, the emergency shipbuilding programs, problems of labor and materials, design, and construction and management of shipyards. Lane devotes entire chapters to the Liberty ship and Victory ship types and includes other major and minor types of vessels constructed during the war. While the book encompasses the entire American shipbuilding effort, it provides also valuable information about Bay Area yards and production. No longer in print, *Ships For Victory* is available in many public libraries, including those of the San Francisco Maritime NHP, the Richmond Library and Sausalito Historical Society.

Western Shipbuilders in World War II, edited by Marshall Maslin (Shipbuilding Review Publishing Association, Oakland, California, 1945). Another valuable account of Bay Area shipbuilding, produced in 1945 just before the war ended. The book includes many photos of local yards and shops, gives descriptions of their management and types of vessels built, and covers the Pacific Coast from Puget Sound to San Diego.

The Use and Disposition of Shipyards at the End of World War II: A report Prepared for the United States Maritime Commission (United States Government Printing Office, 1945). A fascinating discussion about American wartime shipyards and their future was put together by the Graduate School of Business of Harvard University in 1945.

Home Front, U.S.A. by A.A. Hoehling (Thomas Y. Crowell Company, New York, 1996). This book puts the shipbuilding program in perspective with other home-front activities during World War II.

Shipbuilding for Beginners by A.W. Carmichael (The Industrial Service Department, Emergency Fleet Corporation, Washington, D.C., 1918). Despite its title, this isn't a self-help book for someone who wants to build a ship. It was intended to acquaint inexperienced World War I shipyard workers with the complexities of ship construction. Included are several informative glossaries of shipyard terms, parts of ships, and the various trades involved. A good description of building riveted ships.

A Handbook of Practical Shipbuilding, by J.D. MacBride (D. Van Norstrand Company, New York, 1921). Another excellent guide to World War I shipbuilding for the uninitiated. It covers shipyard organization, divisions of work, tools, operations, launching, hull engineering and ship nomenclature.

The "Hog Islanders": The Story of 122 American Ships, by Mark H. Goldberg (The American Merchant Marine Museum, New York, 1991). A definitive study of the famous emergency fleet vessels of World War I, built at the Hog Island Shipyard in Maryland. Many important lessons about mass-producing ships were learned at Hog Island the program that influenced shipbuilding twenty years later during World War II.

From America to United States, In Four Parts: The History of the Merchant Ship types built in the United States of American under the Long-Range Programme of the Maritime Commission, by L.A. Sawyer and W.H. Mitchell (World Ship Society, London, 1979). The lengthy subtitle is self-explanatory. Included are detailed vessel-type descriptions, list of individual vessels and shipyards nationwide.

More Liberty ships were produced during the war than any other merchant type. Several good books describe these vessels and their history in great detail. Among them are:

The Liberty Ships: The History of the 'Emergency' type Cargo ships constructed in the United States during the Second World War, by L.A. Sawyer and W.H. Mitchell (Lloyd's of London Press, Ltd. In conjunction with The National Liberty Ship Memorial, the SS Jeremiah O'Brien, San Francisco, 1970).

Liberty Ships: The Ugly Ducklings of World War II, by John Gorley Bunker (Naval Institute Press, Annapolis).

Several Bay Area wartime shipyards are the subjects of books and published materials. These include Bethlehem, Mare Island Naval Shipyard, Moore Dry Dock Company, Kaiser and Marinship.

A Long Line of Ships: Mare Island's Century of Naval Activity in California, by Arnold S. Lott (United States Naval Institute, Annapolis, 1954). Written during Mare Island's centennial year, this comprehensive history contains a list of all vessels launched at the shipyard.

Sidewheelers to Nuclear Power; A Pictorial Essay Covering 123 Years At The Mare Island Naval Shipyard, by Sue Lemmon and E.D. Wichels (Leeward Publications, Annapolis, Maryland, 1977). Essentially a photographic record of the yard's history, this book comprises four parts, ships, people, places and "everything else." It covers the World War II period in detail.

Marinship at War: Shipbuilding and Social Change in Wartime Sausalito, by Charles Wollenberg (Western Heritage Press, Berkeley, California, 1990). The focus of this book is on social interaction of the workers, shipyard management, labor and residents of the area. An excellent depiction of an emergency wartime shipyard, with photos.

Marinship: The History of a Wartime Shipyard, edited by Richard Finnie (Marinship Corporation, San Francisco, 1947). This is a history of the yard compiled and produced by some of the people who participated in its brief life. It contains a complete breakdown of the components of shipyard administration, operation and production. Illustrated with photos and drawings.

The Story of Moore Dry Dock Company: A Picture History, by James R. Moore (Windgate Press, 1994). A privately produced company history, this book is unavailable except in selected libraries, notably the J. porter Shaw Library of the San Francisco Maritime NHP. The book covers production and operations of the yard during both world wars and the periods before and after. In an appendix are photographic profiles of the types of vessels built by the yard.

Henry J. Kaiser, Western Colossus: An Insider's View, by Albert P. Heiner (Halo Books, San Francisco, 1991). In this complete history of Kaiser and his construction empire is a comprehensive look at the wartime shipyards in Richmond, and Kaiser's interaction with the Maritime Commission.

The Second Gold Rush: Oakland and the East Bay in World War II, by Marilynn S. Johnson (University of California Press, Berkeley, 1993). Johnson describes the impact of wartime construction on the land and people of the East Bay. Chapters include discussions of labor, migrant ghettos, politics and the lives of migrant families.

The Secret Blue-Collar War: A History of Floating Drydocks of WWII, by John Donald Hartney (Insta Print, 1985). A fascinating account of the floating dry docks essential to victory in World War II, the shipyards that built them, how they worked and the men who operated them. Many photographs and drawings.

Many good books provide detail of Naval and Merchant Marine history during World War II. "*A Careless Word... A Needless Sinking,*" by Captain Arthur R. Moore, gives a ship-by-ship account of maritime losses and damage.

Excellent sources of information about wartime shipyards can be found in Bay Area Libraries including the Bancroft Library in Berkeley, public libraries in Richmond, San Francisco, San Rafael, Vallejo and Alameda. In addition, documents and photos are housed in several Bay Area institutions. The photographs in this book are reproduced through the courtesy of the following museums:

THE HAGGIN MUSEUM in Stockton, California, opened to the public in 1931. Its art collections feature 19th century French and American painting, while its history collections focus on the history of the Stockton-San Joaquin County area of California's northern Central Valley. The museum's library/archive houses an extensive collection of photographs, books and ephemera relating to the history of this region. Extensive archival holdings document the history of shipbuilding, Stockton's oldest industry dating back to 1850. Hundreds of photographs record the dramatic expansion of this industry during World War II.

THE RICHMOND MUSEUM OF HISTORY, founded in 1952, is a local history museum located in a 1910 Carnegie Library building on the east side of San Francisco Bay. A small town profoundly changed by the shipbuilding industry that sprung up during World War II on the community's waterfront, Richmond has become an increasingly culturally diverse community. To represent such a community is a commanding mission for a small museum. Among its holdings of everyday objects, the museum maintains a large collection of photographs. In addition to its on-site holdings the museum has accepted a 1944 Richmond-build victory ship, the *Red Oak Victory*, which was conveyed by Congress in 1996. The museum presents a variety of exhibits and programs throughout the year for both adults and children.

THE SAN FRANCISCO MARITIME NATIONAL HISTORICAL PARK collects, preserves, and interprets the maritime heritage of the Pacific Coast, its trades, technology, traditions, and peoples. Founded in the 1950s, the Park maintains a fleet of historic vessels and a major collection of library materials, archival documents, objects, and small craft. The Historic Documents Department manages the Park's archival and manuscript collections containing some 250,000 photographic images, 1,200 linear feet of manuscripts and business records, 120,000 marine architectural and engineering drawings, and some 5,000 charts and maps. The Park library holds over 22, 000 volumes.

THE SAUSALITO HISTORICAL SOCIETY was founded in 1975. Located on the second floor of Sausalito City Hall, its purpose is to collect, preserve, manage, maintain, properly store and display all objects of historical value to Sausalito and its immediate vicinity. It maintains a well-organized record system of marine and railroad oriented historical documents, pictures, rare books, paintings by local artists and other social and cultural records which are open for public inspection at set hours. As a strictly volunteer organization, it produces two special exhibits a year which are preceded by two historical publications entitled "Moments in Time."

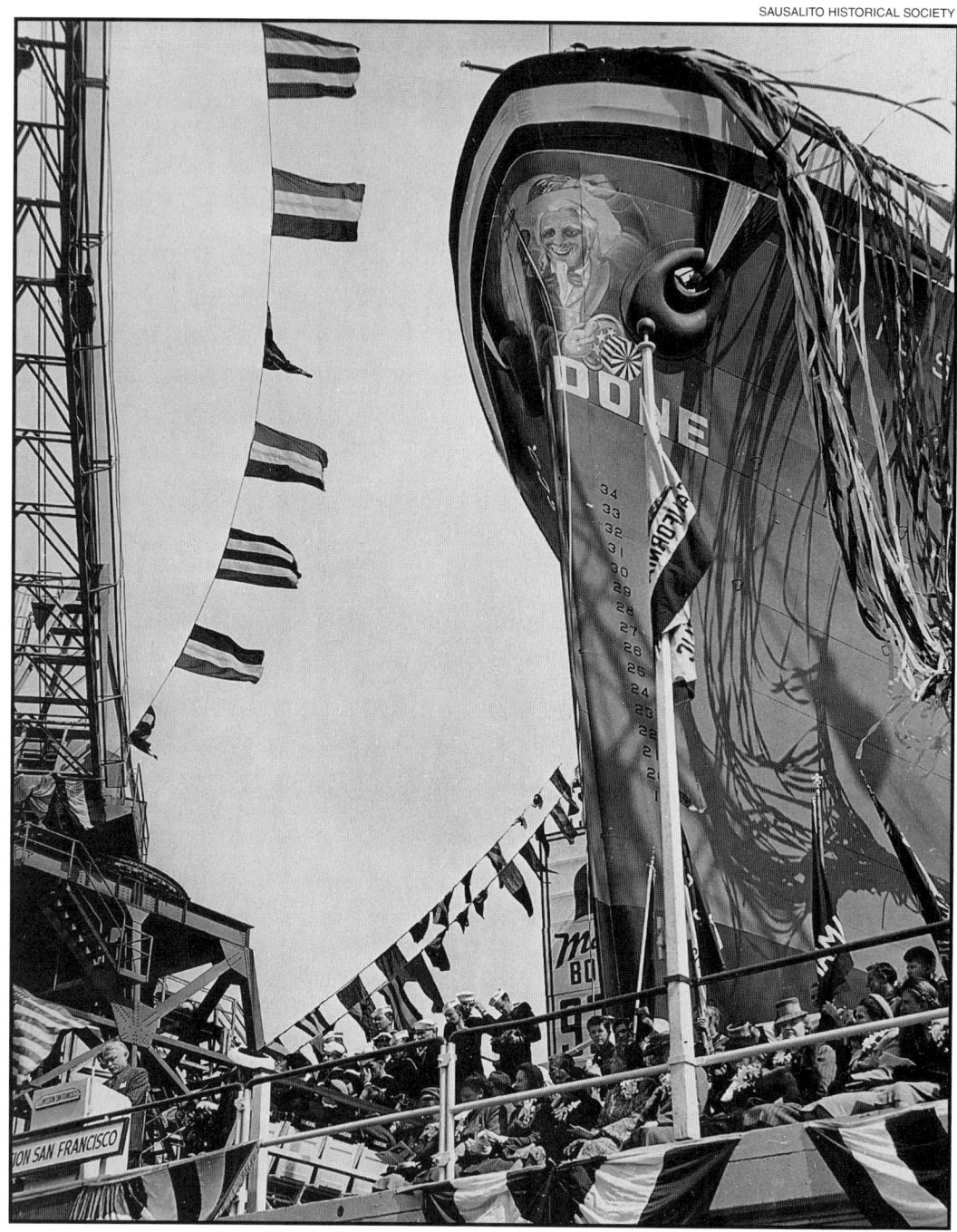

Launch of *Marin Hills*, final ship, Marinship, September 8, 1945.

"Done"